A Foreign Flavour

Rose Elliot became a cookery writer by accident. She was planning to take a history degree when she met and married her husband and became involved in cooking, entertaining and having babies. It was while looking after the latter that she began scribbling down her recipes. These led to her first book, *Simply Delicious*, which in turn brought requests for cookery demonstrations. It was the invention of new recipes which led to her second book, *Not Just a Load of Old Lentils*, and patient research into recipes using pulses resulted in *The Bean Book*.

As well as writing regularly in the leading vegetarian newspaper *The Vegetarian*, Rose Elliot broadcasts and appears on television. When she is not writing and testing recipes, she enjoys studying astrology – which she uses in counselling – and caravanning with her husband and three daughters.

Simply Delicious, *Not Just a Load of Old Lentils*, *The Bean Book* and her latest book, *Your Very Good Health*, are all available from Fontana.

ROSE ELLIOT

A Foreign Flavour

VEGETARIAN DISHES OF THE WORLD

FONTANA/COLLINS

First published by William Collins Sons & Co. Ltd 1981
First issued in Fontana 1982

Copyright © Rose Elliot 1981

Filmset by Northumberland Press Ltd,
Gateshead, Tyne and Wear and
printed in Great Britain by Richard Clay
(The Chaucer Press) Ltd, Bungay, Suffolk

Originally published in hardback as
Vegetarian Dishes of the World.

For Katy, Margaret and Claire

Contents

Introduction

Although I was brought up as a vegetarian, when I started to cook for people who were used to eating meat I found that, unlike me, they did not relish with delight the thought of nut roast. So I began to look for alternatives which they would enjoy more. I soon realized that nearly every country has in its cuisine at least one or two traditional dishes that do not contain meat or fish yet which are still good to look at, good to eat and very satisfying. Over the years I have gradually built up a collection of these recipes and this book is the result; it contains over 250 recipes from more than 30 different countries.

From Britain there are a couple of traditional cheese dishes, including Welsh rabbit; a creamy leek pie and pease pudding, which I've included because although really intended as an accompaniment to meat it is nutritious enough to eat as a main course, and probably often was when times were hard. It's good with vegetables and one of the piquant sauces – mint sauce or apple sauce – which Britain does so well. But the real strength of the British contribution lies in the baking – there are some excellent breads, scones and cakes, including Madeira cake and Dundee cake – and some quite surprisingly superb puddings such as trifle, gooseberry fool and *crème brûlée*, which sounds and tastes as though it ought to be French, but isn't.

France itself has any number of delectable vegetarian dishes. The French just seem to have the knack of putting together a few simple, yet high quality ingredients and finishing up with something that's exactly right. Add to this a love of and respect for vegetables and you come up with such wonderful mixtures as red cabbage cooked with butter, chestnuts and red wine, or aubergines stuffed with mushrooms, parsley and cheese. This book contains many examples of this type of flair as well as those great French vegetarian classics, omelettes, soufflés and savoury flans with their mouthwatering combination of crisp pastry and

9

creamy filling. Then there are the dishes which to me exemplify the thrifty, inventive side of French cookery, the light stuffed pancakes and the golden puffed up savoury choux pastry ring, or *gougère*, which help make the precious vegetables go further. Finally there are one or two slightly frivolous cakes and some good simple puddings.

Italy, with its pizza, pasta and rice dishes, is another country which has a great deal to offer the vegetarian and it's just the type of food that is so useful and popular – cheap and tasty, quick to make and quick to eat. I've often thought it strange that the Italian cuisine, which is the oldest in Europe, should in many ways be the one with the most contemporary appeal and practicality. There is certainly plenty of scope for the vegetarian: as well as cereal and pasta dishes there are also vegetable dishes, including a rich-tasting aubergine casserole and stuffed onions; then there's that cheesy golden bake, *gnocchi alla Romana*, as well as delicate spinach *gnocchi* and some tasty fritters. From Italy also come some refreshing puddings including again the one with perhaps the most appeal for today, ice cream.

German cookery is rather like that of Great Britain in that it seems to be very much orientated towards meat, but there are some interesting vegetable dishes and I particularly like the German way of mixing fruit with vegetables – haricot beans or carrots with apples, fried potato cake with cranberry or apple sauce. The Germans also have a split pea purée rather like the British pease pudding except that they add vegetables which makes a good variation. And they use dried fruits for a compote which makes a pleasant winter pudding.

Austria does not seem to be a very rich source of vegetarian dishes – here again the emphasis is on meat – but the Austrians do have a good way of serving those light little cheesy dumplings, *gnocchi,* in a velvety mushroom sauce, and also of course that marvellous almond and raspberry tart. *Linzertorte.*

Much of the cookery of Spain and Portugal includes fish or meat in one form or another but I have allowed myself the indulgence of including a vegetarian version of perhaps the most famous Spanish dish of all, paella. Although fish is usually among the ingredients, it's a very variable dish and so I hope a vegetarian version will be considered valid. As well as this there is that well-known cold Spanish soup, gazpacho, and some simple stuffed vegetables, also a red kidney bean dish from Portugal; and from Spain perhaps one of the most luxurious puddings of all, chocolate and orange mousse.

Some useful cheese dishes are to be found in both Holland and Switzerland, including one of the best cheese dishes of all, surely a classic, cheese fondue. I have attributed this to Switzerland, although I believe a rather similar dish is made in Holland and in my recipe I have perhaps rather cheekily suggested Dutch Edam cheese as a good alternative to more expensive Gruyère and Emmenthal! Also from Switzerland come what I consider to be a particularly successful cheese flan, a couple of vegetable dishes and a moist fruit bread.

The main contribution from Scandinavia seems to be in the puddings section. From Denmark there's red fruit pudding made from raspberries and redcurrants, and the rice and almond pudding which is traditionally served at Christmas; there's apricot and almond pudding from Sweden, ways with rhubarb and prunes from Norway and with apples from Finland. But the Scandinavians also have some unusual ways of serving vegetables to make them a bit special. I especially like the two Finnish mushroom recipes and the Norwegian cabbage and new potatoes. And then of course there are open sandwiches – ideal for a buffet meal – and also Danish pastries, for which I've developed a wheatmeal version.

Although the countries of Eastern Europe are not vegetarian, they do have a number of national dishes that do not contain meat and so are ideal for vegetarians. In Rumania, for instance, there is a mixed vegetable stew called *ghiveci* and while this can sometimes contain meat it by no means always does, and so I have given an all-vegetable version of that, also a protein-rich cheesy dip. Then from Bulgaria there are a couple of stews, one based on lentils and the other made from red kidney beans; from Hungary come a couple of vegetable stews enlivened with soured cream and paprika, and from Poland a vegetable and bean salad which is pretty to look at and very filling.

Russian cookery offers the vegetarian an ingenious dip with smoky mock caviar; then there's beetroot soup, or borsch, and to eat with it some little curd cheese tartlets, *vatrushki*, and a protein-rich pudding, that traditional Easter dish made from curd or cream cheese, called *pashka*.

I love the easy-going, inventive feel of American cookery; it's exciting and it's fun. The Americans seem to be particularly good with salads – to them we owe coleslaw and Waldorf salad, also some cooked vegetable dishes, including glazed sweet potatoes and sweetcorn fritters; and perhaps the best chilled soup of all, vichyssoise, which was invented by a chef in America although admittedly he was French. But then one of the strengths of American cookery seems to be the way it can contain the cuisines of so many different nationalities yet retain a recognizable character of its own. There are also some substantial puddings; I've included those American favourites, cheese cake and pumpkin pie and also a less well-known flan, raisin and sour cream pie.

In the cookery of South America and the Caribbean there are several vegetarian dishes; a red bean rice dish from the Caribbean, as well as pumpkin soup and banana fritters, and from South America chilled avocado soup and that creamy avocado dip, *guacamole;* also an unusual hot potato salad with a peanut and chilli dressing which sounds strange but works well. In South America, as in India, unleavened breads play an important part in the diet; here they are called tortillas and usually made from maize flour. You will find a recipe for making these and two recipes for stuffing and baking them like pancakes, and also how to make them into *tostadas* by frying them and using them as a base for salad mixtures.

The national cereal of North Africa is couscous, which consists of pellets of semolina (or other grains) and is served with spicy sauces. These sauces generally contain meat of some type, but nearly always have chick peas in the mixture too, which in fact provide excellent protein without the meat when eaten with the couscous. I have therefore given a vegetarian version based on chick peas, vegetables and spices. Cooling side salads are served with couscous meals and there are some typical mixtures in the salads section.

I think the Middle East offers some of the best vegetarian dishes of all. There are dreamy dips – smooth chick pea *hummus*, of course – as well as some less well-known ones made from aubergine and sesame cream and from dried beans. These make first courses or fillings for sandwiches or for the pocket-shaped Middle Eastern bread, pitta, of which I've evolved a wholewheat version. Then there are some unusual salads, among them the famous bulgur wheat, tomato and parsley one called *tabbouleh*, and a cold cooked spinach one which sounds odd but which is particularly cooling on a hot day. But perhaps the most important Middle Eastern contribution to vegetarian cookery is the stuffed vegetables that look so appetizing: tomatoes stuffed with rice, little stuffed aubergines, stuffed vine leaves baked in tomato sauce. There are some splendid pies, too; I think the spinach pie, with its smooth filling and flaky crust is one of the best. And when it comes to puddings, there's an easy uncooked yoghurt tart, a honey cheese cake and a chilled ground rice and rosewater pudding which are nutritious and therefore useful in menu planning, as well as being good to eat.

India has a large proportion of vegetarians in its population and so is as you might expect one of the best sources of vegetarian food – and what colourful, tasty food it is! I think there are few foods as appetizing as a really well-cooked curry or spicy rice dish and you will find a number of recipes for these including *khitchari*, that mixture of lentils and rice from which our present-day kedgeree originated. The Indians are also excellent at making unleavened breads and these are lovely for eating not only with curries, but also with salads and dips as a change from ordinary bread. One of these unleavened bread mixtures is also rolled out thinly, wrapped around a vegetable filling then deep-fried to make *samosas*, little Indian pastries.

China is another country which has plenty to offer the vegetarian. The Chinese were making their own versions of textured protein from wheat flour long before it was ever thought of in the West. I have included a sweet and sour way with this wheat

13

protein, also a recipe using that other high-protein vegetable product, *tofu,* which is made from soya beans and which you can sometimes buy very cheaply in Chinese shops. There are also a couple of the crunchy stir-fried vegetable dishes that the Chinese do so well.

I think most people like to try something new sometimes and there are occasions when even the most dedicated meat eater feels like a change, so I hope this book will prove interesting and helpful and that you will be tempted to cook the recipes and will enjoy the results.

Note on Measurements

Throughout this book I've given both metric and Imperial measurements. As long as you keep to either one set of measurements or the other in a recipe you should find that all is well. I have used the standard equivalents, listed below, but as you will see, for some of the Imperial measurements there are two possible metric equivalents and sometimes I have used one and sometimes the other, depending on which is the more accurate for a particular recipe. This mainly applies to sauces and pastries, where proportions are important.

With liquids I have generally used pints and fractions of a pint as the Imperial equivalent to millilitres, but again, in one or two recipes, where accuracy is particularly important, or where there is no near fractional equivalent, I've used fluid ounces as the equivalent. Measuring liquids is easy with a good measuring jug marked in millilitres, pints and fluid ounces.

The tablespoons and teaspoons used in the recipes are standard size, 15 ml and 5 ml respectively, and level unless otherwise stated.

The eggs used are always standard, size 3.

Grams (g)	Ounces (oz)	Millilitres (ml)	Fluid ounces (fl oz)
25	1	25	1
40	1½	50	2
50	2	75	3
60	2½	125	4
75	3	150	5 (¼ pint)
100	4 } (¼ pound)	175	6
125	4	200	7
150	5	225	8
175	6	250	10 } (½ pint)
200	7	275	10
225	8 (½ pound)	300	11

A Foreign Flavour

Grams (g)	Ounces (oz)	Millilitres (ml)	Fluid ounces (fl oz)
250	9	350	12
275	10	375	13
300	11	400	15 } ($\frac{3}{4}$ pint)
350	12 ($\frac{3}{4}$ pound)	425	16 }
375	13	450	16
400	14	475	17
425	15	500	18
450	16 (1 pound)	550	20 } (1 pint)
475	17	575	20 }
500	18	850	(1$\frac{1}{2}$ pints)
700	24 (1$\frac{1}{2}$ pounds)	1000 (1 litre)	35
1000 (1 kilo)	2–2$\frac{1}{4}$ pounds	1·2 litres	(2 pints)

Oven Temperatures

Temperature	Centigrade (°C)	Fahrenheit (°F)	Gas Mark
	70	150	
	80	175	
	100	200	
Very Cool	110	225	$\frac{1}{4}$
	120	250	$\frac{1}{2}$
	140	275	1
Cool	150	300	2
Warm	160	325	3
Moderate	180	350	4
Fairly Hot	190	375	5
	200	400	6
Hot	220	425	7
	230	450	8
Very Hot	240	475	9
	260	500	9

Equivalents for North American Readers

Ingredients

Aubergine	Egg plant
Beetroot	Beet
Biscuits	Cookies
Black treacle	Molasses
Caster sugar	Fine sugar
Cornflour	Cornstarch
Courgette	Zucchini
Double cream	Heavy cream
Grill	Broiler
Hazel nuts	Filberts
Icing sugar	Confectioner's sugar
Marmite	Savita
Marrow	Squash/very large zucchini
Single cream	Light cream
Spanish onion	Bermuda onion
Spring onion	Scallion

Measurements

1 pint (20 fl oz/575 ml)	$2\frac{1}{4}$ cups
25 g (1 oz) chopped nuts	2 tablespoons
25 g (1 oz) fat/butter/margarine	2 tablespoons
25 g (1 oz) flour	2 tablespoons
25 g (1 oz) grated cheese	4 tablespoons
25 g (1 oz) caster sugar	2 tablespoons
450 g (1 lb) fresh breadcrumbs	8 cups
450 g (1 lb) large beans	3 cups
450 g (1 lb) small beans	2 cups
450 g (1 lb) bulgur wheat	2 cups
450 g (1 lb) cottage/cream/curd cheese	2 cups

450 g (1 lb) grated whole nuts	4 cups
450 g (1 lb) macaroni	3 cups
450 g (1 lb) mashed potato	2 cups
450 g (1 lb) cooked/uncooked rice	2 cups
450 g (1 lb) semolina	2 cups
450 g (1 lb) wholewheat flour	4 cups

Centimetres to Inches

Centimetres	*Inches*
6 mm	$\frac{1}{4}$ in
1 cm	$\frac{1}{2}$ in
2·5 cm	1 in
5 cm	2 in
7·5 cm	3 in
10 cm	4 in
12·5 cm	5 in
15 cm	6 in
18 cm	7 in
20 cm	8 in
23 cm	9 in
25 cm	10 in
28 cm	11 in
30 cm	12 in

Note on Special Ingredients

Most of the recipes are self-explanatory and nearly all the ingredients are easy to get; when something scarce or exotic is called for I've tried to give substitutes where possible so that even if you can't get it you can still make the dish. But here are just one or two notes that might be helpful.

Fats and Oils

You will notice that I generally suggest butter in the recipes because very often that is the fat traditionally used and therefore the one which gives the most authentic flavour. You could substitute a pure vegetable margarine if you prefer and of course make it an unsaturated one if you wish.

It's difficult to decide whether butter or polyunsaturated margarine is better from the health point of view because opinions differ depending on which expert you consult. I must admit that I'm veering towards margarine although I do still use butter sometimes at the table and in some cookery. I also use corn oil, which is low in saturated fat, for frying, and olive oil, which is neutral, for salad dressings. If you want to use a white fat (high in saturated fat) for pastry, choose a pure vegetable one.

Whatever your feelings about the butter versus polyunsaturated margarine controversy, I think the most important thing is to keep a check on the amount of *any* fat used in cooking (including cream and egg yolks) and try to plan a day's – and a week's – meals carefully, balancing eggs, cheese and fats with plenty of cereal and vegetable protein, low-fat cheeses such as cottage cheese and quark (a lovely smooth white cheese which is readily available and which I find very useful) and yoghurt, vegetables and salad.

Flour

The flour I normally use is plain 100% wholewheat, which I find excellent for nearly all my cooking. If you're new to wholewheat flour it's often helpful to start with to mix it with a proportion of plain unbleached white flour; I've given suggestions for this in the recipes where applicable. I also use unbleached plain white flour for all sauces which require a flour thickening.

You will notice in the recipes where wholewheat flour is sifted I say 'add the sifted flour and the residue of bran left in the sieve' or similar. People sometimes ask me why I bother to sift the flour and then add the bran that's been sifted out. The flour is sifted to aerate it and make it light, not to remove the bran, so, having sifted the flour the bran can then be put back.

Sugar

This is another controversial subject and my own feelings are that it's not so much the colour of the sugar that makes a dish healthy or not, but the quantity used. Brown sugar 'feels' healthier to use but I've found this tends to make me a bit more lavish with it! I use brown sugar in breads and in cakes such as Dundee cake, parkin and chocolate brownies, also sometimes in shortbreads and cookies. But there are times when I prefer to use a small quantity of caster sugar or honey because they give the dish a better flavour and appearance. This is particularly true, I feel, when a delicate vanilla flavour is called for and for this I think there is nothing better than vanilla sugar which is so easy to make. All you do is break a vanilla pod in half and bury the halves in a canister of caster sugar, topping up the sugar as it is used.

Salt

I'm afraid I'm very addicted to sea salt which I know is more expensive than ordinary table salt but I like it because it's natural and pure. The trouble is it also makes food taste so much better that once you've used it it spoils you for anything else.

Herbs and Spices

It's often the use of a herb or spice that makes food taste of a particular country: dill immediately gives a Scandinavian or Eastern European flavour, paprika a Hungarian one. I've tried, however, to keep the recipes as simple and straightforward as possible (while still, I hope, keeping their authenticity) and the only spice that I think you could have difficulty in obtaining is fresh ginger root (unless there is a large Asian community where you live). But it's much easier to find than it used to be and I've discovered that the root will keep beautifully in the deep freeze, just wrapped in foil or polythene. You can grate it straight from the freezer, so it's worth buying up a few knobbly pieces of root when you see it or if you have to go some distance to get it.

Pulses

These days it's not usually difficult to find dried beans, peas and lentils and I've been delighted to see dried red kidney beans, chick peas and continental lentils appearing in my local supermarket alongside the more familiar split red lentils and butter beans. Instructions for using these pulses appear in the individual recipes but as a general rule it's worth remembering that if you rinse pulses after soaking, before cooking, it helps to make them more digestible. Also it's best not to add salt to the cooking water as this can toughen the skin before the inside is cooked. In the recipes I've given approximate cooking times for the pulses but these can vary according to how long the pulses have been stored so it's best to keep an eye on them and adjust the timing a little if necessary; do make sure the pulses are thoroughly cooked. I've gone into this whole question of pulse cookery in detail in *The Bean Book*.

RED KIDNEY BEANS – A WARNING

You may have heard that, under certain conditions, it can be dangerous to eat red kidney beans. The toxic factor is most probably a haemagglutinin which may lead to acute gastroenteritis if not destroyed by adequate cooking. Soaking and rinsing the beans prior to cooking reduces the haemagglutinins by two thirds (to about the level present in other dried beans, soaked or unsoaked). The danger can be eliminated entirely by *ensuring that the beans are allowed to boil vigorously for 10 minutes* before lowering the heat and letting the beans cook gently until tender. It is safe to use a slow cooker *provided they are boiled for 10 minutes* as above, before being put into the slow cooker.

Menu Planning

Planning a vegetarian meal is not complicated or difficult – all you have to do is to decide on your source of protein, just like you would with meat or fish, and build the rest of the meal around that. So you could have something like, say, cheese soufflé with new potatoes and French beans followed by a refreshing pudding like tangy orange salad. If you wanted a first course as well you could have a salady one, like stuffed tomato salad or mushrooms *à la Grecque*, or a dip such as mock caviar with crisp Melba toast, or a vegetable purée soup, like French tomato soup or lettuce soup – as you can see there is plenty of scope!

Other examples of this type of simple menu planning based around a protein-rich main course are: Caribbean courgettes stuffed with cheese and onion, with tomato sauce, new potatoes (or cooked rice) and spinach or baby carrots, preceded by pumpkin soup (also from the Caribbean) if you like, and perhaps followed by exotic fruit salad or banana fritters. Or from Italy, gorgeous tomato and mushroom pizza with green salad, with perhaps stuffed cucumber as a starter and pineapple sorbet for pudding. There are plenty of high-protein dishes like these in the book and plenty of scope for many different combinations. Although I've given suggestions for more than one course, if you want to be simpler and more economical the first courses and puddings can of course be left out as long as you've included some protein in the main course.

I think, however, that part of the pleasure of vegetarian cookery and a great deal of satisfaction, as far as I'm concerned, comes from the fact that it gives the opportunity to be very fluid and creative in meal planning. This also enables you to enjoy dishes that you probably wouldn't otherwise. Take for instance luscious French red cabbage stuffed with chestnuts and baked in red wine. This really makes a lovely main dish but it only contains

23

a minimal amount of protein; however there's no reason why the protein should always be in the main dish. You can make a beautifully balanced meal by serving a protein-rich first course, such as the creamy chick pea and vegetable salad *aigroissade*, with warm rolls; or little individual cheese soufflés which make a wonderfully impressive starter; or a nutritious dip, like goat cheese and herb spread, or *hummus*, with fingers of hot buttered or Melba toast.

You could boost the protein level still further if you wanted to by concluding the meal with a pudding like little coffee custards or *coeurs à la crème*, or biscuits and cheese. Another way of introducing protein into a meal is by including it in a vegetable dish, such as potatoes Anna layered with grated cheese or green salad with Gruyère cheese or haricot bean salad.

Here are some of the ways in which you can provide protein for the meal when it is not in the main dish.

1. *Serve a protein starter* such as lentil soup with crusty rolls, French onion soup, or chilled cucumber soup; or tomatoes stuffed with cheese, individual cheese soufflés or individual asparagus tartlets.
2. *Offer a milk-based or cheesy sauce with the meal* – this is particularly good with some of the stuffed vegetable dishes such as the tomatoes à la Provençale or stuffed onions.
3. *Have grated cheese for people to add to their meal* – this is a useful and simple way of increasing the protein with some pasta dishes or vegetable stews such as ratatouille or the mixed vegetable stew from Bulgaria.
4. *Garnish the dish with slices of hardboiled egg* – again, if you like egg, this is a good simple way of adding protein to some vegetable casseroles, salads, curries or rice dishes.
5. *Serve the meal with rice and even add some nuts, sunflower seeds or sesame seeds to the rice to increase the protein further* – this works well with vegetable mixtures like the red peppers with tomatoes and onions and some of the stuffed vegetable dishes.
6. *Have a protein-rich vegetable or salad with the meal* – this is a nice easy way of adding nourishment. Potatoes Anna, layered with cheese, are good, or jacket potatoes with a dollop of

curd cheese or smooth low-fat cheese like quark (see page 19), or the German haricot beans with apples. Or, green salad with Gruyère cheese, haricot bean salad or tomato, cheese and olive salad are all excellent and go with lots of different dishes.

7. *Provide protein with a nutritious pudding* – perhaps this is one time when you can indulge with a relatively easy conscience! Examples of such puddings are ice cream (home-made with egg custard), yoghurt tart, *crème brûlée*, coffee *ricotta* pudding, cheese cake, special ground rice pudding or even biscuits and cheese – and possibly also one of the protein-rich dips – or bowls of assorted nuts and raisins.

As you will see some of these ideas are really very simple, others take more time and organization, but I think you'll agree the idea is quite feasible and practical and it really is fun to experiment with creative menus.

Here are just a few examples of how this planning works – there are lots more ideas with the recipes.

Stuffed tomato salad – fondue with French bread – pear bread (*birnbrot*).

Chick pea soup – paella with Spanish green salad – chocolate and orange mousse.

Individual cheese soufflés – aubergines *à la duxelles* with wine sauce – *gratin dauphinoise* – French beans – fresh peach salad.

Bean pâté with fingers of hot toast – stuffed vine leaves – tomato salad – Greek honey pie.

Avocados with vinaigrette – mushroom soufflé – green salad – *Linzertorte*.

Aubergine and sesame pâté or mock caviar with hot toast – Russian beetroot soup with little cheese tartlets – fresh fruit.

French onion soup – tomatoes à la Provençale with noodles and French beans – *crème brûlée*.

Hummus – tomatoes stuffed with rice – green salad with Gruyère cheese (or you could serve cheese sauce) – orange fruit salad.

Red cabbage and chestnut casserole – jacket potatoes filled with low-fat quark or soured cream and chopped chives – little coffee custards.

Chilled cucumber soup – red pepper stew with brown rice – green salad with Gruyère – chilled yoghurt.

Biriani – curry sauce – tomato side salad – chopped hardboiled eggs, roasted peanuts, poppadums, mango chutney – special ground rice pudding.

Small portions haricot bean salad with bread and butter – ratatouille with potatoes Anna (with layers of cheese) – crêpes suzette.

If you follow the suggestions I've given in the book you certainly needn't worry about missing out on any essential nutrients. The dairy foods, cheese, eggs, milk and milk products such as yoghurt are as rich in protein as meat, whilst the other forms of protein, nuts and seeds, pulses and cereals, are all nourishing if you mix ingredients from two or more of the categories at the same meal – I've given lots of suggestions with the individual recipes. If you want to go into this question of vegetarian nutrition more deeply you will find I've explained it in more detail in my book *Not Just a Load of Old Lentils* and also in *The Bean Book*. But honestly, there really isn't a problem and you needn't worry that you'll be undernourished!

Soups

A bowl of home-made soup makes a very welcoming start to a meal. It can even become the main part of the meal if it's a filling soup: one of our favourite weekend lunches in winter is a good lentil soup with hot rolls and cheese and fresh fruit. There are other hearty soups to choose from besides lentil; French onion soup, with its cheesy bread topping is another favourite, and vivid beetroot soup from Russia is cheering to look at as well as filling to eat on a cold day.

For serving before other more substantial dishes there are some lighter soups made from puréed vegetables, fresh-tasting and delicious, as well as some chilled soups. I know some people find the idea of chilled soups rather strange, but they make a beautifully refreshing start to a summer meal. Both the chilled avocado soup and the chilled cucumber soup are also very easy to do if you've got a liquidizer.

Personally I consider a liquidizer to be almost essential for soup making, but you could use a Mouli-légumes for nearly all the soups in this section if you prefer.

In most of the soups the thickening comes from the vegetables themselves after they have been puréed. This usually seems to be sufficient, especially if a little potato is included in the ingredients. Quite often I liquidize half or three-quarters of the mixture to give the soup a thick, smooth base, and leave the rest as it is to supply some texture and add interest, but this is something you can vary according to how you feel and the effect you want to achieve.

You will notice in the recipes that sometimes I suggest using vegetable stock, sometimes just water and sometimes a choice. I think some soups, like French onion soup, for instance, need stock to give a good flavour; you can use home-made stock, or vegetarian stock cubes or powder from a health shop. There are other soups, however, particularly the simple vegetable soups, for which I don't think it is so important to use stock, and

27

sometimes I think you can even get a better effect by just using water which allows the full flavour of the vegetables to come through, so don't feel guilty if you haven't got any stock.

I've also found it a mistake to think that the longer soups cook the tastier they'll be. This may be true of meat soups, but with vegetable soups once the vegetables are tender there's no point in further cooking and the soup tastes fresher if it's not over-cooked.

Soups are fun to serve because it doesn't take much extra trouble to make them look really pretty. A few fresh green herbs snipped over a pale soup, a swirl of cream on a deep-coloured tomato or beetroot soup or some crunchy little cubes of fried bread topping a smooth-textured soup take only moments and make the soup look and taste extra good.

BEETROOT SOUP

This soup looks very warming and appetizing, its rich ruby red swirled with soured cream. Although borsch, to give it its Russian name, is usually made with beef stock and may contain meat as well, there are numerous versions throughout Russia, the only consistent ingredient being beetroot. So I don't think my vegetarian one is too far-fetched. In Russia borsch is often accompanied by little cottage or curd cheese tartlets, *vatrushki*, which turn it into a complete lunch or supper.

2 large onions
2 large carrots
2 stalks celery
125 g (4 oz) cabbage
2 tablespoons vegetable oil
1 litre (1¾ pints) water or
  vegetable stock
225 g (8 oz) can tomatoes
Serves 4–6

450 g (1 lb) cooked beetroot
  (not beetroot in vinegar)
Sea salt
Sugar
150 ml (5 fl oz) carton
  soured cream (optional)
Fresh dill or chives (optional)

Peel and chop the onions; scrape and dice the carrots and slice the celery and cabbage. Heat the oil in a good-sized saucepan and add the prepared vegetables; stir them so that they all get coated with the oil, then leave them to fry over a gentle heat for about 10 minutes, stirring from time to time. Stir in the water or vegetable stock and tomatoes, bring up to the boil, then cover the saucepan and leave the soup to simmer for about 20 minutes until all the vegetables are tender. (I sometimes use a pressure-cooker for this in which case it takes about 5 minutes.)

  While this is happening rub the peel off the beetroot and cut them into dice. Add the beetroot to the soup and season well with salt and a little sugar. Bring the soup up to the boil again and let it simmer gently for 3–4 minutes. You can serve the borsch like this, but I prefer to liquidize about half of it, which makes the soup slightly thicker while still retaining a nice texture. If using the soured cream whisk it lightly with a fork to make it creamy, then swirl a little into each bowl. Sprinkle with chopped dill if you've got some; or you can use chopped chives.

CHEESE AND ONION SOUP   ITALY

Although the ingredients used in this soup are very similar to those of French onion soup, the result is quite different because it is white with a smooth texture, and the cheese is stirred in just before serving to thicken and flavour it. If you've got time to do them it's very nice with some crunchy cubes of fried bread on top. It's a filling, protein-rich soup, lovely before a salad meal, or buttery pasta and green salad.

700 g (1½ lb) onions	125-175 g (4-6 oz) grated cheese
850 ml (1½ pints) water	25 g (1 oz) Parmesan cheese
25 g (1 oz) butter	Croûtons of crunchy fried
Sea salt	bread
Freshly ground black pepper	

Serves 4

Peel and chop onions, then put them into a large saucepan with the water and simmer them gently until tender – 15–20 minutes. Liquidize the soup, then return it to the rinsed out saucepan and add the butter and a little seasoning. When you're ready to serve the soup reheat it until bubbling hot. Take it off the heat and stir in the cheeses. Check the seasoning and serve the soup immediately.

If you reheat the soup once the cheese has been added don't let it boil or it might get stringy. Also be careful not to over-season the soup before you add the cheese because the cheese will make it taste saltier.

CHESTNUT SOUP
ITALY

The starchy texture and slightly sweet flavour of chestnuts go well with hot vegetables and make this a very warming winter soup. You can use fresh chestnuts if you've got time to prepare them but I must admit I usually use the dried ones which you can get easily now in health shops and some supermarkets.

700 g (1½ lb) fresh chestnuts or 225 g (8 oz) dried chestnuts.
1 large onion
2 large carrots
1 turnip

2 celery stalks
25 g (1 oz) butter
1 litre (1¾ pints) stock or water
1 tablespoon chopped parsley
Sea salt
Freshly ground black pepper

Serves 4–6

If you're using fresh chestnuts make a little cut in them with a sharp knife, then simmer them in boiling water until the cut opens – about 10 minutes. Remove the skins with a sharp, pointed knife – keep the chestnuts in the water until you're ready to peel them because the skins will firm up as they cool. If you're using dried chestnuts soak them in cold water for an hour or so then simmer them gently in plenty of water until they're really tender. I find this takes a good hour or more. Drain the cooked dried chestnuts, saving the liquid.

Peel and chop the onion, carrots and turnip; wash and dice the celery. Melt the butter in a large saucepan and fry the onion for 5 minutes, then add the rest of the vegetables and cook for a further 5 minutes before pouring in the stock. (If you're using dried chestnuts, make the reserved cooking liquid up to a litre (1¾ pints) with water or stock and use this.) Simmer the soup for about 40 minutes until the chestnuts and vegetables are tender. Stir in the parsley and season the soup with salt and pepper.

CHICK PEA SOUP

I think chick peas have a very special savoury sort of flavour, and here they are used to make a tasty soup. If possible you need to allow time for them to soak before cooking as this does speed up the cooking time. This is a useful soup for serving before the Spanish paella or stuffed peppers because it supplies plenty of protein.

225 g (8 oz) chick peas – you can get these easily from health shops
1 onion
2 carrots
50 g (2 oz) butter

1 tablespoon lemon juice
1 bay leaf
Sea salt
Freshly ground black pepper
A few croûtons of fried bread

Serves 4

Soak the chick peas in cold water for several hours or overnight, then drain and rinse them. Put them into a saucepan with plenty of cold water and simmer gently until they are tender – this can take as long as an hour or even more. Then drain the chick peas, keeping the liquid. Measure this and make it up to 1·2 litres (2 pints) with some water or stock.

Peel and chop the onion; scrape the carrots and cut them up into dice. Melt half the butter in a large saucepan and fry the onion and carrot for 5 minutes, letting them get golden brown. Stir them often so that they don't stick, then add the chick peas, liquid, lemon juice and the bay leaf and simmer the soup gently until the vegetables are tender – about 20 minutes. Take out the bay leaf and liquidize the soup. Put it into a clean saucepan, stir in the remaining butter and season to taste. Serve topped with croûtons of fried bread.

CHILLED AVOCADO SOUP

This soup is a good way of making two avocados feed six people. It's very easy to make (with a liquidizer) and comes out a creamy very pale green colour. It's best not to make it more than about 45 minutes in advance in case it discolours.

2 large ripe avocado pears – make sure they feel slightly soft all over when you hold them in the palm of your hand
1 tablespoon lemon juice

850 ml (1½ pints) ice-cold creamy milk
Sea salt
Freshly ground black pepper
2 tablespoons chopped chives

Serves 6

Cut the avocados in half, then twist the two halves apart and remove the stones. Carefully peel off the skin. Cut the avocados into chunks and put these into the liquidizer goblet with the lemon juice and milk. Blend at medium speed until the mixture is smooth. Season with salt and pepper. Put the soup into the fridge to chill until it's needed; if there's room it's a good idea to put the soup bowls in too.

When you're ready to serve ladle the soup into the bowls and sprinkle generously with chopped chives.

CHILLED CHERRY SOUP

No one finds it odd to start a meal with melon and really a fruit soup is only taking this a stage further! Anyway, this black cherry soup looks so delicious with its topping of soured cream that I don't think you'll have much trouble persuading people to try it. I usually use frozen or canned morello cherries but of course fresh ones would be better if you can get them.

450 g (1 lb) frozen or fresh
  morello cherries
850 ml (1½ pints) water
225 g (8 oz) caster sugar
  (or use two 425 g (15 oz) cans
  black cherries and omit
  the above)

2 tablespoons arrowroot
150 ml (¼ pint) dry red wine
A little lemon juice (optional)
A little soured cream

Serves 6

Stone the cherries by halving them and digging out the stones with a sharp knife; or use a cherry stoner if you've got one.

If you're using fresh or frozen cherries put them into a saucepan with the water and sugar and heat gently to dissolve the sugar, then bring them up to the boil and simmer gently until tender. If you're using canned cherries just stone them, put them into a saucepan and bring them up to the boil. Mix the arrowroot with a little cold water to make a smooth paste, then stir a ladleful of the hot cherry liquid into the arrowroot mixture. When blended add it to the saucepan and simmer for 2–3 minutes. Take the saucepan off the heat and pour the soup into a bowl. When it's cool stir in the wine, then chill it before serving. Taste and add a little more sugar if necessary or possibly a drop or two of lemon juice if you've used canned cherries and need to sharpen the flavour slightly; it should be sweet but refreshing. Swirl soured cream on top before serving.

CHILLED CUCUMBER SOUP   BULGARIA

Yoghurt, cucumber, walnuts and dill sound like rather a strange mixture but actually the combination of smooth creamy yoghurt and chewy walnut with refreshing cucumber and dill works well and this soup makes a lovely protein-rich starter for a summer meal.

1 large cucumber
1 garlic clove, peeled and
  crushed in a little salt
425 ml (15 fl oz) natural
  yoghurt
25 g (1 oz) walnut pieces
Sea salt

Freshly ground black pepper
1 tablespoon chopped fresh dill
  weed or parsley (or 1 teaspoon dried dill weed and
  2 teaspoons chopped fresh
  parsley)

Serves 4

Peel the cucumber (if you leave the skin on it can make the soup taste rather bitter), then cut it into rough chunks. Put the chunks into the liquidizer with the garlic, yoghurt, walnuts, about half a teaspoonful of sea salt and a grinding of pepper and blend until you've got a smoothish purée. Taste the mixture and add some more salt and pepper if you think it needs it, then pour the soup into a bowl and chill it thoroughly.

To serve the soup ladle it into individual bowls and sprinkle each with the chopped green herbs.

CHILLED CUCUMBER SOUP   TURKEY

This soup is rather similar to the preceding one but milder in flavour – no walnuts, garlic or dill, just mint and parsley. It's very refreshing and delicious in hot weather and also beautifully low in calories, so ideal for slimmers.

1 cucumber
425 ml (15 fl oz) natural
  yoghurt
8 sprigs of mint

4 sprigs of parsley
1 teaspoon sea salt
4 sprigs of mint to garnish

Serves 4

Peel the cucumber, then cut it into rough chunks. Put the chunks into the liquidizer goblet with the yoghurt. Wash the mint and parsley and remove the stalks; add the leaves to the cucumber and yoghurt together with the salt. Blend at medium speed until you've got a smooth purée. Transfer the purée to a bowl and place it in the fridge until it's really cold. Check the seasoning and add more salt if necessary – chilling tends to dull the flavour – then serve the soup in individual bowls with a sprig of mint floating on top.

If you want a richer-tasting soup for a special occasion you can replace some of the yoghurt with single cream but it's not so good for slimmers then!

GAZPACHO
SPAIN

Most people know of this chilled Spanish 'salad soup' and there are many versions of it. The method I've evolved is very quick and easy: you just liquidize canned tomatoes then stir in chopped fresh vegetables and herbs. If you keep a can of tomatoes in the fridge in the summer you can make this soup in a matter of moments. It's nice served with some crunchy cubes of fried bread.

1 large onion, peeled and cut into rough chunks

2 large garlic cloves, peeled and crushed in a little salt

792 g (1 lb 12 oz) can tomatoes

4 tablespoons olive oil

2 teaspoons wine vinegar

1½ teaspoons sea salt

Freshly ground black pepper

About 10 cm (4 in) cucumber

1 small green or red pepper

1 tablespoon chopped fresh chives

1 tablespoon chopped fresh mint

A few cubes of bread fried in oil

Serves 6

Put the onion and garlic into the liquidizer goblet together with the tomatoes, olive oil, vinegar, salt and a grinding of pepper and blend to a purée. (If you haven't got a liquidizer, grate the onion finely and pass the tomatoes through a vegetable mill, then mix them together and add the garlic, oil, vinegar and seasoning.) Chill the mixture.

Just before you want to serve the soup dice the cucumber and de-seed and finely chop the pepper. Stir the cucumber and pepper pieces into the soup, together with the freshly chopped herbs, then ladle the soup into individual bowls and hand round the croûtons of fried bread separately.

GREEN SPLIT PEA SOUP   HOLLAND

I must admit that this soup is a bit of an adaptation because it usually contains pork and sausages which are cut up and added at the end, but we think this vegetarian version tastes good and it makes a lovely warming winter soup. It's useful for serving before a main course when you want to add more protein to the meal but it's also nice for lunch or supper with just some wholewheat bread, cheese and fruit.

175 g (6 oz) green split peas –
   you can get these at health
   shops and you needn't soak
   them before cooking
1·2 litres (2 pints) water
1 onion
2 medium-sized potatoes

2 celery stalks
2 small leeks
½ teaspoon dried savory or
   marjoram
Sea salt
Freshly ground black pepper

Serves 4

Wash the split peas and put them into a large saucepan with the water. Peel and slice the onion and potatoes; wash and slice the celery and leeks. Add all these vegetables to the saucepan. Bring up to the boil and simmer gently until the peas are tender – about 40 minutes. Stir in the savory or marjoram and season the soup carefully with salt and pepper. You can serve the soup as it is but I think it's best to liquidize it or to liquidize half of it to make a good base and leave the remainder to give some texture.

LENTIL SOUP

I think this is one of the most comforting soups of all and as you don't have to prepare lots of vegetables it's also one of the easiest to make. It takes about 5 minutes to get everything into the saucepan, followed by 15–20 minutes gentle simmering, then a quick blend in the liquidizer and it's ready. Quite often when we get in late and the childen are milling around me in a hungry way I make the soup in a pressure cooker which cuts the cooking time to 5 minutes. (If you do use a pressure cooker, add a couple of tablespoons of oil to the mixture to prevent the water from frothing up as it comes to the boil.)

It makes quite a filling meal on its own with bread and fruit, or serve it before the low-protein Middle Eastern dishes such as rice-stuffed tomatoes or stuffed vine leaves to make a well balanced meal.

225 g (8 oz) split red lentils
1·2 litres (2 pints) stock or
   water
1 large onion, peeled and
   chopped

2 garlic cloves, peeled and
   crushed
1 teaspoon ground cumin
25 g (1 oz) butter
Salt and pepper

Serves 4

Wash the lentils, then put them into a large saucepan with the stock or water, onion, garlic and cumin; bring up to the boil and simmer gently for 15–20 minutes until the lentils are cooked. Liquidize the soup until smooth, then add the butter and seasoning to taste and re-heat the soup gently. This makes a thickish soup but you can of course thin it down with a little milk or water if you want to.

LETTUCE SOUP

I like this soup because it's such a good way of using up those outer lettuce leaves you feel so guilty about throwing away. It's also got a nice fresh summery flavour. For a special occasion it's lovely with the single cream added but for everyday you can leave it out and use extra milk instead.

1 onion	400 ml (¾ pint) milk
450 g (1 lb) potatoes	150 ml (5 fl oz) single cream
Outside leaves of 2 or 3 lettuces	Sea salt
	Freshly ground black pepper
25 g (1 oz) butter	Nutmeg
575 ml (1 pint) water	

Serves 4

Peel and chop the onion and potatoes. Wash the lettuce leaves and cut them up. Melt the butter in a large saucepan and fry the onion and potato gently for 5 minutes, but don't brown them. Then add the lettuce leaves and stir them for a minute or two so that they get all buttery. Add the water and milk and let the soup simmer gently for 15–20 minutes, until the vegetables are cooked.

Liquidize the soup and stir in the cream if you're using it. Season it with salt, pepper and a grating of nutmeg. Reheat it but don't let it boil after you've added the cream.

MUSHROOM SOUP

You can vary the character of this soup according to the type of mushrooms you use. Open mushrooms, or wild field mushrooms make a dark, richly-flavoured soup, while little white button mushrooms give a delicate, pale, creamy result. In either case, if you want to make the soup really special, add a tablespoonful of sherry at the end.

225 g (8 oz) mushrooms
Small piece of onion, peeled
1 bay leaf
1 garlic clove, peeled and
    sliced
A few parsley stalks
575 ml (1 pint) stock
50 g (2 oz) butter

40 g (1½ oz) flour
About 575 ml (1 pint) milk
Sea salt
Freshly ground black pepper
Nutmeg
Cayenne pepper
1 tablespoon sherry (optional)

Serves 4

Wash the mushrooms and remove the stalks. If you're using field mushrooms take off the skins too – but this isn't necessary with cultivated mushrooms. Put the stalks (and skins if you've removed them) into a medium-sized saucepan together with the piece of onion, bay leaf, garlic, parsley stalks and stock and bring up to the boil, then leave to simmer for 10 minutes to extract the flavours. Strain the liquid into a measuring jug and make the quantity up to 850 ml (1½ pints) with the milk. (You won't need the mushroom stalks, etc.)

Melt three-quarters of the butter in the saucepan and stir in the flour. After a moment or two, when it looks bubbly, pour in a quarter of the milk mixture and stir over a fairly high heat until it has thickened. Repeat the process with the rest of the milk in three more batches. Now chop or slice the mushrooms, fry them lightly in the remaining butter and add them to the thickened milk, together with salt, pepper, a grating of nutmeg, a pinch of cayenne pepper and the sherry if you're using it. Let the soup simmer for 3-4 minutes to give the flavours a chance to blend before serving.

ONION SOUP

FRANCE

Although French onion soup is usually made with brown meat stock, I've found that it's possible to make a surprisingly rich-tasting vegetarian version. The important part is the preliminary careful frying of the onions in the butter – and the sherry, if you can spare it, makes all the difference too. This soup is splendid served as a protein-rich starter before a light vegetable main course; it's also filling enough to make a lovely late night supper with just a little fruit to follow.

700 g (1½ lb) onions	Sea salt
40 g (1½ oz) butter	Freshly ground black pepper
1 tablespoon flour	Slices of wholemeal or French
850 ml (1½ pints) vegetable	bread
stock or water	125–175 g (4-6 oz) grated
3 tablespoons cheap sherry	cheese

Serves 4

Peel the onions and slice them into fairly fine rings. Melt the butter in a large saucepan and fry the onions slowly for 15–20 minutes until they're golden, stirring them from time to time, then mix in the flour and cook for a few seconds before adding the stock or water, sherry and a seasoning of salt and pepper. Bring the mixture up to the boil, then let it simmer gently with the lid on the saucepan for 30 minutes. Just before the soup is ready warm heatproof soup bowls and lightly toast a slice of bread for each; put the toast roughly broken into the bowls. Prepare a moderately hot grill. When the soup is ready check the seasoning, then ladle it into the bowls, scatter the grated cheese on top and place the bowls under the grill to melt the cheese; serve immediately.

If you have a large grill I find it's a help to stand the bowls on a metal tray or baking sheet – then they're easier to withdraw from the grill when ready. Alternatively you can put all the soup in a large ovenproof dish or soup tureen – in this case you'll probably need to use the oven to melt the cheese. Or another way of doing it is to prepare the bread and cheese separately under the grill and then pop it on top of the soup just before you serve it!

POTATO SOUP FRANCE

This is a velvety soup with a delicate creamy flavour. You can make it even better by adding a little cream at the end for special occasions but it's very good just as it is.

225 g (8 oz) onions
350 g (12 oz) potatoes
25 g (1 oz) butter
275 ml ($\frac{1}{2}$ pint) milk

575 ml (1 pint) water
Sea salt
Freshly ground black pepper
Fresh chives (optional)

Serves 4

Peel and chop the onion; peel the potatoes and cut them into small dice. Melt the butter in a large saucepan and put in the onion; fry it for 5 minutes, stirring often. Don't let it brown. Add the potato and cook for a further 2–3 minutes until the potato looks nice and buttery, then stir in the milk and water and a teaspoon of sea salt. Bring the soup up to the boil and let it simmer gently for 20–30 minutes, until the vegetables are tender. Liquidize the soup to a smooth creamy consistency then return it to the rinsed out saucepan and check the seasoning. Reheat the soup gently. It's nice served with a scattering of chopped chives on top to provide a little colour.

PUMPKIN SOUP JAMAICA

Pumpkin makes a very delicious soup, golden in colour with a delicate yet distinctive flavour. It's lovely sprinkled with chopped parsley and served with garlic bread at Hallowe'en.

1 kilo ($2\frac{1}{4}$ lb) pumpkin (this
   weight includes the skin and
   pips)

1 litre ($1\frac{3}{4}$ pints) stock
Sea salt
Freshly ground black pepper

2 large onions
2 large garlic cloves
25 g (1 oz) butter

150 ml (5 fl oz) single cream
   or top of the milk
Fresh parsley

Serves 6

Cut the skin off the pumpkin and scoop out the seeds; cut the flesh into even-sized pieces. Peel and chop the onion; peel and crush the garlic.

Melt the butter in a heavy saucepan and cook the chopped onions for about 5 minutes, then put in the garlic and pumpkin and cook for a further 5 minutes. Add the stock and some salt and pepper; bring to the boil and simmer until the pumpkin is tender – this takes about 15 or 20 minutes. Sieve or liquidize the soup then stir in the single cream or top of the milk. Reheat the soup gently. Serve in individual bowls with some chopped parsley on top.

TOMATO SOUP

FRANCE

This is a lovely light soup with a buttery tomato flavour. I think it's best when you can make it with fresh tomatoes in the late summer but I use canned tomatoes in the winter and it's still very good.

1 onion
350 g (12 oz) potatoes
25 g (1 oz) butter
450 g (1 lb) tomatoes or a
   425 g (15 oz) can
1·2 litres (2 pints) water
Sea salt

Freshly ground black pepper
Sugar
Chopped fresh green herbs –
   basil is best if you can get it,
   otherwise use chives or
   parsley

Serves 4–6

Peel and chop the onion; peel and cube the potatoes. Melt the butter in a large saucepan and fry the onion for about 5 minutes, until it's beginning to soften, but not brown, then put in the potato and stir over the heat for a minute or two until it is well coated with butter. With fresh tomatoes wash and quarter them – there's no need to skin them as the soup is first liquidized then strained at the end. If you're using canned tomatoes drain them and keep the juice. Add the tomatoes to the vegetables in the saucepan, mix them round and then pour in the water, or reserved tomato juice and water to make 1·2 litres (2 pints) in all. Bring up to the boil and let the soup simmer for 20–30 minutes, until the vegetables are tender. Liquidize the soup then pour it through a sieve into a clean saucepan. Season it with salt, pepper and about half a teaspoonful of sugar which helps to bring out the flavour of the tomatoes. Reheat and serve with a sprinkling of finely chopped fresh green herbs on top.

VICHYSSOISE   USA

I've often thought it surprising that you can make such good chilled soup from what are really winter vegetables – leeks and potatoes! It's rather a pity really that these vegetables start coming into season just when the days are getting crisp and you're thinking more of soups to warm you up than cool you down. But vichyssoise is so creamy and delicious that it always seems to be popular. If the weather gets really cold you can always serve it hot, when I think it's every bit as good.

1 onion, peeled and chopped	Sea salt
25 g (1 oz) butter	575 ml (1 pint) milk
225 g (8 oz) potatoes	Freshly ground black pepper
700 g (1½ lb) leeks	150 ml (5 fl oz) single cream
575 ml (1 pint) water	2 tablespoons chopped chives

Serves 6

Fry the onion in the butter for about 5 minutes in a large saucepan but don't let it get at all brown. While it's cooking peel the potatoes and cut them into smallish chunks. Cut the roots and most of the green top off the leeks, slit them down the side, open them out and rinse them thoroughly under the cold tap then cut them up into small rings. Add the potato and leek to the onion and mix so that everything gets coated in the butter, then let it all cook gently for a further 4–5 minutes but be very careful you don't let it brown. Stir in the water and a teaspoonful of sea salt and bring up to the boil; then put a lid on the saucepan and leave the soup to simmer for 20–30 minutes until the vegetables are tender. Liquidize the soup, adding some of the milk if you like, to make the process easier, then tip the soup into a bowl or jug which will fit your fridge and add the remaining milk. Taste and season the soup then chill it.

You can stir the cream into the soup before you serve it, or swirl some over the top of each bowlful then sprinkle with the chopped chives. It looks very pretty – palest green with the darker chives on top. It's a good idea to check the seasoning after you've chilled the soup and add some more salt and pepper if necessary, as chilling seems to dull the flavour a little.

WATERCRESS SOUP   FRANCE

I think this is one of the best soups because it's got such a lovely flavour and the ingredients are easy to get and don't take much preparation. My own special tip is to cook only the watercress stalks with the potatoes and add the chopped leaves at the end, just before you serve the soup. This makes the soup look and taste very fresh and inviting.

2 bunches of watercress

1 onion

450 g (1 lb) potatoes

25 g (1 oz) butter

575 ml (1 pint) water

Serves 6

275 ml ($\frac{1}{2}$ pint) milk

Sea salt

150 ml (5 fl oz) single cream
   or top of the milk

Wash the watercress carefully, then separate the tough stalks from the leaves; chop the stalks roughly. Peel and slice the onion and potatoes. Melt the butter in a large saucepan and add the onion; cook gently for 5 minutes (but don't brown it), put in the potato and watercress stalks (keep the leaves on one side for later). Stir the vegetables over a gentle heat for a minute or two so that they all get coated with the butter, then pour in the water and milk, bring the mixture up to the boil and let it simmer gently for about 15 minutes or until the potato is soft. Put the soup in the liquidizer goblet together with the watercress leaves and a little salt and blend until smooth. Stir in the cream or top of the milk and check the seasoning; reheat the soup gently.

Although the cream gives the final touch to the recipe and makes it suitable for extra special occasions, you can make a nice everyday version without it – just increase the quantity of milk to 400 ml ($\frac{3}{4}$ pint).

_____

YELLOW SPLIT PEA SOUP   CZECHOSLOVAKIA

This is quite a simple soup but it has a good flavour and is lovely on a cold day. The split pea purée is thickened slightly with some butter and flour which gives the soup a nice smooth texture and a buttery flavour.

225 g (8 oz) yellow split peas
1·7 litres (3 pints) water
25 g (1 oz) butter
1 large or 2 medium onions,
  peeled and finely chopped

1 garlic clove, peeled and
  crushed
25 g (1 oz) wholewheat flour
Sea salt
Freshly ground black pepper

Serves 4–6

Put the split peas into a saucepan with the water; let them simmer gently for 40–50 minutes until they're tender then liquidize them. Melt the butter in the rinsed out saucepan and fry the onion until it's golden, then stir in the garlic and flour. Cook for a minute or two, then gradually pour in the split pea purée, stirring until you have a smooth mixture. Let the soup simmer for 5–10 minutes to cook the flour, then season with salt and pepper to taste. This makes quite a thick soup; if you want it thinner you can always add more liquid.

You will need to use a large saucepan for boiling the split peas because of the way they bubble up as they cook. Adding a couple of tablespoonfuls of oil to the cooking water helps, or if your saucepan isn't quite big enough you can cook the peas using only 1·2 litres (2 pints) of water and add the rest when you liquidize the soup.

Sauces and Salad Dressings

These sauces and salad dressings are the ones which I find useful in practice and which go with the foods in this book. Some of them such as the milk-based white sauces and cheese sauce, also the sweet pouring egg custard, are an easy and delicious way of including more protein in the meal. Others, particularly the fruit sauces and the English mint sauce are good for adding piquancy and colour to the meal and seem to go with many vegetarian dishes just as well as the meat ones with which they are traditionally served.

APPLE SAUCE   GREAT BRITAIN

This sauce is also very popular in Germany where it's often served with crisp potato fritters – a delightful combination. It's also good with bean and lentil dishes.

225 g (8 oz) cooking apples   Sea salt
15 g ($\frac{1}{2}$ oz) butter
25–50 g (1–2 oz) granulated
   sugar

Serves 4–6

Peel and core the apples then cut them up into smallish pieces. Put the apple into a heavy-based saucepan with the butter and 25 g (1 oz) sugar. Cover the saucepan and set it over a fairly gentle heat for about 10 minutes, until the apple has softened and collapsed to a soft purée. Beat the mixture a bit with a wooden spoon then taste it and add a little more sugar and some salt if necessary. I think this sauce is nicest served warm.

CHEESE SAUCE   FRANCE

This cheese sauce, *sauce Mornay*, is useful both for incorporating into other dishes before baking or grilling them and for serving with vegetables to make them into more of a meal. Strictly speaking this sauce should be made with half Gruyère cheese and half Parmesan. The Gruyère makes it creamy and the Parmesan gives it a good flavour, but both are expensive and for day-to-day cooking I use a cheaper substitute plus a good seasoning of mustard, cayenne and freshly ground black pepper.

25 g (1 oz) butter
25 g (1 oz) plain white flour
1 bay leaf
250 ml (½ pint) milk
50 g (2 oz) grated cheese –
   Cheddar, or I like double
   Gloucester as it's creamy-
tasting and gives the sauce a
   pretty colour
1 teaspoon mustard powder
Cayenne pepper
Sea salt
Freshly ground black pepper

Makes 250 ml (½ pint)

Melt the butter in a medium-sized saucepan and stir in the flour; cook for a few seconds until the flour bubbles round the edges, then add the bay leaf, turn up the heat and pour in about one-third of the milk. Stir hard until the sauce is very thick and smooth, then repeat the process twice with the remaining milk so that you finish with a smooth, medium-thick sauce. Take the saucepan off the heat and beat in the grated cheese, mustard, a tiny pinch of cayenne pepper and salt and pepper to taste. Don't let it get too hot once the cheese has been added or it may go stringy and spoil.

CRANBERRY SAUCE
USA

Red cranberry sauce with its sweet yet slightly astringent taste is one of the most delicious parts of the traditional American Thanksgiving dinner, and of our British Christmas, of course. It goes surprisingly well with vegetable dishes such as the German potato fritters and the sweetcorn pudding from the USA.

175 g (6 oz) cranberries
4 tablespoons water
75 g (3 oz) sugar

Sort out the cranberries and remove any bruised ones; take off any little stems. Wash the berries and put them into a saucepan with the water. Cook gently until the berries begin to 'pop' and are tender – 7–10 minutes on rather a high heat. Add the sugar and simmer for a further few minutes. This makes quite a thick mixture, you can thin it with a little more water (or some red wine) if you like.

CURRY SAUCE INDIA

This spicy sauce is useful for serving with Indian rice dishes like *biriani* or with the spicy little Indian pastries, *samosas*. It also provides the basis of a quick curry – you just add some vegetables, simmer them in the sauce until they're tender then serve with fluffy boiled rice.

1 large onion
2 tablespoons oil, butter or ghee
1–2 garlic cloves, peeled and crushed
225 g (8 oz) can tomatoes
½ teaspoon ground ginger

1 teaspoon ground cumin
2 teaspoons ground coriander
1 bay leaf
275 ml (½ pint) water
Sea salt
Freshly ground black pepper

Serves 4–6

Peel and chop the onion and fry it in the butter, oil or *ghee* in a fairly large saucepan for 10 minutes, until it's tender but not browned. Add the garlic, tomatoes, spices and bay leaf to the onion, mixing them around so that they all get coated with the fat. Pour in the water and bring up to the boil, then turn the heat down, partially cover the saucepan and leave the mixture to simmer for about 20 minutes. Taste and season with salt and pepper. Take out the bay leaf and liquidize the sauce if you want it smooth; or serve it as it is if you would like some texture.

POURING EGG CUSTARD   ENGLAND

This is a sweet sauce, a real egg custard that is delicious with
puddings when you don't want to have cream; it's useful too
because it's a way of adding protein to the meal.

2 eggs	275 ml ($\frac{1}{2}$ pint) milk
25 g (1 oz) caster sugar – or use vanilla sugar if you've got it	A little extra vanilla flavouring

Serves 4–6

Whisk the eggs in a medium-sized bowl. Put the sugar into a
saucepan with the milk and bring just to the boil, then pour
on to the beaten eggs. Strain this mixture back into the saucepan
and stir over the heat for a minute or two until the sauce thickens.
This will happen very quickly and you need to be ready to take
the saucepan off the heat immediately. If, in spite of all your care,
it does overheat and curdle, I've found it's usually all right again
if I liquidize it, just like one would any lumpy sauce! Flavour
with a few drops more vanilla if you like. It's also nice flavoured
with grated orange or lemon rind. Serve this sauce hot or cold.

GRAVY   GREAT BRITAIN

I have to admit that this is not quite a traditional British gravy
because that's usually made with the fat and juices from meat,
but I hope you'll agree that this vegetarian version is also very
tasty. You can buy vegetarian stock cubes and powder from health
shops and these make a good basis for the gravy; so does Marmite
or one of the other vegetable yeast extracts. The preliminary
browning of the flour is important because this gives the gravy
a lovely nutty flavour and dark colour.

1 onion	A bouquet garni or a bay leaf
2 tablespoons vegetable oil	and $\frac{1}{2}$ teaspoon mixed herbs
25 g (1 oz) flour	Sea salt
1 garlic clove	Freshly ground black pepper
575 ml (1 pint) well-flavoured	
stock	

Serves 6

Peel and finely chop the onion and fry it in a saucepan in the oil for 5 minutes, then stir in the flour and continue to cook until the flour and onion are well browned. Add the garlic, stock and the bouquet garni or bay leaf and herbs. Bring up to the boil and let the mixture simmer for 10–15 minutes without a lid on the saucepan. Take out the bouquet garni or the bay leaf and season the gravy well with salt and pepper. You can serve the gravy as it is, with the bits of onion in it, or sieve or liquidize it to give a smooth consistency. For a special occasion it's delicious with a tablespoon of sherry stirred in.

MAYONNAISE   FRANCE

If you use a liquidizer to make mayonnaise it really is a quick and easy process. I find that mayonnaise keeps very well in a jar in the fridge.

1 whole egg	2 teaspoons lemon juice
$\frac{1}{4}$ teaspoon salt	200 ml (7 fl oz) olive oil or a
$\frac{1}{4}$ teaspoon dry mustard	mixture of olive oil and
2 or 3 grindings of black	other good quality oil such
pepper	as corn oil or sunflower oil
2 teaspoons wine vinegar	

Makes 200 ml (7 fl oz)

Break the egg straight into the liquidizer and add the salt, mustard, pepper, vinegar and lemon juice. Blend for a minute at medium speed until everything is well mixed, then turn the speed up to high and gradually add the oil, drop by drop, through the hole in the lid of the liquidizer goblet. When you've added about half the oil you will hear the sound change to a 'glug-glug' noise and then you can add the rest of the oil more quickly, in a thin stream. If the consistency of the mayonnaise seems a bit on the thick side you can thin it with a little boiling water or some milk.

MINT SAUCE   ENGLAND

Sharp-tasting yet sweet as well, mint sauce is lovely for serving with many lentil and bean dishes. It's particularly good with pease pudding.

Enough fresh mint leaves to make 2 tablespoons when chopped	1 tablespoon sugar 1 tablespoon boiling water 4 tablespoons cider vinegar

Serves 4–6

If you've got a liquidizer just wash the mint leaves and take off any stalks, then put the leaves into the goblet with all the other ingredients and blend until the mint is all chopped. Pour into a jug to serve.

If you'd rather make the sauce by hand, wash and chop the mint leaves, then put them into a bowl, add the sugar, boiling water and cider vinegar and mix well.

TOMATO SAUCE   ITALY

With canned tomatoes and a liquidizer this sauce really couldn't be easier and is one of my standbys. I find it best not to let the tomatoes cook for very long; this way the sauce seems to have a much fresher flavour.

1 onion	425 g (15 oz) can tomatoes
2 tablespoons vegetable oil	Sea salt
1 garlic clove	Freshly ground black pepper

Serves 4–6

Peel and chop the onion and fry it gently in the oil in a medium-sized saucepan until it's soft but not browned – about 10 minutes. Peel the garlic, crush it in a little salt with the blade of a knife and add it to the onions along with the tomatoes.

Liquidize or sieve the mixture, then put it back in the saucepan and reheat it. Taste the sauce and season with salt and pepper.

That's the basic recipe but you can vary it in lots of ways. Try putting a bay leaf with the onions to draw out its lovely flavour as the onions soften, or add a little chopped or dried basil, thyme or powdered cinnamon to the finished sauce; or stir a couple of tablespoons of red wine into the liquidized mixture before you reheat it. Another addition which I sometimes make, and which I'm rather ashamed to admit, is a little Heinz tomato ketchup; used discreetly it perks up the flavour without being at all obvious!

VINAIGRETTE FRANCE

The secret of a good vinaigrette lies almost entirely in the ingredients. If you use a really top quality olive oil, wine vinegar, sea salt and freshly ground black pepper and remember the proportions three or four parts oil to one of vinegar you really can't fail!

| 1 tablespoon wine vinegar – I think red wine vinegar has the best flavour | 3 or 4 tablespoons olive oil Sea salt Freshly ground black pepper |

Serves 4–6

Mix together the vinegar and 3 tablespoons of oil. Add a good seasoning of salt and pepper – remember the dressing will be weakened by being put with other ingredients so it needs to be well seasoned. Taste the dressing and if it's too vinegary add the remaining oil until you get the flavour just right. Pour the dressing into a small jug and stir it again before you serve it. This is also nice with a tablespoon of chopped herbs added, or a little mustard, depending on what you're going to serve it with. It's fun to experiment once you've got the basic mixture right.

WHITE SAUCE AND VARIATIONS   FRANCE

Strictly speaking a proper *sauce Béchamel* is made from milk which has been delicately flavoured by being heated in a saucepan with a clove, a piece of onion, a slice of carrot and a bay leaf, covered and left to infuse and then strained. I must admit that for normal cookery I generally use ordinary milk plus a bay leaf, and rely on good seasoning for the flavouring, but if you do go to the trouble to infuse the milk first, the sauce will be that much more delicate and delicious.

When making a sauce I always used to let it simmer for 10 or 15 minutes after I'd added the milk, to cook the flour. This was a nuisance because it was all too easy to burn it and also one had to remember to make the sauce a bit on the thin side to allow for it to reduce. Then one day when I hadn't got my milk measured out properly I added it in 2 or 3 instalments and I found the sauce had no floury-taste and needed no extra simmering. I realized that if you add the milk in batches and let the sauce thicken over a good heat before adding more, by the time you've added all the milk the flour has cooked and the process is much quicker. So I always make sauces by this 'batch' method now.

Sauce making is easy if you can remember the basic quantities. I find it difficult to hold figures in my head so I remember just one quantity and relate everything to that. 25 g (1 oz) each of butter and plain (white) flour and 250 ml ($\frac{1}{2}$ pint) liquid makes a

medium-thick sauce – the type you would use to cover cauliflower
or stuffed pancakes, commonly called a coating sauce. If you
want it thicker or thinner you simply decrease or increase the
quantity of milk: 400 ml (¾ pint) milk gives a thickish pouring
sauce, 575 ml (1 pint) gives a thin pouring sauce.

25 g (1 oz) butter or margarine	1 bay leaf
25 g (1 oz) plain white flour	Sea salt
250 ml (½ pint) milk – ordinary	Freshly ground black pepper
milk or milk that you have	Nutmeg
flavoured as above	

Makes 250 ml (½ pint)

Put the butter or margarine into a medium-sized saucepan and
melt it gently over quite a low heat, then stir in the flour and add
the bay leaf. Let the flour cook for a few seconds, then turn up the
heat, pour in one-third of the milk and stir vigorously until you've
got a very thick, smooth sauce, then add another third of the milk.
At first the sauce will look lumpy but don't worry, continue
stirring over a high heat and soon the sauce will be beautifully
smooth again.

Repeat the process with your final batch of milk, then when
the sauce is smooth turn down the heat and season the sauce with
salt, pepper and a grating of nutmeg. It's now ready to serve,
but if you want to make it look extra good and glossy for a
special occasion you can beat in about 15 g (½ oz) extra butter
at the last minute.

If you're making the sauce in advance and want to prevent a
skin forming you can dot this extra butter over the surface, then
beat it in when you reheat it. Alternatively a circle of damp
greaseproof paper pressed down on to the surface of the sauce
also stops it getting a skin.

MUSHROOM SAUCE

This is good with vegetables and for serving with pasta and

gnocchi. To make it, wash and finely slice 125 g (4 oz) button mushrooms and add them to the basic Béchamel sauce. Some people fry the mushrooms lightly in butter before adding them to the sauce but I prefer the less rich version I've given.

WHITE ONION SAUCE

Another useful variation, good when you want to add more flavour to a meal. Make it by peeling and finely chopping an onion; fry the onion in the butter before adding the flour. I I think this is nice flavoured with a pinch of ground cloves.

PARSLEY SAUCE

For this fresh-tasting variation add 1 or 2 tablespoons of finely chopped parsley to the Béchamel sauce. Or, an easier way, take the stalks off a few sprigs of parsley and put the sprigs into the liquidizer with the sauce; blend for a few seconds.

WINE SAUCE
FRANCE

This sauce always makes a meal taste special. You can either use a cheap wine for the sauce or buy a little extra to have with the meal and use some to make the sauce.

400 ml ($\frac{3}{4}$ pint) stock
400 ml ($\frac{3}{4}$ pint) red wine
1 bay leaf
A piece of onion, peeled
1 garlic clove, peeled and sliced
A pinch of dried thyme
$\frac{1}{2}$ teaspoon black peppercorns

2–3 parsley stalks
1 tablespoon redcurrant jelly
Sea salt
Freshly ground black pepper
40 g ($1\frac{1}{2}$ oz) butter, softened
20 g ($\frac{3}{4}$ oz) flour

Serves 6

Put the stock and red wine into a saucepan with the bay leaf, onion, garlic, thyme, peppercorns and parsley stalks and bring to the boil. Let the mixture boil vigorously for 10–15 minutes so that the amount of liquid reduces to half. Strain the liquid into a clean saucepan and mix in the redcurrant jelly and some salt and pepper. Next make a *beurre manié:* mash half the butter with the flour to make a paste and add this, in small pieces, to the still-warm sauce, mixing well after you've added each piece. Put the sauce back over the heat and stir it gently until it has thickened slightly. Then let the sauce simmer gently for a few minutes to cook the flour. Check the seasoning again and beat the remaining butter into the sauce just before serving to make it look glossy and appetizing.

If you want to prepare the sauce in advance, after you've added the *beurre manié* and simmered the sauce for a few minutes, take it off the heat and dot the remaining butter over the top of the sauce to prevent a skin forming. When you're ready heat the sauce gently and stir the butter in.

Dips and Spreads

These dips and spreads are really the vegetarian alternative to pâtés and meat pastes. If you serve them with something crisp like fingers of hot buttered toast they make a delicious first course; or for a party you can spread them on little crackers and garnish them with pieces of olive, gherkin or parsley.

One of these dips with a bowl of home-made soup and some hot rolls or toast makes a welcoming late supper or winter lunch. In the summer they're also nice served very cold from the fridge with some crisp salad.

Some of the dips contain protein which makes them useful for serving as a starter when you want to increase the nourishment of a meal, or for putting in sandwiches for packed lunches.

As with soups, I think you really need a liquidizer for making dips; you can get such a deliciously smooth and creamy texture that way.

In my view dips should have a slightly salty, tangy flavour to whet the appetite, so they need careful seasoning, and it's worth using good quality olive oil and wine vinegar if possible.

The sesame cream or *tahini* that's used in two of the recipes can be bought from health shops. It's very nourishing indeed, and an excellent source of calcium. It's quite expensive but it keeps for ages.

AÏOLI WITH CRUDITÉS   FRANCE

Crisp raw vegetables dipped in smooth garlic-flavoured mayonnaise make a delicious starter or can become a complete salad meal with a lentil or vegetable soup and some wholewheat bread or rolls.

If you want to serve aïoli but hesitate on account of all the calories it contains you might like to do what I usually do and use half mayonnaise and half natural yoghurt; or add some garlic to the dressing given for the Russian cucumber salad with soured cream and hardboiled eggs and use that instead of the mayonnaise. It tastes surprisingly like mayonnaise but contains no oil.

The *crudités* can be a gloriously colourful selection of whatever fresh vegetables are available: crunchy red radishes served whole with some of the green part still attached; bright orange carrot cut into matchsticks; red or green pepper de-seeded and cut into strips; tiny crimson cubes of raw beetroot; sprigs of pearly cauliflower; small very fresh mushrooms; baby green Brussels sprouts served whole or bigger ones (as long as they're firm) cut into halves or quarters; spring onions, shiny white and just trimmed; pieces of crunchy fennel bulb; juicy cucumber in chunks; crisp leaves of chicory or sticks of celery; quarters of firm red tomatoes.

For the crudités
A selection of vegetables as above; about 4 or 5 different types.

For the aïoli:

1 egg	$\frac{1}{4}$ teaspoon pepper
2–4 garlic cloves, peeled and crushed	2 teaspoons wine vinegar
	2 teaspoons lemon juice
$\frac{1}{4}$ teaspoon sea salt	200 ml (7 fl oz) salad oil
$\frac{1}{4}$ teaspoon dry mustard	

Serves 4–6

Break the egg into the liquidizer goblet and add the garlic, salt, mustard, pepper, vinegar and lemon juice. Blend at medium speed for about 1 minute. Then turn the speed to high and gradually add the oil, drop by drop, through the top of the goblet lid. When about half the oil has been added and you hear the sound of the mixture change you can add the oil more quickly in a thin stream. If the mixture is very thick you can thin it by stirring in a little hot water; or if you're doing the yoghurt version add this now, stirring it gently into the mayonnaise. Spoon the aïoli into a bowl and stand it on a large plate or small tray with the *crudités* arranged around it. People can then help themselves to a spoonful of the aïoli and some of the vegetables and eat them together.

AUBERGINE AND SESAME PÂTÉ   MIDDLE EAST

In this pâté, *baba ghannooj*, the intense, subtle flavour of the aubergine goes well with the rich, earthy taste of the sesame cream and the texture is substantial without being at all heavy. I think it's nice with fingers of crisp toast or some warm pitta bread. It makes a good light lunch dish after lentil soup.

2 medium aubergines – about 450 g (1 lb)	Freshly ground black pepper
2 heaped tablespoons sesame cream *(tahini)*	Crisp lettuce leaves
1 tablespoon lemon juice	Olive oil
1 large garlic clove, peeled and crushed	Sesame seeds, if available
Sea salt	Fresh parsley and chives
	Fingers of hot wholewheat toast or some warm pitta bread

Serves 4–6

Prick the aubergines, then place them on a baking sheet and bake in a fairly hot oven – say 200°C (400°F), gas mark 6. But don't heat it specially; the aubergines will bake with something else and adapt to any temperature from about 160°C (325°F), gas mark 3 to 230°C (450°F), gas mark 8. They'll take about 20–30 minutes, depending on the temperature, and are done when they can be pierced easily with the point of a sharp knife. Let them cool, then remove the stalks. Chop the aubergine flesh as finely as you can then mix it with all the other ingredients, or put the aubergine into the liquidizer goblet with the sesame cream, lemon juice and garlic and blend until fairly smooth. You will probably have to do this in several short bursts, stopping the machine and stirring the mixture in between, as it is fairly thick. Season the mixture with salt and pepper, then chill it.

To serve, spoon the pâté into little dishes and smooth the tops, or arrange a bed of lettuce leaves on small plates and spoon it on top. Pour a little olive oil over the pâté, sprinkle with some whole sesame seeds, if you have them, and snip some parsley and chives over the top of everything. Hand round hot fingers of whole-wheat toast or warm pitta bread.

AVOCADO DIP   MEXICO

In Mexico this creamy pale green avocado mixture, *guacamole*, would probably be served as a sauce or as a filling for tortillas but we think it makes a lovely starter either served on a base of crisp lettuce heart or with some crunchy Melba toast. It's also another good way of making two avocados feed six people.

2 large ripe avocado pears	Freshly ground black pepper
2 tablespoons lemon juice	Paprika pepper
1 garlic clove	Crisp lettuce leaves or Melba
Sea salt	toast
Tabasco sauce	

Serves 6

Cut the avocados in half, twist the halves in opposite directions to separate them and remove the stones. Carefully peel off the

67

skins – they should come away quite easily if the avocados are really ripe. Put the avocado into a bowl, sprinkle it with lemon juice and mash it with a fork. Peel the garlic and crush it in a little salt with the blade of a knife; add the garlic to the avocado together with a drop or two of Tabasco (go carefully as it's hot) and some pepper. Taste and add more salt, pepper and Tabasco as necessary. Either spoon the *guacamole* on to a plate, decorate the top with the prongs of a fork and sprinkle with paprika pepper to give a nice touch of scarlet against the pale green, or arrange lettuce leaves on small individual plates and spoon the *guacamole* on top.

Guacamole is best made just before you need it; don't keep it waiting more than 1 hour or the avocado will begin to discolour.

BEAN PÂTÉ
MIDDLE EAST

You're supposed to use *ful medames* or dried broad beans for this dip but these are hard to get and I find it tastes good with other types of bean. British field beans have the right earthy sort of flavour and so have continental lentils, which I like best of all for this recipe because you don't need to sieve them like the beans. This is a protein-rich dish, so it makes a useful starter before a salad or vegetable meal. It is also good as a sandwich filling or as a spread for little biscuits.

175 g (6 oz) *ful medames* beans, British field beans or continental (whole) lentils
2 tablespoons olive oil
1 tablespoon lemon juice
1 garlic clove, peeled and crushed
1 tablespoon finely chopped parsley

Sea salt
Freshly ground black pepper
Sugar
4 black olives·
Fingers of hot brown toast
Butter

Serves 4

Cover the beans generously with boiling water and leave them to soak for 4–5 hours if possible (not so long if you're using lentils), then drain and rinse them, put them into a good-sized saucepan with plenty of cold water and simmer them over a gentle heat until they're tender – $1\frac{1}{4}$–$1\frac{1}{2}$ hours for beans, 30–45 minutes for lentils. Drain the beans or lentils, reserving the liquid. Pass the beans through a vegetable mill or mash the lentils with a fork, then mix in the olive oil, lemon juice, garlic, parsley, salt and pepper and, if necessary, enough of the reserved cooking liquid to make a thick creamy pâté. Taste the mixture and add a little sugar if you think it needs it.

Spoon the pâté into 4 small ramekin dishes, smooth the surface and decorate each with an olive. Serve the pâté chilled and hand round fingers of hot toast for people to spread first with butter and then with the pâté.

CREAM CHEESE AND SOURED CREAM DIP

USA

An American friend gave me this recipe which she serves on Thanksgiving Day as a first course. Like the aïoli, it's superb with a colourful selection of crisp fresh vegetables for dipping into the creamy mixture. The recipe as I've given it makes a luxurious-tasting dip; for an even richer version you could use cream cheese (which was used in the original recipe); alternatively, for a less calorific dip, you could use natural yoghurt in place of the soured cream.

For the dip:

225 g (8 oz) low-fat quark
Two 150 g (5 fl oz) cartons
  soured cream
1 garlic clove, peeled and
  crushed

2 tablespoons finely chopped
  chives
Sea salt
Freshly ground black pepper

For the crudités:

A selection of about 5 different vegetables of contrasting colours, like those described for the aïoli on page 65.

Serves 6

Put the quark into a bowl and break it up with a fork, then stir in the soured cream, garlic and chives and mix to a smooth consistency. Season with salt and pepper. Spoon the dip into a serving dish and chill it until required. Arrange the colourful vegetables around the dip and let everyone help themselves to a spoonful of the creamy mixture and some crisp *crudités*.

GOAT CHEESE AND HERB SPREAD   RUMANIA

If you can't get goat cheese I find that crumbly white Wensleydale makes a good alternative, although it's not as salty. You can serve this spread in a pâté dish or if you want to be more Rumanian heap it up into a cone shape in the centre of a serving dish and surround it with tangy black olives, whole radishes, crunchy spring onions and quartered tomatoes.

125 g (4 oz) brynza or feta cheese (or use crumbly white Wensleydale)
125 g (4 oz) unsalted butter, softened
1 tablespoon chopped chives

1 tablespoon chopped green fennel, if available
1 tablespoon chopped parsley
Pinch each of paprika and caraway seeds

Serves 4 as a starter

Crumble the cheese finely. Put the butter into a bowl and cream it with a wooden spoon, then gradually beat in the crumbled cheese and the herbs and spices. Chill the spread, then serve it as suggested above or use it as a sandwich filling or a topping for savoury biscuits.

70

HUMMUS
MIDDLE EAST

If I, as a vegetarian, told you that one of my favourite dishes consisted of a purée of chick peas and sesame cream you might well be forgiven for thinking it was some strange vegetarian concoction, certainly too adventurous to be tried. Yet the dish I've described is of course *hummus*, one of the best known and most popular dips in the Middle East. It's interesting too, because it contains two complementary proteins and therefore represents excellent nourishment as well as being delectable. The sesame cream, *tahini*, can be bought from health shops. It tastes like rather earthy, slightly bitter peanut butter, but once you come to appreciate the flavour it's very more-ish.

225 g (8 oz) chick peas
8 tablespoons olive oil
3 garlic cloves, peeled and
  crushed
4 tablespoons lemon juice

4 tablespoons sesame cream
 (*tahini*)
Sea salt
Paprika pepper
Lemon wedges

Serves 4 as a main meal, 8 as a starter

Soak the chick peas in plenty of cold water for several hours, then drain and rinse them. Put them into a saucepan, cover them with fresh cold water and simmer them for 1–1½ hours until they're tender, then drain them, keeping the cooking water. You can pass the chick peas through a vegetable mill, then mix in half the olive oil and all the other ingredients, but I find the easiest way to make *hummus* is to use the liquidizer. Put the chick peas into the goblet with half the olive oil, the garlic, lemon juice, sesame cream and some salt and blend to a smooth, fairly thick purée. You may need to add some of the cooking liquid to enable the liquidizer to cope with this process and to bring the *hummus* to a nice creamy consistency. Chill the *hummus*, then serve it on a flat dish, with the rest of the olive oil spooned over the top and a good sprinkling of paprika. Garnish with lemon wedges. Or, if you're serving the *hummus* as a starter, it's probably easiest to cope with if you put individual portions on to medium-sized plates and top

71

each one with some olive oil and paprika. Serve it with extra olive oil and plenty of soft bread – pitta bread if you can buy or make it (see page 330); this is the usual accompaniment in the Middle East.

LIPTAUER CHEESE HUNGARY

This mixture of cottage cheese, soft butter and flavourings is popular in Austria, Hungary, Yugoslavia and Holland. It makes a good starter with hot fingers of toast. You don't need extra butter with it and it's quick to spread, so it's also good in sandwiches or on little cracker biscuits.

50 g (2 oz) butter, softened
225 g (8 oz) low-fat quark or
  cottage cheese
1 teaspoon paprika pepper

1 teaspoon chopped capers
1 tablespoon chopped chives
½ teaspoon French mustard
Salt and pepper

Serves 4–6

Beat the butter until it's soft and light, then gradually mix in the quark or cottage cheese and continue to beat until it's well blended. Add the paprika, capers, chives and mustard, then season to taste with salt and a grinding or two of black pepper. Put the mixture into a small bowl or pottery crock and serve it chilled; people can take a portion from the bowl and eat it with hot toast.

MOCK CAVIAR RUSSIA

This always popular Russian dip is made from aubergines. It has a luscious, slightly smoky taste and a lovely creamy consistency which goes beautifully with rye bread or wholewheat toast. It makes an unusual starter for when you're entertaining adventurous friends!

1 large aubergine – about
   450 g (1 lb)
1 large garlic clove, peeled and
   crushed

3 tablespoons olive oil
1 tablespoon lemon juice
Sea salt
Freshly ground black pepper

Serves 4–6

Before you make this dip you need to char the aubergine – this gives the dip its slightly smoky flavour. The easiest way to do it is to put the aubergine on the prongs of a fork and turn it over a gas flame until the skin is black and the inside is soft. Or you can place it under a hot grill or in the oven, turning it round from time to time so that it gets evenly burnt. Then carefully scrape off the skin (you don't need this!) and mash, chop or liquidize the aubergine. Put this purée into a bowl and stir in the garlic, oil, lemon juice and a seasoning of salt and pepper. Mix everything well together, then spoon the mixture into a small dish – or individual dishes – and chill until required.

Salads

The salads in this section can be divided into two types, those which contain protein and those which don't, and I've mentioned this in the individual recipes. Most of the protein salads can be made into complete meals, perhaps with some bread and another lighter salad, like green or tomato salad to accompany them. The butter bean salad from the Middle East, the haricot bean salad, chick pea and vegetable mayonnaise and *salade Niçoise* from France and the vegetable and bean salad from Poland are all examples of this type of substantial salad; there are others too. These protein salads are also useful for serving as a first course if the main dish is something which is rather low in protein, like a vegetable casserole; alternatively they can be served with the main dish as a side salad. The tomato, cheese and olive salad and the green salad with Gruyère cheese are particularly useful for this.

The non-protein salads make excellent side salads too, and these I serve alongside main dishes which contain plenty of protein, such as cheese flans or stuffed pancakes. They are often quicker to prepare than a cooked vegetable and very refreshing. Some of these salads also make good first courses before a substantial main dish; I particularly like the stuffed tomato salad, from Switzerland, which is good before a fondue, and the spicy mushrooms *à la Grecque*, from France, which are good before something like a soufflé.

AVOCADO AND CARROT SALAD   MIDDLE EAST

This mixture of pale green buttery avocado, crisp orange carrot and sweet raisins is very pleasant. If you serve the salad with some bread and butter and soft cheese or hardboiled egg wedges it makes a good lunch or supper.

1 large ripe avocado pear
A little fresh lemon juice
225 g (8 oz) coarsely grated
  carrot

Juice of 1 orange
50 g (2 oz) seedless raisins,
  washed
Parsley sprigs

Serves 2 as a salad, 4 as a starter

Cut the avocado pear in half, twist the halves in opposite directions to separate them, then remove the stone. Carefully peel off the outer skin of the avocado halves, using a sharp pointed knife to prise it up – it should then come away quite easily if the avocado pear is really ripe. Cut the avocado into long, thin slices and sprinkle them with lemon juice, making sure that the cut surfaces are completely coated.

Mix together the grated carrot, orange juice and raisins. Arrange the avocado slices on individual plates, top with the grated carrot mixture and garnish with parsley sprigs.

BEETROOT AND HORSERADISH SALAD AUSTRIA

A curiously pleasant mixture of flavours and textures, this salad makes a good accompaniment to cold savoury dishes.

700 g (1½ lb) cooked beetroot
1 eating apple
1 teaspoon caraway seeds

1 tablespoon sugar
2 tablespoons wine vinegar
1–2 tablespoons horseradish
  sauce

Serves 4

Peel and dice the beetroot and the apple. Put them into a bowl with the caraway seeds, sugar, vinegar and horseradish sauce and mix them all together lightly. Chill before serving.

BULGUR WHEAT, TOMATO AND PARSLEY SALAD   MIDDLE EAST

In this Middle Eastern salad, *tabbouleh*, parsley is used rather like a vegetable to provide the basis of the dish, and it's surprising what a big bunch you'll need to weigh 125 g (4 oz). If you haven't got enough I find you can use a bunch of watercress or some tender young spinach leaves instead. The bulgur wheat is quite easy to get in health shops.

225 g (8 oz) bulgur wheat
125 g (4 oz) parsley
25 g (1 oz) mint leaves
1 onion
3 tomatoes
2 tablespoons olive oil

Juice of 1 lemon
1 garlic clove, peeled and
   crushed in a little salt
Sea salt
Freshly ground black pepper

Serves 4

Cover the wheat with boiling water and leave it to soak for 15 minutes, then drain it thoroughly and put it into a bowl. Meanwhile wash the parsley and mint and chop them up fairly finely; peel and chop the onion and tomatoes, then add them to the wheat, together with the oil, lemon juice and garlic. Mix everything together and season with salt and pepper to taste.

Spoon the mixture on to a flat serving dish and press it down with the back of a spoon. Serve it chilled. You can sprinkle a little extra olive oil over the top if you like to make it look shiny. Or serve it simply, in a salad bowl or heaped up on crisp lettuce leaves.

BUTTER BEAN SALAD   MIDDLE EAST

Serve this substantial, protein-rich dish with a fresh vegetable salad such as the Middle Eastern cabbage salad or a platter of lettuce and juicy sliced tomato for a complete meal, along with soft wholemeal bread rolls or pitta bread.

175 g (6 oz) butter beans	1 tablespoon lemon juice
6 spring onions	3 tablespoons olive oil
2 tablespoons chopped fresh parsley	Sea salt
	Freshly ground black pepper

Serves 4

Cover the butter beans with water and leave them to soak for several hours if possible. Then drain and rinse the beans and simmer them gently in plenty of water until they're tender; drain them thoroughly (the liquid makes good stock). Put the beans into a bowl.

Wash and trim the spring onions, retaining as much of the green part as seems reasonable, then chop them up and add them to the butter beans, along with the parsley, lemon juice, oil and a seasoning of salt and pepper. Stir the mixture gently, being careful not to break up the beans, then leave it to cool. I think the salad is nicest served really cold.

CABBAGE SALAD WITH MINT   MIDDLE EAST
AND POMEGRANATE

Those large white cabbages make a good basis for winter salads when lettuce is scarce and expensive, but I think they need additional ingredients to make them really interesting. Here in this Middle Eastern salad the cabbage is flavoured with mint and topped with a flush of red pomegranate seeds. When you can't get fresh mint I find you can get a good flavour by omitting some of the lemon juice from the recipe and replacing it with the same amount of mint sauce – this makes a nice dressing for other salads, too.

450 g (1 lb) hard white cabbage (about a quarter of a small/medium white cabbage)
1 garlic clove
Sea salt
2 tablespoons lemon juice

3 tablespoons oil
Freshly ground black pepper
2 tablespoons chopped fresh mint
1 pomegranate
A few sprigs of fresh mint if available

Serves 4–6

Cut the cabbage into fine shreds with a sharp knife. Put these into a colander, rinse them under the cold tap then drain them well. Peel the garlic and crush it in a little salt with the blade of a knife; put it into a large bowl and gradually add the lemon juice, oil and a grinding of black pepper, stirring until it's all well blended. Put the cabbage into the bowl together with the mint and mix everything gently so that the cabbage all gets coated with the dressing and the mint gets distributed throughout.

Next prepare the pomegranate; cut it in half and carefully ease out the juicy red seeds using the point of a sharp knife or a pointed skewer or cocktail stick – catch the juice on a plate as you work. Arrange the cabbage salad on a shallow dish with the pomegranate seeds and juice poured over the top. Garnish with a few sprigs of fresh mint if available.

If you prepare the cabbage an hour or more before you need it you will find that it will soften considerably in the dressing; do not add the pomegranate until just before serving.

CAULIFLOWER AND APPLE SALAD
USA

This is useful for serving as a side salad with cooked dishes, particularly those containing cheese, and it's quick and easy to make.

1 small cauliflower
2 large sweet apples

Juice of 1 orange
Sea salt

Serves 4

Wash the cauliflower then break it into florets and slice fairly finely. Dice the apples, discarding the cores. Mix the cauliflower and apple together in a large bowl; pour in the orange juice and turn the salad so that everything gets coated with the juice. Season with a very little salt if you like.

You can add a tablespoonful or so of oil to the dressing if you like but I think orange juice makes a very refreshing dressing on its own.

CELERIAC SALAD
FRANCE

Celeriac, that knobbly root with the delicious celery flavour, makes a good salad. In some ways I prefer it to celery itself, although the texture is not as crisp. It's very nice prepared the French way in a mustardy vinaigrette, and makes a pleasant side salad to accompany either a hot or cold protein dish.

1 smallish celeriac – about
    450 g (1 lb)
½ teaspoon mustard powder
½ teaspoon sugar
¼ teaspoon sea salt
Freshly ground black pepper

1 tablespoon wine vinegar
3 tablespoons olive oil
1 bunch of watercress, washed
    and trimmed
Paprika pepper

Serves 4

81

Peel the celeriac and cut it into quarters. Keep the pieces under cold water while you make the dressing as celeriac quickly discolours. Put the mustard, sugar and salt into a shallow dish with a good grinding of black pepper and add the vinegar. Mix to a paste then gradually stir in the oil. Grate the celeriac straight into the dish, turning it over in the dressing as you do so to coat it well and prevent it from discolouring. I think it's best to use a fairly coarse grater as it gives the salad a nice texture. Taste the mixture and add a little more seasoning if you think it needs it. If possible leave it for 30 minutes or so to give the celeriac a chance to soak up the flavour of the dressing, then pile it into a serving dish, arrange the watercress round the edge and sprinkle the top with a little red paprika pepper.

CHICK PEA AND VEGETABLE MAYONNAISE   FRANCE

This combination of chick peas, cooked tender young vegetables and smooth garlic-flavoured mayonnaise, called *aigroissade*, is delicious. It makes a beautiful protein-rich starter or main salad dish with just some crisp lettuce or watercress. You can use all mayonnaise for the dressing but I prefer this lighter version.

175 g (6 oz) chick peas
700 g (1½ lb) tender new
  vegetables – potatoes,
  carrots, french beans,
  shelled broadbeans –
  cooked, drained and cooled
400 g (14 oz) can artichoke
  hearts, drained

1–2 large garlic cloves, crushed
6 rounded tablespoons mayonnaise
6 rounded tablespoons natural yoghurt
Sea salt
Freshly ground black pepper
A little chopped fresh parsley

Serves 4 as a main meal, 6–8 as a starter

Cover the chick peas with cold water and leave them to soak for several hours, then drain and rinse them, put them into a saucepan with a good covering of water and simmer them for about 1–1½ hours, until they're tender. Drain the chick peas thoroughly – the cooking water makes good stock for soups and sauces.

Cut the cooked vegetables and the artichoke hearts into chunky pieces and put them into a bowl with the chick peas. Mix together the garlic, mayonnaise and yoghurt then add this to the vegetables in the bowl, turning them over gently until they're all coated with the creamy mixture. Season carefully with salt and pepper. Cool, then chill the salad. Serve it heaped up in a serving dish, or spoon the salad on to crisp lettuce leaves arranged on individual plates. Sprinkle the top with chopped parsley to give a pleasant colour contrast. It's nice with warm soft rolls, French bread or pitta bread.

COLESLAW   USA

'Cole' is the general term for all members of the cabbage family and coleslaw is a delicious cabbage salad mixture. It's best made with firm white 'salad' cabbage in the winter and in the summer a compact, hearty cabbage such as Primo. If it's made an hour or so in advance the cabbage will soften a little which makes it easier to eat. It's useful as a side salad.

350 g (12 oz) white cabbage   3–4 tablespoons mayonnaise
2 medium carrots   Sea salt
1 small onion   Freshly ground black pepper
Serves 4

Wash and very finely shred the cabbage; scrape or peel and coarsely grate the carrots; skin and finely slice the onion. Put all the prepared vegetables into a bowl and stir in the mayonnaise so that you have a nice creamy mixture. Season the salad with a little salt and pepper.

This is the basic coleslaw but you can vary it by adding other ingredients such as chopped red or green peppers, raisins, chopped dates, roasted peanuts, sunflower seeds, cress, sprouted seeds, sliced apple or other fruits and green herbs. You can also use half mayonnaise and half natural yoghurt for a less rich, lower-calorie version.

CUCUMBER SALAD WITH SOURED CREAM AND HARDBOILED EGGS
RUSSIA

This refreshing salad makes a useful protein-rich starter accompanied by thinly sliced brown bread and butter. Traditionally the dressing is made with soured cream, but yoghurt can also be used for a low-calorie dressing which incidently makes an excellent slimmer's substitute for mayonnaise.

1 large cucumber
Sea salt
Whites of 4 hardboiled eggs
1 tablespoon chopped fresh dill weed or ½ teaspoon dried dill and 2 teaspoons chopped parsley
4 crisp nicely shaped lettuce leaves

For the dressing
Yolks of 4 hardboiled eggs
2 teaspoons wine vinegar
1 teaspoon caster sugar
1 teaspoon mustard powder
Sea salt
Freshly ground black pepper
150 ml (5 fl oz) carton soured cream or natural yoghurt

Serves 4

Wash the cucumber and remove the peel if you want to, then slice the cucumber into thin rounds, put them into a colander, sprinkle with salt and put a weight on top. Leave them for 30 minutes to draw out the excess water. Meanwhile chop the egg whites and leave them on one side. Make the dressing: put the egg yolks into a medium-sized bowl with the vinegar, sugar, mustard and some salt and pepper and mash them all together. Add a little of the soured cream or yoghurt and mix well to make a smooth creamy consistency; gradually add the remainder, beating well. Taste and season. Drain the cucumber rings and mix them with the egg white and dill; chill if possible.

When ready to serve arrange a lettuce leaf on each serving dish, divide the cucumber mixture between them and spoon the dressing over the top.

STUFFED CUCUMBER SALAD   ITALY

This is an unusual dish with a fresh, tangy flavour. It makes a good protein-rich starter or can be the basis of a simple lunch. It's nice served with thin slices of brown bread and butter and if you don't like onions use chopped chives or spring onion green instead.

1 large cucumber	1 tablespoon olive oil
150 ml ($\frac{1}{4}$ pint) water	$\frac{1}{2}$ teaspoon mustard powder
2 tablespoons wine vinegar	1 small onion, peeled and
Sea salt	chopped
Freshly ground black pepper	Sprigs of watercress
2 hardboiled eggs	A few radishes

Serves 2 as a salad meal, 4 as a starter

Trim the cucumber then cut it into 4 equal-sized chunks. Peel the chunks then halve them lengthwise and with a teaspoon scoop out the seeds to leave a cavity for the stuffing – you won't need the seeds. Put the pieces of cucumber into a saucepan with the water, wine vinegar and a little salt and pepper and bring up to the boil, then put a lid on the saucepan and leave the cucumber to simmer gently for about 5–7 minutes until it feels tender when pierced with a knife. There won't be much liquid left in the saucepan so watch it towards the end of the cooking time. Drain and cool the cucumber.

To make the filling shell the eggs and mash them with a fork, then mix in the olive oil, mustard, onion and salt and pepper to taste. Arrange the cucumber in a serving dish and spoon the filling neatly into the cavities. Decorate the dish with the watercress and radishes.

CUCUMBER AND YOGHURT SALAD
MIDDLE EAST

The combination of cucumber, yoghurt and herbs is very refreshing, making this a good salad to serve on a hot day, either accompanying a main dish, or as a starter.

1 cucumber
Sea salt
1 tablespoon chopped fresh
 parsley
1 tablespoon chopped fresh
 chives
2 teaspoons chopped fresh dill
 or fennel if available

275 ml (10 fl oz) natural
 yoghurt
Freshly ground black pepper
1 crisp lettuce heart, cut into
 4 or 6 pieces, one for each
 person; or warm wholewheat
 rolls

Serves 4–6

Wash the cucumber and slice it finely or grate it fairly coarsely. Put the pieces into a colander, sprinkle them with salt, place a weight on top and leave for about 30 minutes to draw out the excess moisture. Then squeeze the cucumber to extract as much liquid as possible and place it in a large bowl. Stir in all the other ingredients and season with pepper and some more salt if you think it's necessary.

This salad is nicest served really cold so put it into the fridge to chill for an hour or so if you can. You can serve each portion of the salad spooned over a crisp wedge of lettuce heart, or put it into small bowls and accompany it with fresh warm wholewheat rolls.

FENNEL AND CUCUMBER SALAD   ITALY

Raw fennel, with its crisp texture and slightly aniseed flavour, combines well with cool juicy cucumber and makes a refreshing first course or side salad.

1 cucumber	1 tablespoon olive oil
Sea salt	1 tablespoon chopped fresh
2 fennel bulbs	mint
6 crisp lettuce leaves	1 teaspoon caster sugar

For the dressing:
1 tablespoon lemon juice

Serves 4–6

Wash the cucumber then cut it into small dice and put these into a colander, sprinkling each layer with a little salt. Put a saucer on top and weigh it down with something heavy: leave for about 30 minutes, then pat dry. Meanwhile wash the fennel and trim off the root ends and tough stalks, but keep any tender stems and little bits of feathery leaf, then cut the fennel into neat slices and put them into a bowl.

Mix up a dressing: put the lemon juice, oil, mint and sugar into a bowl and beat them together until blended. Add the cucumber and the dressing to the fennel and mix everything together gently so that it all gets coated with the dressing. Taste and add a bit more salt if necessary (you may not need to because of the preliminary salting of the cucumber). Arrange the lettuce leaves in the base of a salad bowl, or put one on each individual serving dish, and spoon the salad on top.

GREEN SALAD

FRANCE

A well-made green salad goes with so many dishes; it's quick and easy to do and ideal for entertaining because you can serve it instead of a vegetable and then don't have to worry about last minute cooking. You can serve it with the main dish or, as is often done in France, afterwards, as a palate-cleansing course on its own, before the cheese.

1 large lettuce
1 bunch watercress

For the dressing:
1 garlic clove
1 tablespoon wine vinegar –
   red or white

3 tablespoons olive oil
Sea salt
Freshly ground black pepper
Fresh green herbs – parsley
   and chives, and others such
   as tarragon, chervil, lovage
   and fennel as available

Serves 4

Wash the lettuce and watercress, discarding tough stalks and damaged leaves. Dry the salad in a salad shaker, salad spin-drier or by patting gently in a clean tea-towel. Keep the salad in a polythene bag in the base of the refrigerator until you're almost ready to serve it. Meanwhile make the dressing – you can make it in a screw-top jar but I think it's easier to put the ingredients directly into the salad bowl and mix it in that. Peel the garlic, and either cut it in half and rub the salad bowl thoroughly with the cut surfaces, if you like a delicate garlic flavour, or for a stronger taste, crush the garlic to a paste in a little salt with the blade of a knife, and put it into the salad bowl. Add the vinegar, oil, some salt and pepper and mix well with the salad servers or a wooden spoon. Scatter the herbs on top of the dressing and leave in a cool place until just before the meal, then put in the lettuce and watercress, tearing them into manageable pieces as you go. Turn the salad in the dressing at the last moment so that it won't go soggy – I usually do this at the table.

A green salad is easy to make but its success depends on the quality of the ingredients: really crisp lettuce and watercress, the best wine vinegar and olive oil, sea salt and freshly ground black pepper. Make sure that you dry the salad carefully or the water clinging to it will dilute the dressing and spoil it.

GREEN SALAD   SPAIN

This Spanish-style green salad makes a useful accompaniment to dishes such as the paella and the Portuguese kidney bean stew.

1 large lettuce	Freshly ground black pepper
1 bunch watercress	1 large tomato
1 tablespoon lemon juice	1 large onion, preferably
1 tablespoon olive oil	Spanish
Sea salt	A few olives

Serves 4

Wash the lettuce and watercress, discarding any damaged leaves and tough stems; dry the salad in a salad drier or by patting it gently in a clean tea-towel. Tear the lettuce leaves into even-sized pieces and put them into a bowl with the watercress.

Make the dressing by mixing together the lemon juice, olive oil and a seasoning of salt and pepper. Add this to the lettuce and watercress in the bowl and turn the salad gently, so that all the leaves get coated in the dressing and are glossy-looking; arrange the salad in a mound on a large plate. Slice the tomato into thin rounds; peel and thinly slice the onion; arrange these on top of the green salad, together with a few olives. Serve at once.

GREEN SALAD WITH GRUYÈRE CHEESE

FRANCE

This delicious variation on the basic green salad makes a useful accompaniment to a low-protein main dish such as vegetable rice or stuffed peppers. Traditionally Gruyère cheese is used, but it's also nice with other smooth, firm cheeses such as Edam or Gouda.

1 lettuce
1 bunch watercress
125–175 g (4–6 oz) Gruyère
  cheese

For the dressing:
1 garlic clove
1 tablespoon wine vinegar

3 tablespoons olive oil
Sea salt
Freshly ground black pepper
1 tablespoon chopped fresh
  summer savory if available,
  otherwise use chives or
  tarragon

Serves 4

Wash the lettuce and watercress and shake them dry, then if possible put them into a polythene bag and pop it in the fridge to chill for a while. Cut the cheese into little dice and leave on one side. Peel the garlic clove, and crush it in a little salt with the blade of a knife and put it into the salad bowl together with the vinegar, oil, a little sea salt and a grinding of pepper and mix them round with the salad servers. Sprinkle the herbs on top and leave until just before the meal, then put in the lettuce and watercress, breaking them up with your fingers, and the cubes of cheese. Just before serving turn the salad over with the servers so that it all gets coated with the dressing.

HARICOT BEAN SALAD   FRANCE

Served with one or two other salad dishes, such as a green
salad and a tomato salad, and some nice soft wholewheat rolls,
this makes a delicious main dish for a light meal. It's also good as a
starter. The important thing is to cook the beans so that they're
just right: catch them when they're tender but before they start
to break up, because they get firmer as they cool and if they're
at all underdone it makes for a very chewy salad. I think the
mustard and sugar in the dressing go well with the beans but it's
really the chopped fresh herbs which make all the difference and
enable you to vary the flavour. If you can't get any fresh green
herbs, one or two chopped spring onions (including as much of the
green part as possible) are also good.

225 g (8 oz) dried haricot beans
1 teaspoon caster sugar
1 teaspoon mustard powder
1 tablespoon wine vinegar
4 tablespoons olive oil
Sea salt

Freshly ground black pepper
3 tablespoons chopped
   fresh green herbs; parsley,
   chives, mint, chervil,
   tarragon or fennel

Serves 4

Soak the beans in plenty of cold water for 2–3 hours if possible,
then drain and rinse them, put them into a saucepan with plenty of
cold water and let them simmer gently for 1–1¼ hours or until
they're very tender but not soggy. Drain. Put the sugar, mustard,
vinegar and oil into a salad bowl and mix together; season with
salt and pepper, then stir in most of the herbs and the hot beans.
Turn the beans gently in the dressing so that they all get well
coated. Leave them to get cold, then chill them. Serve sprinkled
with the remaining herbs.

LENTIL SALAD   FRANCE

You need continental (whole) lentils for this salad because they hold their shape when they're cooked. Combined with a good fruity olive oil, lemon juice and some crisp onion rings they make a delicious salad. If you serve it with some bread – soft wholewheat rolls, French bread or pitta bread – and a lettuce or other green salad it makes a complete meal.

225 g (8 oz) continental lentils	Sea salt
1 tablespoon lemon juice	Freshly ground black pepper
3 tablespoons olive oil	1 onion

Serves 4

Soak the lentils in water for a couple of hours or so if possible, then drain and rinse them, put them into a saucepan with fresh water and simmer them gently until tender – about 45 minutes. Drain the lentils thoroughly (keep the cooking liquid, it makes good stock) and put them into a bowl with the lemon juice, olive oil and some salt and pepper. Peel the onion and cut it into thin rounds then add these to the lentils and mix everything gently together. Cool, then chill the salad. It looks nice in a white bowl which contrasts with the rich brown lentils.

MUSHROOM SALAD   FINLAND

This salad differs from mushrooms *à la Grecque* in that the mushrooms are not cooked, so you need to use very fresh white button mushrooms. It makes a pleasant starter particularly if accompanied by soft warm wholewheat rolls.

225 g (8 oz) fresh white button
  mushrooms
1 tablespoon lemon juice
Sea salt
Freshly ground black pepper

2 tablespoons lightly whipped
  double cream, soured cream
  or natural yoghurt
Lettuce leaves
Fresh chives

Serves 4 as a starter

Wash the mushrooms, then pat them dry and slice thinly. Put
the slices into a bowl and sprinkle them with lemon juice and
some salt and pepper. Add the double cream, soured cream or
natural yoghurt and stir gently. Chill, then check the seasoning.
To serve the salad, spoon it on to lettuce leaves on individual
plates and sprinkle some chopped chives over the top.

    The mushrooms will give off some liquid after you've sprinkled
them with the lemon juice and salt and this will blend with the
cream to make a thin dressing. If you would prefer a thicker
dressing, sprinkle the lemon juice and salt on the mushrooms an
hour or so before the meal, then drain off the juice which will
have accumulated and fold the mushrooms through the cream
just before serving them, checking the seasoning. (The mushroom
liquid makes good stock.)

MUSHROOMS À LA GRECQUE   FRANCE

These coriander-flavoured mushrooms make an excellent starter
before a non-spicy main meal.

450 g (1 lb) small white button
  mushrooms
4 tablespoons olive oil
2 teaspoons ground coriander
1 bay leaf
2 garlic cloves, peeled and
  crushed

2 tablespoons lemon juice
Freshly ground black pepper
Sea salt
Lettuce leaves
Fresh parsley

Serves 4

Wash the mushrooms, halving or quartering any larger ones, then fry them in the olive oil with the coriander, bay leaf and garlic for about 2 minutes, stirring all the time. Turn the mushrooms straight into a large bowl to prevent further cooking, then add the lemon juice and a grinding of black pepper. Leave the mixture to cool, then chill it. Check the seasoning before serving the mushrooms piled up on lettuce leaves on individual plates and sprinkled with chopped parsley. They're also nice served in a bowl as part of a selection of different salads for a buffet lunch or supper.

SALADE NIÇOISE
FRANCE

I don't suppose purists would call this a *salade Niçoise* at all as it doesn't contain tuna fish and anchovies. But as there's no exact recipe and it's open to many variations I'm putting forward my vegetarian version which is a mixture of the other usual ingredients – tomatoes, cooked French beans, black olives and hardboiled eggs – all bound together in a good vinaigrette and served in a glossy, colourful heap. It makes a very filling starter or an excellent main lunch dish with soft warm wholewheat rolls or crunchy French bread.

1 large lettuce
450 g (1 lb) tomatoes
6 hardboiled eggs
450 g (1 lb) cooked French
  beans
12 black olives
2 tablespoons chopped fresh
  parsley

For the dressing:
1 large garlic clove, peeled
  and crushed
2 tablespoons wine vinegar
6 tablespoons olive oil
Sea salt
Freshly ground black pepper

Serves 4

Wash the lettuce and dry it in a salad shaker or by patting it dry with a clean tea-towel. Spread the leaves out on a flat serving dish. Slice the tomatoes, quarter the hardboiled eggs and cut the green beans into even-sized lengths. Put them all into a bowl together with the olives and parsley.

Next make the dressing: put the garlic into a bowl and gradually mix in the wine vinegar, then add the oil and some salt and pepper and beat it all together until it's smooth. Pour the dressing over the bean and tomato mixture and turn it gently so that it all gets coated with the dressing but doesn't get broken up. Heap the salad on top of the lettuce leaves and serve at once.

ORANGE AND RADISH SALAD NORTH AFRICA

Bright red radishes and golden segments of orange make a colourful salad. I find it's a useful salad for early summer when lettuce is still scarce but the first radishes have appeared and there are plenty of juicy oranges in the shops.

2 bunches of radishes   Sea salt
6 large oranges   1 bunch of watercress

Serves 4

Wash the radishes then cut them into rings. Using a sharp knife cut the skin and pith from the oranges and then cut the segments away from the white skin. Mix the oranges with the radishes and season to taste with a very little salt. Chill, then serve the salad in a border of watercress.

POTATO SALAD USA

For this salad you need firm potatoes which won't break up and go mushy when you mix them with the mayonnaise. In the summer new potatoes are ideal but in the winter I use King Edwards or Desirée. As with the chick pea and vegetable salad, and the Waldorf salad, I prefer to use a mixture of mayonnaise and yoghurt which is lighter and less fattening, but of course you could use just mayonnaise. You could also use the dressing given for the Russian cucumber salad with soured cream and hardboiled eggs.

700 g (1½ lb) new potatoes or firm-cooking old potatoes
Sea salt
2 rounded tablespoons mayonnaise

2 rounded tablespoons yoghurt
2 tablespoons fresh green herbs – parsley, chives, tarragon, fennel – whatever is available

Serves 4

Scrub the potatoes then cook them in their skins in boiling, salted water until they're tender. Let them get cool enough to handle then slip the skins off using a small pointed knife. (Cooking the potatoes in their skins like this really does make a surprising difference to the flavour.) Cut the potatoes into chunky pieces and put them into a bowl with the mayonnaise, yoghurt and herbs. Turn the mixture gently with a spoon until all the potatoes are coated with the dressing but be careful not to break them up. Check the seasoning, adding pepper and salt if necessary.

Cool, then chill the mixture and serve it heaped up on a dish: it looks good in a shallow glass one or on a base of crisp lettuce on a flat plate.

HOT POTATO SALAD WITH PEANUT DRESSING

SOUTH AMERICA

This is one of those dishes which sounds very strange but tastes really good. It's a mixture of hot and cold, bland and spicy, and it is rich in protein too. You can use ordinary salted peanuts but if you can get the plain roasted kind from a health shop they're better.

225 g (8 oz) roasted peanuts
150 ml (¼ pint) milk
50 g (2 oz) finely grated cheese
½–1 teaspoon chilli powder, or
  a small green chilli

700 g (1½ lb) potatoes
1 lettuce
1 bunch of watercress
4 tomatoes
1 onion

Serves 4

First put the peanuts and milk into the liquidizer goblet and blend until they're thick and fairly smooth – add a little more milk if necessary to give the consistency of whipped cream. Turn the mixture into a bowl and stir in the grated cheese. Add chilli powder to taste, or, if you're using a fresh chilli remove and discard the seeds and chop the flesh very finely – add it to the mixture a little at a time, tasting to get the right degree of hotness.

Peel the potatoes and cut them into even-sized pieces, then boil them in salted water until they're just tender; drain. Wash the lettuce, watercress and tomatoes; peel the onion. Slice the onion and tomatoes into thin rounds.

To serve pile the hot potatoes into the centre of a serving dish (or individual plates) and arrange the lettuce, watercress, tomatoes and onion round the edge. Spoon the peanut sauce over the potatoes and serve at once.

RED BEAN SALAD   USA

This salad looks particularly appetizing, with its shiny red beans and slivers of white onion. You can make it taste spicier if you want to by adding some chilli powder and cumin to the dressing. It makes a lovely lunch with home-made wholewheat bread and some lettuce and watercress.

225 g (8 oz) red kidney beans, soaked, cooked (see p. 22) and drained;
or use 2 cans of beans, drained
1 small onion, peeled and cut into thin slices
Fresh parsley if available

1 garlic clove, peeled and crushed
Sea salt
Freshly ground black pepper
1 tablespoon tomato purée
1 tablespoon red wine vinegar
3 tablespoons olive oil

For the dressing:
½ teaspoon mustard powder
½ teaspoon sugar

Serves 4

Put the beans into a bowl with the onion. For the dressing put the mustard, sugar and garlic into a small bowl with a little salt and a grinding of pepper. Mix to a paste with the tomato purée and vinegar then gradually add the oil and stir until everything is blended. Pour this dressing over the beans, turning them gently until they're all coated with it and look glossy. Check the seasoning and add more salt, pepper and sugar if necessary.

This salad looks pretty in a glass or white china bowl with chopped parsley sprinkled over the top.

RED CABBAGE SALAD   POLAND

This is a useful winter salad and the warm mauve colour is cheerful on a cold day.

It makes a nice side salad or accompaniment to a protein-rich dish such as a cheese flan. Because of its unusual colour it's also a good salad to include when you're making several for a buffet lunch or supper.

You can leave out the caraway seeds if you don't like them though they do give a lovely spicy flavour. I don't think the raisins are very authentic in this salad but we like them and I'm giving you the version I usually make – you can leave them out, too, if you prefer!

450 g (1 lb) red cabbage	2–3 tablespoons oil
2 eating apples	2–3 teaspoons caraway seeds
50 g (2 oz) raisins	Sea salt
1 tablespoon lemon juice or red wine vinegar	Freshly ground black pepper

Serves 4

Wash the cabbage then grate or shred it as finely as you can. I think it's best grated because then it makes a nice soft mixture which blends well with the other ingredients and isn't too chewy. Cut the apples into small dice discarding the cores and wash the raisins, then add these to the cabbage together with the lemon juice or vinegar, oil, caraway seeds and a little salt and pepper. Stir well so that everything is thoroughly mixed together.

RICE AND ARTICHOKE HEART SALAD   FRANCE

This makes a complete meal if you serve it with one or two other vegetable salads such as a bowl of crisp lettuce and herbs and a juicy tomato salad. If you serve it with the green salad with Gruyére cheese or the tomato salad with cheese and olives they will supply the extra protein needed; or the salad can be garnished with wedges of hardboiled egg. Alternatively you could start or end the meal with a protein dish such as a lentil soup or home-made ice cream.

225 g (8 oz) long-grain brown
  rice
575 ml (1 pint) water
Sea salt
400 g (14 oz) can artichoke
  hearts, drained
1 garlic clove
1 tablespoon wine vinegar
3 tablespoons olive oil

Freshly ground black pepper
1 tablespoon chopped fresh
  parsley
1 tablespoon chopped fresh
  chives
Extra parsley to garnish
3 hardboiled eggs, quartered
  (optional)

Serves 4

Wash the rice then put it into a heavy-based saucepan with the
water and half a teaspoon of salt and bring to the boil, then put
a lid on the saucepan, turn the heat down low and leave the rice
to cook very gently for 40–45 minutes. You should find that the
rice is tender and all the water has been absorbed. If there is still
a little water, put the lid back on the saucepan and leave it to
stand (off the heat) for 10–15 minutes.

While the rice is cooking cut the artichoke hearts into slices
and peel the garlic and crush it in a little salt with the blade
of a knife. Put the garlic into a small bowl and mix in the vinegar,
olive oil and a grinding of pepper, then stir this mixture gently
into the hot rice, together with the parsley, chives and sliced
artichoke hearts, using a fork to avoid mashing the rice. Check
the seasoning – rice can take quite a lot of salt – then leave the
mixture to cool.

Serve the salad heaped upon a shallow dish with a sprinkling
of chopped parsley on top and the hardboiled eggs, if you're
using them, tucked round the edge.

SPINACH SALAD USA

This is different from the Middle Eastern spinach salad because here tender young spinach leaves are used uncooked and they make a surprisingly good mixture. In this recipe from the USA they're combined with tomatoes and button mushrooms and tossed in a garlic-flavoured French dressing.

225 g (8 oz) very fresh tender spinach
2 tomatoes
125 g (4 oz) fresh white button mushrooms

1 tablespoon red wine vinegar
3 tablespoons olive oil
Freshly ground black pepper
Sugar

For the dressing:
1 garlic clove
Sea salt

Serves 4

Wash the spinach thoroughly then dry it in a salad drier or clean tea-towel and tear it into rough pieces, discarding any tough stems. Wash and chop the tomatoes and mushrooms.

Peel the garlic then crush it in a little salt with the blade of a knife. Put the garlic into a large bowl – you can use the bowl in which you're going to serve the salad – and add the vinegar, mixing it with the garlic to make a paste, then gradually add the oil. Season with a little pepper and a pinch of sugar, then put in the spinach, tomatoes and mushrooms and turn them lightly so that they all get coated with the dressing and look glossy. Serve at once.

COLD SPINACH SALAD

MIDDLE EAST

I know some people find the idea of a salad made from cold cooked spinach very off-putting, but I think the mixture of the soft, dark green spinach, the fruity olive oil and the sharp-tasting lemon juice is delicious. There are versions of this salad throughout the Middle East. Yoghurt can be included in the dressing or served with the salad, as in this recipe; cooked chick peas can be added, providing a pleasant contrast of colour and texture as well as protein. I also like it with a topping of slivered almonds fried golden and crisp in butter.

1 kg (2¼ lb) spinach	1 garlic clove
1 tablespoon lemon juice	275 ml (½ pint) natural yoghurt
3 tablespoons olive oil	Fresh mint, parsley or chives;
Sea salt	or 50 g (2 oz) slivered
Freshly ground black pepper	almonds fried in butter

Serves 4

Wash the spinach well then cook it in just the water clinging to it. When it's done drain it thoroughly and leave to cool. Chop the cold spinach and put it into a bowl with the lemon juice, olive oil, some salt and pepper and turn it gently so that the oil and lemon juice get well distributed.

Peel and crush the garlic then mix it with the yoghurt and add some salt and pepper. Put the spinach salad on to a flat plate and spoon some of the yoghurt mixture on top; garnish with chopped green herbs or fried almonds. Serve the rest of the yoghurt separately.

THREE-BEAN SALAD USA

This attractive salad shows off the contrasting shapes and colours of three different types of bean: red kidney beans, haricot or other white beans and chick peas. Other beans could of course be used; the aim is to get as much variety as possible. It's advisable to soak and cook the red kidney beans separately as the colour can stain the others slightly pink, but you can cook them all in one saucepan if you wish.

125 g (4 oz) red kidney beans
125 g (4 oz) haricot or other
   white beans
125 g (4 oz) chick peas
2 tablespoons chopped fresh
   green herbs

2 tablespoons wine vinegar
6 tablespoons olive oil
Sea salt
Freshly ground black pepper

Serves 4 as a main meal, 6–8 as a starter

Soak the red kidney beans in water in one bowl and the other two types together in another, then drain, rinse and cook them in fresh water until they're tender, again keeping the red ones separate if possible. Drain the beans well, put them all into a bowl together and add the herbs (you don't need to cool the beans). Mix the vinegar, oil and some salt and pepper in a small bowl, then stir this dressing into the bean mixture, turning the beans until they're coated with it and all look glossy. Leave the mixture to cool, stirring it from time to time, then chill it.

   Three-bean salad looks pretty served in a shallow glass bowl or white dish to show off the colours of the beans, or it can be spooned over crisp lettuce leaves and garnished with extra chopped fresh green herbs if you prefer.

TOMATO SALAD   FRANCE

One of the joys of late summer is getting firm, fragrant, orange-red tomatoes and then using them extravagantly, as in this juicy salad which I like to serve with pasta dishes.

700 g (1½ lb) tomatoes	1 tablespoon olive oil
1 small onion	Sea salt
1 teaspoon red wine vinegar	Freshly ground black pepper

Serves 4

Wash the tomatoes and cut them into slices. Peel and finely slice the onion. Put the tomato and onion into a bowl and gently stir in the vinegar, oil and salt and pepper to taste. Serve as soon as possible.

TOMATO, CHEESE AND OLIVE SALAD   FRANCE

If you serve this as a side salad with a plain pasta or rice dish it will supply the extra protein; accompanied by bread or rolls it also makes a delicious lunch, simple yet good. The type of cheese you use is up to you; the Brie or Camembert are delicious but I find a cheaper white cheese like Caerphilly is very good too.

450 g (1 lb) firm tomatoes	Sea salt
1 onion	Freshly ground black pepper
8 black olives	175 g (6 oz) soft white cheese
2 tablespoons olive oil	such as Brie or Camembert
1 tablespoon wine vinegar	or use Caerphilly

Serves 4 as a side salad, 2–3 for lunch

Wash the tomatoes and cut them into fairly thin slices; peel and finely slice the onion. Put them into a bowl with the olives, oil, vinegar and some salt and pepper and mix them lightly together. Just before you want to serve it cut up the cheese and add it to the salad. This looks good in a shallow glass bowl or white china dish. If possible don't make it more than about 30 minutes in advance or the juices will run and it could be a bit too wet.

STUFFED TOMATO SALAD SWITZERLAND

Stuffed tomato salad from Switzerland makes a refreshing starter in late summer when tomatoes are large and cheap; or it can make a light salad lunch after a substantial soup.

6 good-sized tomatoes – about
   450 g (1 lb)
Sea salt
2 eating apples
4 stalks of crisp, tender celery

1 tablespoon mayonnaise
1 tablespoon natural yoghurt
Freshly ground black pepper
Lettuce leaves

Serves 6

Halve the tomatoes round their middles and, using a teaspoon, scoop out the centres – you won't need them for this recipe. Sprinkle a little salt inside each tomato half and leave them upside down on a plate or in a colander to drain off any excess liquid.

   Wash the apples and celery then cut them into small dice and add the mayonnaise, yoghurt and a little salt and pepper to taste. Arrange the tomatoes, right way up, on a base of lettuce. Spoon the celery and apple mixture into the tomato halves, piling it up attractively.

VEGETABLE AND BEAN SALAD   POLAND

This salad, *salata mehania* from Poland, makes a lovely filling meal. It's nice with home-made brown bread or pitta bread. You can really use any dried beans but I prefer the red kidney beans as they're nice and colourful.

125 g (4 oz) frozen peas
125 g (4 oz) frozen green beans
125 g (4 oz) red kidney beans, soaked, cooked and drained, or use a 424 g (15 oz) can
225 g (8 oz) cooked potatoes, cubed
125 g (4 oz) fresh firm button mushrooms
1 celery heart
225 g (8 oz) firm cabbage, red or white

2 tablespoons chopped chives, if available
1 garlic clove
Sea salt
Freshly ground black pepper
½ teaspoon mustard powder
½ teaspoon sugar
1 tablespoon wine vinegar
3 tablespoons olive oil

Serves 4–6

Cook the peas and green beans together in a little fast-boiling salted water until they're just tender, then drain them. Put them into a bowl with the kidney beans and potatoes. Wash and slice the mushrooms and celery; wash and shred the cabbage and add these all to the bowl, together with the chives.

Peel the garlic and crush it in a little salt, then put it into a small bowl and add a grinding of pepper, the mustard, sugar and vinegar. Mix well, then gradually stir in the oil. Put this dressing over the vegetables in the bowl and turn them lightly so that they all get coated with it and look glossy and appetizing. Serve the salad in a glass bowl or on a base of crisp lettuce on a flat plate.

WALDORF SALAD USA

This salad contains a very pleasant mixture of flavours and textures: crisp celery, sweet apple and crunchy walnuts bound together in a creamy mayonnaise (I use half mayonnaise, half natural yoghurt). The only problem is the colour which can be rather dull so I try to use red-skinned apples which don't need peeling. Accompanied by crisp lettuce leaves, Waldorf salad makes an excellent lunch, and is also delicious as a protein-rich starter.

1 celery heart – about 225 g (8 oz) after it's been trimmed
2 red-skinned apples – about 225 g (8 oz)
125–175 g (4–6 oz) walnuts, roughly chopped
3–4 rounded tablespoons mayonnaise
3–4 rounded tablespoons natural yoghurt
Sea salt

Serves 4 as a main salad, 6–8 as a starter

Wash the celery thoroughly then slice it fairly finely. Quarter the apples and remove the cores, then cut the quarters into dice. Put the apple and celery into a bowl and add the walnuts. Stir in enough mayonnaise and yoghurt to bind everything lightly and give a creamy consistency. Taste and season with a little salt if necessary. The salad looks nice piled up in a shallow glass bowl and garnished with a few extra pieces of walnut, or heaped on to crisp lettuce leaves.

If you don't like the slightly bitter flavour of walnuts you can of course use other nuts for this salad. My family likes it best made with whole roasted hazel nuts: I spread 175 g (6 oz) of hazel nuts on a dry baking tray and roast them in a moderate oven – 180°C (350°F), gas mark 4 – for about 20 minutes or until the skins will rub off easily, then I cool them and remove the skins by rubbing the nuts gently in a soft dry cloth before mixing them with the apple and celery. You could also used roasted peanuts or toasted flaked almonds.

Accompanying Vegetables

These recipes are for the vegetables that you serve alongside the main dish, and some of them make good hot starters, too. They are mostly fairly simple ideas for making ordinary vegetables a bit different, or for preparing some of the more exotic vegetables like okra, fennel, pumpkin and sweet potatoes that you can sometimes find these days. One or two of the recipes contain protein – the Brussels sprouts with cheese, haricot beans with apples and potatoes Anna, for instance – which makes them another useful way of increasing the nourishment of a meal.

BRUSSELS SPROUTS WITH CHEESE   HOLLAND

This is really a very simple way with Brussels sprouts but it's useful if you want to add a little extra protein to the meal. It's also good for a dinner party because it means you don't have to deal with the sprouts at the last minute.

700 g (1½ lb) Brussels sprouts	125–175 g (4–6 oz) finely
Sea salt	grated Edam cheese
A little butter	Freshly ground black pepper

Serves 4

Set the oven to 160°C (325°F), gas mark 3. Wash and trim the sprouts. Leave them whole if they're tiny, otherwise halve or quarter them – that way they cook well and don't get soggy. Put 1 cm (½ in) water and a little salt into a saucepan and bring to the boil; add the sprouts, bring up to the boil again and cook for 2 minutes. Drain the sprouts immediately. Grease an oven-proof dish quite generously with butter and put in the sprouts; sprinkle the grated cheese over them and grind over a little pepper. Dot with a little more butter, cover with foil or a lid and bake the sprouts in the oven for about 20 minutes until the cheese has melted and they're piping hot.

If you want to keep the sprouts warm for longer I find they will stay nice and fresh-looking for quite a long time if you prepare them as above and put them in a lower oven – say 140–150°C (275–300°F), gas mark 1–2.

CABBAGE WITH SOURED CREAM   NORWAY

If you cook cabbage until it's just tender, then drain it well and stir in some soured cream you get a delicious mixture: simple, yet good enough for a special occasion. In Norway some caraway seeds would probably be added too, but these are optional.

111

700–900 g (1½–2 lb) firm
  cabbage, washed and
  shredded
Sea salt
150 ml (5 fl oz) soured
  cream

Freshly ground black
  pepper
1 teaspoon caraway seeds
  (optional)

Serves 4

Put about 2·5 cm (1 in) water into a large saucepan, together
with a teaspoonful of salt, bring up to the boil, then add the
cabbage. Let the cabbage simmer gently, with a lid on the saucepan, for about 7–10 minutes, until it is just tender. Drain the
cabbage well and stir in the soured cream, a good grinding of
pepper and the caraway seeds if you're using them. Taste and
add a little more salt if necessary. Reheat for a minute or two,
just to warm through the cream, then serve.

STIR-FRIED CHINESE CABBAGE   CHINA

Chinese cabbage, or 'Chinese leaves' as it's sometimes called,
is quite often found in the shops now and makes a lovely cooked
vegetable dish that's very quickly prepared. I like to stir-fry the
cabbage in the Chinese way; it's good with either an ordinary
Western-style meal or as part of a Chinese meal.

1 Chinese cabbage,
  about 700 g (1½ lb)
1 small onion, peeled and
  chopped
2 tablespoons oil
1 garlic clove, crushed
1 piece of fresh ginger, if
  available, peeled and
  grated to make 1 teaspoonful;

or use ½ teaspoon
  ordinary powdered ginger
1 teaspoon soy sauce
½ teaspoon cornflour
1 tablespoon cold water
Sugar
Sea salt
Freshly ground black pepper

Serves 4

112

Wash the cabbage and shred it – not too finely. Fry the onion in the oil in a large saucepan for about 7 minutes without browning it, then add the garlic and ginger and fry for a further 2 or 3 minutes. Take the saucepan off the heat and leave on one side until just before you want to serve the cabbage. Mix the soy sauce, cornflour and water together in a small cup and keep these on one side too.

When you're ready for the cabbage, reheat the onion in the large saucepan. When it's really hot put in the cabbage and fry it over a fairly high heat for about 2 minutes, stirring all the time. It will quickly soften. Give the cornflour mixture a quick stir then pour it into the saucepan with the cabbage and stir over the heat for about 30 seconds until the juices have thickened. Check the seasoning, adding a little sugar, salt and pepper if necessary, then serve immediately. The cabbage should still be rather crisp and crunchy.

CARROTS WITH APPLES GERMANY

Fruit, both dried and fresh, is used a good deal in German cookery, with some delicious sweet-sour mixtures. Here the soft slightly sharp cooking apples contrast well with the firm sweet carrots. Like the haricots with apples, this is a useful recipe to serve with a dish which would normally require an apple sauce.

700 g (1½ lb) carrots	Sea salt
900 g (2 lb) cooking apples	Freshly ground black pepper
1 large onion	Sugar
2 tablespoons oil	

Serves 4

Peel the carrots and cut them into even-sized pieces; cook them in a little boiling, salted water until they're nearly tender, then drain them, reserving the cooking liquid. While this is happening, peel and slice the apples and the onion. Add the apple to the cooked, drained carrot in the saucepan, together with 4 tablespoons of the reserved cooking liquid and cook over a gentle heat, with a lid on the saucepan, for 5–7 minutes, until the apple has reduced to a soft pulp. Meanwhile fry the onion in the oil until it's crisp and beginning to brown. Taste the carrot and apple mixture and add salt, pepper and sugar to taste.

Serve the carrot and apple with the fried onion poured over the top.

CARROTS À LA VICHY   FRANCE

Although you're supposed to use new baby carrots for this recipe I find it's a marvellous way of making older carrots taste extra special. Some people use Vichy water for cooking the carrots or put a pinch of bicarbonate of soda in with them to give a more authentic-tasting result but I don't think this makes much difference and I just use ordinary tap water. Personally I think it's the butter, sugar and chopped parsley that work the magic, not the water!

450 g (1 lb) carrots	15 g ($\frac{1}{2}$ oz) butter
75 ml ($\frac{1}{8}$ pint) water	Sea salt
1 tablespoon caster sugar	Fresh parsley

Serves 4

Scrape the carrots then cut them into matchsticks. Put the water, sugar, butter and salt into a heavy-based saucepan and bring to the boil, then add the carrots and put a lid on the saucepan. Simmer very gently for about 10–15 minutes, until the carrots are tender and all the water has been absorbed. Watch them carefully towards the end to make sure they don't burn. Serve them sprinkled with a little chopped parsley.

CAULIFLOWER IN TOMATO SAUCE   GREECE

This is an easy and attractive way of cooking cauliflower and the sauce means that you don't have to serve a gravy as well.

1 onion, peeled and chopped
2 tablespoons oil
1 garlic clove, peeled and
   crushed
425 g (15 oz) can tomatoes
275 ml (½ pint) water
Sea salt
Freshly ground black pepper
1 medium cauliflower,
   washed and broken into
   florets
Fresh parsley if available

Serves 4

Cook the onion gently in the oil for 10 minutes until it's soft but not browned, then put it into the liquidizer with the garlic, tomatoes and water and blend to a purée. Put this purée into a fairly large saucepan and add some salt and pepper. Bring the mixture up to the boil then put in the cauliflower and simmer gently, with a lid on the saucepan, for 10–15 minutes, until the cauliflower is just tender. You can take the cauliflower out of the saucepan using a perforated spoon and serve the sauce separately, but I usually serve them together with a little chopped parsley sprinkled over the top.

COURGETTES WITH FRESH HERBS   FRANCE

This is a good way to serve courgettes early in the season when they're young and tender and you want to make the most of their delicate flavour.

700 g (1½ lb) young courgettes
Sea salt
25 g (1 oz) butter
1 tablespoon finely chopped
   fresh parsley
1 tablespoon finely chopped
   fresh chives
Freshly ground black pepper

Serves 4–6

Wash the courgettes and trim the ends. Cut the courgettes into 6 mm ($\frac{1}{4}$ in) slices then cook them in 1 cm ($\frac{1}{2}$ in) boiling salted water for 5–7 minutes, until they're just tender but not soggy. Drain the courgettes well and add the butter, parsley, chives, pepper and a little more salt to taste if necessary.

FENNEL BAKED WITH CHEESE   ITALY

It's quite easy to find crisp white bulbs of Florentine fennel in the shops these days and it makes an interesting vegetable dish. It's very nice steamed and served simply with just a little butter and black pepper or you can boil it then bake it with cheese, as in this recipe, which gives a tasty golden result.

2 large bulbs of fennel – about 700 g (1$\frac{1}{2}$ lb) together	25 g (1 oz) butter
275 ml ($\frac{1}{2}$ pint) water	Freshly ground black pepper
Sea salt	50 g (2 oz) grated cheese

Serves 4–6

Set the oven to 200°C (400°F), gas mark 6. Trim the fennel and slice the bulbs into quarters or eighths. Put the water and a little salt into a saucepan; bring to the boil then put in the fennel and simmer for 20–30 minutes until the fennel is tender. Take the fennel out of the saucepan with a draining spoon and put it into a shallow greased dish. While you're doing this let the water in which the fennel was cooked boil away vigorously until it has reduced to just a couple of tablespoons or so of well-flavoured liquid. Pour this liquid over the fennel, then dot with the butter, grind some pepper over the top and finally sprinkle with the grated cheese. Bake the fennel, uncovered, for 20–30 minutes, until it's heated through and golden brown on top.

The cheese in this dish adds protein of course and so makes it useful for serving when you want to increase the food value of a meal – you could use more cheese if you want to – 125 g (4 oz) or even 175 g (6 oz).

HARICOT BEANS WITH APPLES GERMANY

You might think this is an unlikely combination, but it works well. The apples collapse, bathing the beans in a soft sweet-sour sauce and making this an ideal mixture for serving with a dish which would normally require an apple sauce. The recipe can also be made with pears but I think it's nicest with apples. Obviously with the protein-rich beans it's useful for serving with a low-protein main dish. I like it with the crisp German potato cakes or the Swiss *rösti*.

225 g (8 oz) haricot beans	2 tablespoons caster sugar
450 g (1 Ib) cooking apples	Sea salt
50 g (2 oz) butter or margarine	Freshly ground black pepper

Serves 4

Cover the beans with plenty of cold water and leave them to soak for several hours or overnight. Then drain off the water and rinse the beans under cold running water; put them into a large saucepan, cover them generously with cold water and simmer gently until they're tender – about 1 hour. Drain off the cooking liquor – it won't be needed for this recipe but as it's nutritious it's worth keeping for soups or sauces.

Peel, core and dice the apples. Melt the fat in a fairly large saucepan and fry the apples gently in it, without browning, until they're soft. Then add the beans and cook gently until they're heated through. Stir in the sugar and salt and pepper to taste.

MUSHROOMS IN SOURED CREAM FINLAND

In Finland and Sweden whole families go into the woods in the autumn to gather baskets of fresh earthy-smelling mushrooms and they have quite a number of different ways of cooking them. This is one of the simplest but it makes a luxurious vegetable

117

dish to go with a plainer main course, or it can be served as a delicious starter, in little individual dishes, with fingers of hot toast.

1 medium onion	150 ml (5 fl oz) carton
450 g (1 lb) mushrooms –	soured cream
field ones if you have them,	Sea salt
or else button ones	Freshly ground black pepper
25 g (1 oz) butter	Fresh parsley

Serves 2–3 as a vegetable, 4–6 as a starter

Peel and finely chop the onion; wash the mushrooms. If you're using wild mushrooms, remove the stalk and peel off the skin – this is not necessary with cultivated mushrooms. Cut the mushrooms into even-sized pieces. Melt the butter in a fairly large saucepan and fry the onion, without browning, for about 5 minutes, then add the prepared mushrooms and cook for a further 4–5 minutes until they are tender. If they make a lot of liquid boil them vigorously for a minute or two without a lid on the saucepan to evaporate it. Then stir in the soured cream and salt and pepper and heat through gently. Spoon at once into a warmed dish or individual containers and sprinkle with chopped parsley.

SPICY OKRA INDIA

You can sometimes get okra in Indian shops where it may be called *bhindi* or ladies' fingers. It's an intriguing vegetable, a plump green pod which has a soft, glutinous texture and delicate flavour when it's cooked. You can usually get canned okra at specialist food shops and delicatessens. Prepared like this it's nice as an accompaniment to curries or Caribbean rice dishes.

225 g (½ lb) fresh okra; or
    425 g (15 oz) can okra in
    brine
1 medium onion, peeled and
    chopped
25 g (1 oz) butter
225 g (8 oz) can tomatoes

1 garlic clove, peeled and
    crushed
2 teaspoons ground coriander
3 teaspoons garam masala
Sea salt
Freshly ground black pepper
2 teaspoons lemon juice

Serves 4

Top and tail the fresh okra or drain off the liquid if you're using the canned variety. Fry the onion in the butter for about 10 minutes until it's soft and golden, then add the tomatoes, garlic, coriander, garam masala and a little salt – not too much if you're using canned okra. Bring up to the boil then put in the okra and let it simmer gently for 15–20 minutes (until it's tender) if it's fresh, or about 5 minutes for canned. Check the seasoning and add more salt if necessary and a little lemon juice to taste.

CREAMED ONIONS AND PEAS   USA

An American friend gave me the recipe for this creamy vegetable dish which she serves her family at Thanksgiving. It's useful for serving when you want to add extra protein to a meal.

350 g (12 oz) baby onions –
    the type sold for pickling
Sea salt
450 g (1 lb) frozen peas
40 g (1½ oz) butter

40 g (1½ oz) flour
400 ml (¾ pint) milk
Freshly ground black pepper
Nutmeg
Ground cloves

Serves 6

Peel the onions with a small sharp, pointed knife then boil them in a little salted water for 15–20 minutes until they're almost

119

tender; drain them, reserving the liquid. De-frost the peas by putting them in a colander and rinsing them under hot water.

Melt the butter in a large saucepan and add the flour; cook for a minute or two then stir in the milk in three batches, over a high heat, stirring each time until the mixture is smooth before adding more. When all the milk has been incorporated and you have a smooth sauce taste it and season with salt, pepper, some grated nutmeg and a pinch of ground cloves. Carefully stir in the onions and peas and cook gently for 5 minutes to heat them through. Serve at once.

SUGAR-GLAZED PARSNIPS   FRANCE

This French way of cooking parsnips gently with butter, sugar and just a little liquid leaves them glistening in a buttery syrup which enhances their natural sweetness and makes them delicious. You can cook other root vegetables besides parsnips in this way: carrots, turnips and swedes are all good and so are sweet potatoes.

700 g (1½ lb) parsnips	1 tablespoon soft brown sugar
175 ml (6 fl oz) water or stock	½ teaspoon sea salt
25 g (1 oz) butter	Freshly ground black pepper

Serves 4

Peel the parsnips and cut them into small even-sized pieces, discarding the central 'core' if it is at all tough, though it should be all right if the parsnips are small. Put the parsnips into a heavy-based saucepan with the liquid, butter, sugar, salt and a grinding of black pepper, cover with a lid and simmer over a gentle heat for about 20 minutes until the pieces of parsnip are tender and the liquid reduced to a syrupy glaze.

PEAS BRAISED WITH LETTUCE

FRANCE

If you can get fresh young peas they are superb cooked like this: sweet, tender and juicy. But it's also a marvellous way of making frozen peas taste really good – and it's so simple to do.

450 g (1 lb) frozen peas or
   900 g (2 lb) fresh peas
About 6 outer lettuce leaves
25 g (1 oz) butter

2–3 sprigs of mint or parsley
   if available
½ teaspoon sea salt
½ teaspoon caster sugar

Serves 4

Put the frozen peas into a colander and run them under the hot tap to rinse off the ice. Or, if you're using fresh peas, shell them then rinse them in cold water. Wash the lettuce leaves then tear them roughly and put them in a heavy-based saucepan. Put the peas in on top, then the butter, in pieces, and the mint or parsley, salt and sugar. Cover the saucepan with a lid and set it over a moderate heat; when you hear it start to bubble turn the heat down a bit and let it cook gently until the peas are tender – 5 minutes for frozen peas, 15–20 minutes for fresh. Remove the parsley or mint sprigs before serving.

I find you don't need to add any water if the lettuce leaves are freshly washed when they're put into the saucepan and they really give the peas a lovely flavour. You can also add some spring onions – just the white part – to make a pleasant variation.

POTATOES ANNA

FRANCE

This is another useful potato dish which will cook slowly in the oven and won't spoil. It's rather like the creamy potato dish, *gratin dauphinoise,* except that it's turned out like a cake for serving. You don't have to add cheese, but I often do because it improves the flavour and increases the protein content of the dish making it useful to serve with something like ratatouille, making a complete meal.

50 g (2 oz) butter
700 g (1½ lb) waxy potatoes
  such as Desirée
150 g (6 oz) grated cheese
  (optional)

Salt and pepper
Fresh parsley

Serves 4–6

First line an 18 cm (7 in) cake tin by pressing a piece of foil into the base, extending it up the sides a little. Set the oven to 160°C (325°F), gas mark 3.

Melt the butter in a small saucepan, then use some of it to brush the inside of the foil-lined cake tin. Peel the potatoes, then slice them into thin rounds using a mandolin or the slicing edge of a grater. Put the rounds into a colander and rinse them thoroughly under cold water, then drain them and pat them dry with a clean cloth. Arrange a layer of potato in the base of the tin then sprinkle it with some of the grated cheese and a little salt and pepper; then add another layer of potato and continue in this way until it is all used up, ending with a generous layer of grated cheese. Pour the remaining butter over the top and cover with foil. Bake in the oven for about 2 hours, or until the potato can be pierced easily with the point of a knife. Pour off any excess butter, then slip a knife round the sides of the tin to loosen the potato. Invert the tin over a warmed plate and turn the potato out. Remove the foil. Sprinkle a little chopped parsley over the top of the potato.

BAKED POTATOES   GREAT BRITAIN

There are two ways of doing baked potatoes. You can rub the skins with fat or oil before you bake them, which makes the skin soft and flavoursome; or you can just wash them, prick them and bake them as they are (with the skins still wet), in a hot oven, and this way the skins will get lovely and crisp and crunchy. So you can use one method or the other depending on what people prefer and which goes best with the particular meal you're making.

4 medium unblemished potatoes – about 175 g (6 oz) each	A little oil or butter if liked

Serves 4

Set the oven to 230°C (450°F), gas mark 8. Scrub the potatoes and cut out any blemishes if necessary. Make two or three small cuts or fork pricks on each potato to allow the steam to escape. Rub each potato in a little oil or butter if you're using this, then put them in a baking tin and place them in the oven. Bake the potatoes for 1–1¼ hours until they feel tender when squeezed slightly. Serve them at once, particularly if you want them crisp.

I find the skins get soft if you try to keep the potatoes waiting and it's no good reducing the oven heat – they have to remain at this high temperature to retain their crispness. If you're going to have to keep them waiting it's best to do the soft-skinned variety. These can be cooked at a lower temperature, too, if more convenient – anything from 160°C (325°F), gas mark 3 is all right but of course then they take longer to cook.

Baked potatoes can really make the basis of a simple meal. Of course they're delicious served with grated cheese and a bowl of mixed salad, or you can make quite a festive meal by offering a choice of salads and several different toppings for the potatoes such as *hummus* and the soured cream dip or the goat cheese and herb spread, and bowls of different-coloured grated cheeses – a white one, such as Wensleydale, with for instance orange Leicester and golden Cheddar as well as cottage cheese.

POTATOES BAKED WITH CREAM FRANCE

In this dish, *gratin dauphinoise,* potatoes are sliced very thinly, layered in a shallow casserole with cream and butter and baked in a slow oven until they're meltingly tender. I find it a useful dish for entertaining because it doesn't need any last-minute attention and will keep warm in the oven for a long time without spoiling.

If you want to increase the protein content of a meal you can add some layers of grated cheese, preferably Gruyère, but I think the flavour is better without. Incidentally you can make a nice economical family version by using creamy milk instead of the single cream and my own favourite but unauthentic variation is to substitute tomato juice for the cream. This gives a tasty, less rich result which is very useful for a meal when you want plainly cooked potatoes to contrast with a creamy first course or pudding.

1 garlic clove, peeled and halved	Sea salt
25 g (1 oz) butter	Freshly ground black pepper
700 g (1½ lb) waxy potatoes – the red-skinned Desirée are good	Nutmeg
	275 ml (10 fl oz) single cream

Serves 4–6

First prepare a shallow ovenproof dish by rubbing the inside with the cut clove of garlic then greasing it generously with about half the butter. Set the oven to 160°C (325°F), gas mark 3.

Next peel the potatoes, then slice them very finely, using a mandolin or the slicing edge of a grater. Put the potato slices into a colander and rinse them thoroughly under the cold tap to remove some of the starch; pat them dry on kitchen paper or a tea-towel. Arrange a layer of the potato slices in the prepared dish, season with salt, pepper and a little grating of nutmeg, then add another layer of potato slices, continuing in this way

124

until all the potato is used. Pour the cream evenly over the top and dot with the remaining butter. Cover with a piece of foil and bake in the preheated oven for 1½–2 hours, until the potatoes feel tender when pierced with the point of a knife – sometimes this takes the full two hours so you need to allow this amount of time when planning the meal. Remove the foil and serve the potatoes straight from the dish.

Usually I find I'm baking this dish in the oven with other things and so have to compromise a little over the temperature; it's all right at a hotter temperature if it's near the bottom of the oven.

NEW POTATOES BAKED IN BUTTER   NORWAY

This is such an easy way to cook new potatoes but it really seems to conserve their delicate flavour and they come out tender and buttery. In Norway they would probably be garnished with a sprinkling of chopped fresh dill, which is a very popular flavouring in Scandinavia, but chopped parsley or chives will do just as well.

700 g (1½ lb) baby new
   potatoes – try to choose
   ones that are all the same
   size, the smaller the better

40 g (1½ oz) butter
1 teaspoon sea salt
Freshly ground black pepper
Fresh dill, parsley or chives

Serves 4

Set the oven to 160°C (325°F), gas mark 3. Scrape the potatoes or just scrub them thoroughly and leave the skins on. Put them into an ovenproof casserole with the butter, salt and a little grinding of black pepper. Cover the casserole and place it in the oven for about 45 minutes, or until the potatoes are tender when pierced with a sharp knife. Serve the potatoes sprinkled with chopped herbs.

If you want to cook something else in the oven and need to have it hotter, I find the potatoes are all right if they're put near the bottom.

ROAST POTATOES   GREAT BRITAIN

Quite a number of vegetarian dishes have a fairly soft consistency and so I think need to be served with something crisp. These crunchy golden potatoes are a popular and delicious way of providing that textural contrast.

900 g (2 lb) potatoes   Vegetable oil – I like corn oil
Sea salt   best for this

Serves 4

Set the oven to 220°C (425°F), gas mark 7. Peel the potatoes and cut them into even-sized pieces. With medium-sized potatoes I usually cut them into about four pieces as I think it's nicer to have two or three small crisp potatoes than one larger one. Cook the potatoes in boiling, salted water for 5–6 minutes, then drain them thoroughly.

While the potatoes are boiling put the oil in the oven to heat: pour about 6 mm ($\frac{1}{4}$ in) corn oil into a roasting tin and place it towards the top of the oven. Put the hot, drained potatoes into the hot oil – if the oil is really hot enough it should hiss and splutter as they go in. Turn the potatoes over in the oil so that they get well coated in it then put the tin back in the oven. After about 25–30 minutes have a look at the potatoes and if they're nice and golden underneath turn them over to give the other side a chance to crisp. I find they take about 45 minutes. If they seem to be racing along and you're afraid they'll be done before you're ready, turn the oven down to 160°C (325°F), gas mark 3 and this will keep them in good condition until you're ready. Drain the potatoes with a perforated spoon and serve them in a hot dish.

PUMPKIN BAKED WITH BUTTER AND GARLIC

Pumpkins are a vegetable I find difficult to resist. I don't know whether it's something to do with the time of the year and the magic of Hallowe'en, or whether it's their glorious warm apricot colour and pretty rounded shape, but I always seem to end up buying one. This is my favourite way of cooking pumpkin as a vegetable (it's also good for vegetable marrow).

700 g (1½ lb) pumpkin or vegetable marrow, weighed after skin and seeds have been removed
1 large garlic clove or 2 small ones

Sea salt
50 g (2 oz) butter
Freshly ground black pepper

Serves 4

Set the oven to 180°C (350°F), gas mark 4. Cut the pumpkin or marrow into smallish even-sized pieces. Peel the garlic and crush it into a paste with a little salt, then mix it with the butter. Use half this garlic butter to grease an ovenproof dish generously, then put in the pumpkin or marrow and top with the remaining butter and a good grinding of black pepper. Cover and bake in the oven for about 40 minutes or until the pumpkin or marrow is tender, stirring it once or twice during the cooking so that the butter gets to all the pieces.

STEWED RED CABBAGE

GERMANY

This is a useful vegetable dish because you can more or less forget it while it cooks. It doesn't need any last minute attention; it turns out moist and juicy so you don't need gravy and it can also be reheated if necessary and still tastes good. It's a lovely warming dish for winter but it's also good cold, as a salad.

There are similar recipes for red cabbage in many other European countries and in Scandinavia. In France chestnuts are sometimes added and I've given a recipe for this delicious variation in the stews and casseroles section of the book. In Russia the red cabbage might be served with soured cream which is a lovely addition and in Denmark red cabbage is part of the traditional Christmas feast.

700 g (1½ lb) red cabbage	50 g (2 oz) raisins or sultanas
2 large onions	1 tablespoon sea salt
2 large cooking apples	1 tablespoon brown sugar
3 tablespoons oil	1–2 tablespoons lemon juice

Serves 6

Prepare the cabbage by shredding it fairly finely with a sharp knife, discarding the hard core. Put the cabbage into a large saucepan, cover it with cold water and bring it up to the boil then take it off the heat and turn it into a colander to drain.

Meanwhile peel and chop the onions and apples and fry them lightly in a large saucepan for 5–10 minutes. Add the cabbage together with the raisins or sultanas, salt, sugar and lemon juice. Stir well so that the cabbage gets coated with the oil and everything gets mixed together, then put a lid on the saucepan and leave the cabbage to cook very gently for 1½ hours, stirring from time to time, until it's very tender. Or you can put the cabbage into an ovenproof casserole, cover with a lid and bake it in the oven, at 160°C (325°F), gas mark 3, for about 2 hours.

You can make the cabbage spicier if you want to by adding

some cinnamon, caraway seeds or cloves to the basic mixture –
lots of variations are possible.

SALSIFY WITH PARSLEY, BUTTER AND LEMON

FRANCE

Salsify – and its close relative, scorzonera – look like long, rather
dirty roots when you see them in the shops, but when they're peeled
and cooked they have a most delicate flavour which I think
makes them ideal as a hot first course. They're also nice served
in a well-flavoured cheesy sauce and baked in little individual
dishes; or mixed with a good vinaigrette while still warm and
served cold as a first course or salad.

1 kilo (2¼ lb) salsify or scorzonera – this might seem a lot but you lose a great deal in peeling	Sea salt
	25 g (1 oz) butter
	2 tablespoons chopped fresh parsley
Lemon juice	Freshly ground black pepper

Serves 4–6

Peel the roots, keeping them under cold water to preserve the
colour. Cut them into 2·5 cm (1 in) pieces and put them straight
into a bowl of cold water with a tablespoonful of lemon juice,
again to help keep them white. When they're all prepared, bring
2·5 cm (1 in) of salted water to the boil in a large saucepan and
cook them for about 10 minutes, or until just tender.

Drain and add the butter, a tablespoonful of lemon juice,
the parsley and salt and pepper to taste. Heat gently to melt
the butter then serve at once. Some thinly sliced wholewheat
bread and butter is nice with it.

CREAMED SPINACH   SWEDEN

People who don't normally like spinach might enjoy it done this way because the creamy sauce takes off the acidity and makes it less sharp-tasting. This is a useful dish for when you want to add protein to a meal; you could increase the protein content further by garnishing the creamy spinach with chopped hardboiled egg, which is the Finnish way of serving it.

450 g (1 lb) spinach   Sea salt
25 g (1 oz) butter   Freshly ground black pepper
25 g (1 oz) flour   Nutmeg
275 ml ($\frac{1}{2}$ pint) milk

Serves 4

Wash the spinach very thoroughly: I find the easiest way to do this is to put it into a big bowl full of cold water and swish it round with my hands, then take it out and repeat the process twice with fresh water each time. Put the spinach into a large saucepan. If you have just washed it you won't need to put any water in the saucepan as the spinach will be wet enough not to burn. Cook the spinach over a moderate heat. Have a lid on the saucepan but keep pushing the spinach down into the saucepan with a fish slice, chopping it a bit as it gets softer. It will take about 10 minutes to get really tender. Drain the spinach very well – the easiest way is to turn it into a colander and press it with a spoon to squeeze out all the liquid.

While the spinach is cooking make a sauce. Melt the butter in a medium-sized saucepan and add the flour, cook for a minute or two without browning then add a third of the milk and stir over a high heat until the mixture is thick and smooth; repeat with the rest of the milk, adding it in two batches. When all the milk is in and the sauce is thick and smooth take it off the heat and season it with salt, pepper and some grated nutmeg.

Mix the sauce with the spinach and check the seasoning;

you'll probably need to add some more. I think spinach needs plenty of pepper. Reheat the mixture gently, stirring all the time.

BAKED CREAMED SWEDES   SWEDEN

This is a useful vegetable dish because you can get it ready in advance and just heat it through in the oven when you want it. The crunchy breadcrumb topping contrasts well with the soft creamy swede.

900 g (2 lb swede)	Freshly ground black pepper
25 g (1 oz) butter	Nutmeg
2 tablespoons creamy milk	Soft breadcrumbs
Sea salt	A little extra butter

Serves 4

Peel the swede and cut it into even-sized pieces. Put the pieces into a large saucepan, almost cover them with cold water and then cook gently, with a lid on the saucepan, until tender. Drain off all the water, then return the saucepan to the heat for a minute or two to dry the swede a little. Mash the swede until it's smooth, adding the butter, milk and seasoning and beating well. Lightly grease an ovenproof dish – a shallow one is best as it gives you plenty of crispy topping – and spoon the swede mixture into it, smoothing the surface.

Sprinkle the top fairly generously with soft crumbs and dot with a few little pieces of butter. All this can be done in advance; before the meal bake the casserole in a moderate oven – 180°C (350°F), gas mark 4 – for about 40 minutes, until the inside is heated through and the top golden brown and crisp.

GLAZED SWEET POTATOES

You can sometimes find sweet potatoes at the greengrocer's. They look like large ordinary red-skinned potatoes and have a sweet, chestnutty flavour which I love. You can prick them and bake them in the oven like a jacket potato; par-boil and roast them as you would ordinary potatoes or glaze them as in this American recipe. This brings out the sweetness of the potatoes in a delicious way. Done like this they're good with Caribbean dishes and with the sort of dishes which you'd normally serve with redcurrant jelly or a sweet chutney. They're also very nice just on their own, with some crisp salad.

700 g (1½ lb) sweet potatoes –
  if they're very large the
  greengrocer may sell you a
  piece of potato

25 g (1 oz) butter
25 g (1 oz) brown sugar
2 tablespoons lemon juice
Sea salt

Serves 4

Scrub the potatoes, cut them into even-sized pieces then put them in a saucepan, cover with water and boil gently until tender – about 15–20 minutes. Drain them and peel off the skins. Set the oven to 200°C (400°F), gas mark 6. Use half the butter to grease a shallow ovenproof dish generously; then arrange the potato pieces in the dish and sprinkle them with the sugar, lemon juice and a little salt, dot with the remaining butter and place them, uncovered, in the oven. Bake them for 40–50 minutes, until they're golden brown and glazed, turning them over once or twice during the cooking time.

Vegetable Bakes, Stews and Casseroles

There are some very colourful and delicious mixtures in this section from quite a number of different countries ranging from Great Britain, France, Portugal and Italy to Russia, Hungary and Rumania. Some of these recipes were really originally intended for serving as an accompaniment to meat, but I think they are substantial and delicious enough to be main dishes in their own right with a side salad or cooked vegetables and rice or potatoes.

You will notice that a number of the dishes – the red cabbage and chestnut casserole, ratatouille, the red peppers with tomatoes and onions and the mixed vegetable stew – while being colourful and delicious, don't contain protein, so you need to introduce this into the meal. One way is to serve these stews with fluffy brown rice which has had some cheese or crunchy nuts or sunflower seeds forked into it; alternatively potatoes Anna made with layers of cheese in it is good or you could of course serve a protein starter or pudding, as I've suggested in the section on menu planning. I've also given suggestions with each individual recipe.

ASPARAGUS PUDDING   ITALY

This savoury pudding is called a *sformato* in Italy and is a cross
between a soufflé and a savoury loaf. I think it's best to serve it
straight from the dish and it's nice with something crisp – hot
garlic bread if you're serving it as a first course, triangles of fried
bread or crunchy golden roast potatoes and a good tomato sauce
for a main course.

50 g (2 oz) butter	3 eggs
50 g (2 oz) flour	Two 300 g (10½ oz) cans cut
275 ml (½ pint) milk	green asparagus
2–3 tablespoons grated	1 tablespoon chopped fresh
Parmesan cheese	parsley
Sea salt	Triangles of fried bread
Freshly ground black pepper	

Serves 4 as a main dish, 6 as a starter

Set the oven to 180°C (350°F), gas mark 4. Make a sauce: melt
the butter and stir in the flour; when it's blended add the milk in
three batches, keeping the heat up high and stirring well each
time until the mixture thickens before adding any more. Take the
saucepan off the heat and add the grated Parmesan cheese and
salt and pepper to taste.

Whisk the eggs. Drain the asparagus – you won't need the
liquid for this recipe. Mix the eggs into the sauce then gently stir
in the asparagus and parsley. Check the seasoning, then pour the
mixture into a lightly greased shallow ovenproof dish. Put the
dish into a baking tin containing about 2·5 cm (1 in) of very hot
water and place it in the centre of the oven. Bake for about 1 hour
or until the mixture is set and serve with triangles of fried bread.

AUBERGINE BAKE   ITALY

I love aubergines, with their shiny purple skins and strange subtle flavour, and this Italian dish, *parmigiana*, is one of my favourite ways of cooking them. With crusty bread and a green salad it makes a good lunch or supper, or with creamy mashed potatoes or fluffy brown rice and a cooked green vegetable it is substantial enough to make a main meal.

450 g (1 lb) aubergines
Sea salt
Vegetable oil
450 g (1 lb) onions, peeled
   and sliced
1 glass red wine – you can
   leave this out but it's lovely
   if you've got it
3 large garlic cloves, peeled
   and crushed

792 g (1 lb 12 oz) can
   tomatoes
Freshly ground black pepper
175 g (6 oz) cheese – sliced
   mozzarella plus some
   grated Parmesan if you
   want to be really authentic
   but Cheshire or Lancashire
   are a good cheaper
   substitute

Serves 4

Wash the aubergines and slice them thinly, discarding stalk ends. Put the slices into a colander and sprinkle them with salt. Place a plate and weight on top and leave for half an hour for the bitter juices to be drawn out. Then wash the slices under cold water and pat them dry. Preheat the oven to 180 C (350 F), gas mark 4.

Heat about 4 tablespoons of oil in a large saucepan and fry the onions for about 10 minutes until they're softened but not brown, then remove from the heat and stir in the wine, if you're using it, and the garlic and tomatoes. Season with salt and pepper. Heat some more oil in a frying pan and quickly fry the aubergine slices until they're soft and lightly browned – you may have to do this in two or more batches. Drain the aubergines then lay half of them in the base of a shallow ovenproof dish. Spread with half the tomato mixture, then with half the cheese. Repeat the layers,

136

ending with grated cheese, then bake it for about 1½ hours until crisp, golden brown and bubbly. Serve immediately.

CAULIFLOWER, EGG AND POTATO BAKE

RUSSIA

In Russia soured cream would probably be used for this bake but as this makes it both expensive and rather rich I use a well-flavoured cheese sauce instead, and the result is a filling dish rather like a substantial cauliflower cheese. If you don't like eggs you could put in a layer of sliced fried mushrooms instead – you'll need about 225 g (8 oz).

700 g (1½ lb) even-sized smallish potatoes
Sea salt
1 medium-sized cauliflower

850 ml (1½ pints) cheese sauce
6 hardboiled eggs, sliced
Dried crumbs
A little butter for topping

Serves 4–6

Scrub the potatoes then cook them in their skins in boiling salted water until they're tender; drain and cool them, then slip off the skins with a sharp knife. (Cooking the potatoes in their skins like this makes a big difference to the flavour.) Cut the potatoes into slices. Wash the cauliflower, break it into even-sized sprigs and cook these in a little boiling salted water for about 7 minutes until they're just tender; drain well. Set the oven to 190 C (375 F), gas mark 5.

Grease a large shallow ovenproof dish with butter, then place a layer of the potato slices in the base, followed by some of the sauce, then the cauliflower and the egg slices, then some more sauce. Continue like this until everything has been used, ending if possible with layers of potato and sauce. Sprinkle the top with dried crumbs, dot with a little butter and bake for about 50 minutes, until heated through and golden brown on top.

All this needs as an accompaniment is some lightly cooked

greens – little firm sprouts are ideal, or some buttered cabbage or spinach.

CHOP SUEY CHINA

Although the list of ingredients always makes this dish look rather daunting it's actually very easy to make. You get all the preparation done in advance so you only have to cook the vegetables quickly at the last minute.

1 onion
1 garlic clove
1 piece of fresh root ginger, about 2·5 cm (1 in) if possible; otherwise use $\frac{1}{2}$ teaspoon ground ginger
225 g (8 oz) fresh or canned bean sprouts
125 g (4 oz) button mushrooms
1 small pepper, preferably red
432 g (15$\frac{1}{2}$ oz) can sliced pineapple in its own juice

225 g (8 oz) can wheat protein from health shops or Chinese stores
1 teaspoon soy sauce
1 tablespoon tomato ketchup
1 teaspoon sugar
1 tablespoon cheap sherry
2 tablespoons water
1 egg
Sea salt
A little oil

Serves 4

Peel and chop the onion; peel and crush the garlic, peel and grate the ginger. Wash the bean sprouts if fresh. Wash and slice the mushrooms and the pepper. discarding the seeds from the pepper. Drain the pineapple and the wheat protein; cut both into small pieces. In a cup mix together the soy sauce, tomato ketchup, sugar, sherry and water. Break the egg into a bowl and whisk it with a little salt.

When you're ready to make the meal, heat 2 tablespoons of oil in a large saucepan and fry the onion for 5 minutes, then stir in the garlic and ginger and cook for a few seconds before adding the bean sprouts, mushrooms, pepper, pineapple and wheat protein. Stir and fry over quite a high heat for about 2 minutes, then add the mixture from the cup and stir well. Leave this to cook for just a minute or so while you quickly make an omelette with the beaten egg. Keep the omelette flat. To serve the chop suey pile it up on a hot dish and lay the omelette on top.

Serve with lots of hot, well-cooked rice and some other Chinese dishes if you like.

GREEN PEPPER AND TOMATO STEW   HUNGARY

This spicy Hungarian stew, called *Lecso*, is rather similar to the Italian *peperonata* but it's made with green peppers and has a generous seasoning of paprika. You can serve it Hungarian style with a fried egg on top, but I think it's nicer with fluffy brown rice or warm crusty bread and soft cheese.

450 g (1 lb) green peppers, de-seeded and roughly chopped
2 medium onions
3 tablespoons vegetable oil

2 garlic cloves, crushed
2 tablespoons paprika
425 g (15 oz) can tomatoes
Salt and pepper

Serves 4

Slice the peppers into even-sized pieces, discarding seeds and stalk. Peel and chop the onions, then fry them in the oil in a large saucepan for about 5 minutes until golden brown. Remove from the heat and stir in the garlic, paprika, peppers, tomatoes and a seasoning of salt and pepper. Cover and cook gently for about 30 minutes until all the vegetables are tender. Check seasoning and serve.

KIDNEY BEANS WITH TOMATOES, ONIONS AND CUMIN

PORTUGAL

This Portuguese mixture of glossy red kidney beans, tomatoes, onions and cumin is spicy and delicious.

225 g (8 oz) red kidney beans
6 tablespoons olive oil
Sea salt
Freshly ground black pepper

1 large onion
2 teaspoons cumin seeds
225 g (8 oz) can tomatoes

Serves 4

Soak the kidney beans for 2–3 hours in plenty of cold water then drain and rinse them. Put them into a saucepan with enough cold water to come about 2·5 cm (1 in) above them and add 4 tablespoons of the olive oil. Simmer the beans gently, with a lid on the saucepan, until they're very tender and most of the water has gone. Season them with salt and pepper.

While the beans are cooking peel and chop the onion and fry it lightly in the remaining 2 tablespoons of oil. Cook the onion for about 10 minutes, until is is soft but not brown, then add the cumin seeds and stir them for a minute or two before putting in the tomatoes and some salt and pepper. Let the mixture simmer for about 10 minutes to give all the flavours a chance to blend, then take it off the heat and mix it gently with the beans. Reheat as necessary and serve with fluffy brown rice or warm wholewheat bread and a crisp green salad.

LENTIL AND RED PEPPER STEW

BULGARIA

You can make this stew with all lentils or all beans but I think with this half-and-half mixture you get the best of both; the lentils thicken the sauce and give it body while the beans supply extra interest and texture. One of the nicest things about this is its colour – it comes out a heart-warming vivid red and is really welcoming on a chilly day. Serve it with a dollop of soured cream, some crunchy jacket potatoes and a green side salad; or try creamy mashed potatoes and a cooked green vegetable.

125 g (4 oz) red lentils
125 g (4 oz) haricot beans
2 large onions
700 g (1½ lb) red peppers –
  about 4 large ones
40 g (1½ oz) butter

1 litre (2 pints) unsalted stock
  or water
4 tablespoons tomato purée
Sea salt
Sugar

Serves 4

Put the lentils and beans into a bowl and cover generously with cold water; leave them to soak for several hours or overnight, then drain and rinse them.

Peel and chop the onions; slice the peppers, discarding the cores and seeds. Melt the butter in a large saucepan and fry the onion for about 10 minutes to soften it, then add the red peppers and cook for a further 4–5 minutes before stirring in the drained lentils and beans and the stock or water. Bring the mixture up to the boil and let it simmer gently, with a lid half on the saucepan, until the beans are tender – 1–1¼ hours.

Then mix in the tomato purée, and some salt and sugar to taste, as necessary. If the stew still seems a bit runny, turn up the heat and boil it for a few minutes without the lid on until it's the right consistency.

MIXED VEGETABLE STEW RUMANIA

Unlike so many stews, this one, *ghiveci*, does not have to contain meat but may be just a gloriously colourful mixture of every sort of vegetable you can find. You can really use whatever is available.

In the early autumn I make it with the first of the parsnips, celery and leeks and the last of the vegetable marrows and serve it with jacket potatoes, baked in a hot oven so they've got lovely crunchy skins. As the season progresses I replace the marrow with swede or turnip and at the end of the cooking time I may stir in some cooked butter beans, kidney beans or even, I'm ashamed to admit, some baked beans to make it more filling for the cold weather.

When preparing the vegetables try to cut them up into the sort of sizes which will make them all cook in about the same amount of time.

2 tablespoons oil
2 large onions, peeled and sliced
2 celery stalks, washed and chopped
225 g (8 oz) carrots, scraped and sliced
225 (8 oz) parsnips, peeled and diced
225 g (8 oz) vegetable marrow, de-seeded, peeled if necessary and cut into chunks
450 g (1 lb) leeks, washed,
trimmed and cut into 2·5 cm (1 in) pieces
3 large tomatoes, skinned and quartered
450 g (1 lb) potatoes, peeled and cut into chunks
25 g (1 oz) flour
575 ml (1 pint) water or stock
2 tablespoons tomato purée
2 bay leaves
1 garlic clove, peeled and crushed
Sea salt
Freshly ground black pepper

Serves 4

Heat the oil in a large saucepan and fry the onion for 5 minutes, then put in the celery, carrots, parsnips, marrow, leeks, tomatoes and potatoes and cook for a further 4–5 minutes, turning them often to prevent sticking. Then sprinkle the flour over the vegetables and mix gently to distribute it. Pour in the water or stock, stirring, and add the tomato purée, bay leaves, garlic and a seasoning of salt and pepper. Bring the mixture up to the boil then turn the heat down and leave the stew to simmer very gently, with a lid on the saucepan, for about 25–30 minutes or until the potatoes and other vegetables are tender. Taste the mixture and add more seasoning if necessary.

I often serve this with a bowl of grated cheese or roasted sunflower seeds (just sunflower seeds spread on a baking sheet and baked for about 10 minutes in a moderate oven) for people to help themselves and sprinkle over the top of their portion – but really it's very nice just as it is because it's delicately flavoured with all the vegetables. If you don't serve the cheese or sunflower seeds, though, you need to add protein to the meal, and I think the best way is to serve a pudding such as yoghurt, cheese cake or even *pashka* – or just finish with biscuits and cheese.

MUSHROOMS AND TOFU CHINA

Tofu, or bean curd, is creamy white and extremely high in protein. It is sold in small squares in Chinese shops and other delicatessens. If you can't get it you could use a small can of wheat protein – available from health shops – for this recipe but the result won't be quite the same. If you can get dried Chinese mushrooms they give the dish an excellent flavour, but you can use ordinary fresh mushrooms instead.

6 dried Chinese mushrooms or use 125 g (4 oz) fresh mushrooms
8 squares of *tofu*
Vegetable oil for shallow frying – sesame oil if possible
1 onion, peeled and chopped
Garlic clove, peeled and crushed
1 piece of fresh root ginger

about 2·5 cm (1 in) long, peeled and grated
½ teaspoon soy sauce
½ teaspoon vegetarian stock powder or crumbled stock cube
2 tablespoons water or liquid drained from the dried mushrooms
50 g (2 oz) flaked almonds

Serves 2 or 4 with other Chinese dishes

If you're using dried mushrooms, rinse them under the tap then put them into a small bowl, cover them with boiling water and leave them for 1 hour. Drain the mushrooms, reserving the liquid.

Cut the mushrooms into pieces; if you're using fresh mushrooms wash and slice them. Cut the *tofu* into smallish cubes, heat a little oil in a large saucepan and fry the *tofu* quickly until it is lightly browned on all sides. Take it out of the oil and keep it warm. Heat a little more oil in the saucepan and fry the onions for about 7 minutes, then add the garlic, ginger and mushrooms and fry for about 2 minutes, until the mushrooms are just tender. Stir in the soy sauce, stock powder and water or mushroom liquid. Let the mixture bubble for a moment or two, then put in the *tofu* and cook gently for about 2 minutes, just to reheat the *tofu* and give it a chance to absorb the flavours of the sauce. Sprinkle the almonds over the mixture just before serving it.

Serve this with fluffy cooked rice and Chinese cabbage; or include it as part of a selection of Chinese dishes, adding chop suey and fried wheat protein in sweet and sour sauce as well.

PEASE PUDDING
GREAT BRITAIN

Pease pudding is one of the few traditional British dishes which are vegetarian. Mrs Beeton describes it as 'an exceedingly nice accompaniment to boiled beef' but I think it also makes a very good main dish in its own right. It's quick to make, high in fibre and protein, low in fat and cholesterol and very economical too. We like it with crisp roast potatoes, a vegetable such as sprouts, a savoury brown gravy and some mint or apple sauce which gives a pleasant sharpness that's just right with the sweet-tasting peas.

450 g (1 lb) yellow split peas   Sea salt
2 large onions   Freshly ground black pepper
40 g (1½ oz) butter or
    margarine

Serves 4

If possible soak the peas in cold water for a couple of hours or so – this speeds up the cooking time – then drain and rinse them, put them into a large saucepan with a good covering of cold water and simmer them gently, with the lid half on the saucepan, until they're tender. I find the cooking time of split peas seems to vary quite a bit; sometimes they're done in 30 minutes, other times they can take as long as an hour. Watch the water level and add more if necessary as they cook; when they're done drain off any excess – they should be soft but not soggy.

While this is happening, peel and chop the onions and fry them gently in the butter until they're soft and golden – 10 minutes. Add the onion to the split peas and season with salt and pepper. You can serve the mixture straight away or keep it warm in a covered casserole in a low oven.

You can vary pease pudding in quite a few ways. It's nice with some grated lemon rind added, or some chopped marjoram or sage. Caraway, cumin and fennel seeds also go well with it – add them to the onion when it's nearly done – and a pinch of ground cloves is nice, too.

POTATO BAKE
HOLLAND

A simple savoury dish that's useful for children's suppers because it's quick to make and popular. It's nice with a juicy salad or with grilled tomatoes and a green vegetable. A parsley or tomato sauce goes well with it too.

900 g (2 lb) potatoes
25 g (1 oz) butter or vegetable
  margarine
25 g (1 oz) grated Parmesan
  cheese
125 g (4 oz) grated Edam
  cheese

2 eggs
275 ml ($\frac{1}{2}$ pint) top of the
  milk or creamy milk
Sea salt
Freshly ground black pepper

Serves 4

Set the oven to 190°C (375°F), gas mark 5. Peel the potatoes, cut

145

them into even-sized pieces and boil them in salted water until they're tender, then drain and mash them. Add the butter or margarine, the Parmesan cheese and half the Edam cheese and mix well. Beat together the eggs and milk and gradually add this to the potato mixture, stirring well. Season with salt and pepper. Spoon the mixture into a shallow ovenproof dish, scatter the remaining grated cheese on top and bake for 30–40 minutes, until slightly puffed up and golden brown.

POTATO AND MUSHROOM STEW WITH SOURED CREAM   HUNGARY

A Hungarian stew or *paprikas*, as it's called, doesn't always contain meat but can be based on vegetables, as in this version which makes a lovely vegetarian main dish. The protein can be supplied by serving a protein starter, side salad or pudding or by garnishing the *paprikas* with wedges of hardboiled eggs or grated cheese.

900 g (2 lb) potatoes
I medium onion
1 garlic clove
175 g (6 oz) button
  mushrooms
3 tablespoons oil
1 tablespoon mild paprika –

look for Hungarian 'rose'
  paprika
25 g (1 oz) flour
400 ml ($\frac{3}{4}$ pint) stock
Sea salt
Black pepper
150 ml (5 fl oz) soured cream
  or natural yoghurt

Serves 4

Peel the potatoes and cut them into even-sized chunks, peel and chop the onion, crush the garlic, wash the mushrooms and cut them into halves or quarters if necessary. Heat the oil in a large saucepan and fry the onion for about 5 minutes until golden, then stir in the garlic, potatoes, paprika and flour and cook for a further minute or two. Add the stock and bring up to the boil.

Put a lid on the saucepan and leave it over a gentle heat for about 20 minutes, until the potatoes are very nearly tender, then put in the mushrooms and cook for a further 3–4 minutes.

Put the soured cream or yoghurt into a small bowl and gradually add to it a ladleful of the liquid from the saucepan; mix well then pour this into the saucepan and heat gently until the mixture is very hot. Season to taste. Serve immediately.

RATATOUILLE   FRANCE

In the late summer when courgettes, aubergines, peppers and tomatoes are cheap and plentiful, ratatouille makes the basis of a delicious vegetarian meal. You can serve it with lots of plain fluffy brown rice and a crisp green salad with fresh herbs in it, with a protein starter like individual cheese soufflés or a pudding such as little coffee custards, ice cream or crisp wholewheat biscuits and Brie cheese.

450 g (1 lb) courgettes or
  marrow
450 g (1 lb) aubergines
Kitchen salt
2 large onions
Olive oil or vegetable oil –
  or a mixture

2 large garlic cloves
2 red peppers
4 tomatoes
Sea salt
Freshly ground
  black pepper
Fresh parsley

Serves 4

Cut the courgettes or marrow and the aubergines into small dice. Put them into a colander and sprinkle with kitchen salt. Place a plate with a weight on it on top and leave for at least half an hour for any bitter liquids to be drawn out of the aubergines and excess moisture out of the courgettes.

Peel and slice the onions and fry them in a little oil in a big saucepan until they're beginning to get soft, then add the garlic. Slice the peppers and remove the seeds; add the sliced pepper to the saucepan together with the aubergine and courgette. Cook gently with a lid on the pan for about 30 minutes, then add the tomatoes, skinned and chopped, and cook for another 30 minutes. Season with salt and pepper and sprinkle with chopped parsley.

When marrows are good and cheap I quite often make this with double the amount of marrow and no aubergine.

RED CABBAGE AND CHESTNUT CASSEROLE
FRANCE

Real warming winter food this, a rich burgundy-coloured casserole of succulent red cabbage and sweet-tasting chestnuts cooked with butter, onions and red wine. It's lovely served as a main dish with jacket potatoes which have been split and filled with soured cream and chopped chives. If there's any over it's very good cold as a salad. I rather lazily tend to use dried chestnuts but you could use fresh ones. You'll need about 450 g (1 lb) for this recipe. Prepare them in the way I've described on page 31 and add them to the casserole with the wine and seasoning.

125 g (4 oz) dried chestnuts	275 ml (½ pint) cheap red wine
1 large onion	Sea salt
50 g (2 oz) butter	Freshly ground black pepper
700 g (1½ lb) red cabbage	Sugar

Serves 3–4

Cover the chestnuts with plenty of cold water and leave them to soak for several hours. After that cook them gently until they're tender – this will take 1–1½ hours and you'll need to watch the level of the water and probably add some more so that they don't burn dry. Drain the chestnuts.

Set the oven to 150°C (300°F), gas mark 2. Peel and chop the onion and fry it in the butter for 10 minutes; while it's cooking wash and shred the cabbage, then add this to the onion and turn it so that it gets coated with the butter. Stir in the chestnuts, wine and some salt and pepper. Bring the mixture up to the boil, then transfer it to an ovenproof casserole, cover with a lid and bake slowly for 2–3 hours, until the cabbage is very tender. Check the seasoning – you'll probably need to add more salt and pepper and some sugar to bring out the flavour.

This dish can be made in advance and reheated – in fact I think this actually improves the flavour – and it can also be cooked at the bottom of a hotter oven if you want to bake jacket potatoes at the same time.

RED KIDNEY BEAN STEW   BULGARIA

This warm-coloured stew is lovely with buttery brown rice, baked potatoes or creamy mashed potatoes and a lightly cooked green vegetable. For a short cut you can use two cans of red kidney beans; this makes it a very quick dish to make.

175 g (6 oz) dried red kidney beans	Sea salt
450 g (1 lb) onions	Freshly ground black pepper
50 g (2 oz) butter	Sugar
Two 425 g (15 oz) cans tomatoes	

Serves 4

Soak the kidney beans for 2–3 hours in plenty of cold water then drain and rinse them. Put the beans into a saucepan with a good covering of cold water, boil vigorously for 10 minutes, simmer them gently until they're tender, then drain.

While the beans are cooking peel and chop the onions and fry them in the butter in a good-sized saucepan for about 10 minutes until they're soft but not browned. Add the tomatoes and beans to the onions with a good seasoning of salt, pepper and a little sugar if necessary. Let the mixture simmer gently for 10–15 minutes, then serve.

RED PEPPERS WITH TOMATOES AND ONIONS

ITALY

Although this Italian dish, *peperonata*, doesn't contain protein, you can build some nice meals around it. It's lovely served with rice, noodles or potatoes and protein can be introduced in the starter, side salad or pudding.

450 g (1 lb) red peppers
450 g (1 lb) onions
4 tablespoons oil
425 g (15 oz) can tomatoes
1 garlic clove, peeled and

crushed in a little salt
(optional)
Sea salt
Freshly ground black pepper

Serves 4

Cut the peppers into even-sized pieces, discarding seeds, stalk and core. Peel and slice the onions.

Heat the oil in a large saucepan and fry the onions for about 5 minutes until they're beginning to soften, then add the peppers and cook for a couple of minutes more, stirring so that they all get coated with the fat. Mix in the tomatoes, garlic if you're using it and some salt and pepper. Let the mixture simmer gently for about 30 minutes, stirring it from time to time, until all the vegetables are tender.

Some people let it cook to an almost purée-like consistency, but personally I prefer not to cook it this long as I think the flavour is fresher and sweeter and the texture more interesting if it's slightly under-done.

SWEETCORN PUDDING

USA

Really this is another of those dishes that's supposed to be served as an accompaniment to meat, but I think you'll agree it also makes a good main dish in its own right. I like to serve it with sprouts, gravy, roast potatoes and cranberry sauce – rather a bizarre-sounding combination, I know, but it works.

275 ml (½ pint) milk
25 g (1 oz) butter
125 g (4 oz) bread, weighed
  with the crusts removed
330 g (11½ oz) can sweetcorn
  kernels, drained
1 egg or 2 egg yolks

1 tablespoon chopped fresh
  parsley
½ teaspoon paprika
Sea salt
Freshly ground black pepper
A little grated cheese

Serves 3–4

Set the oven to 190°C (375°F), gas mark 5. Put the milk and butter into a saucepan and heat gently until the butter has melted. Remove from the heat and with your fingers crumble the bread into the milk – don't worry if there are some lumpy pieces. Leave on one side for a few minutes to allow the bread to soften, then mix it round and add the sweetcorn, egg, parsley, paprika and salt and pepper to taste. Spoon the mixture into a greased oven-proof dish and sprinkle with grated cheese. Bake the pudding for 35–40 minutes until set and golden brown.

TIAN   FRANCE

This is a baked vegetable casserole, rather like a savoury loaf except that it is served from the dish. It takes its name from the earthenware casserole dish in which it is cooked in Provence and it can be made from any green vegetable, although spinach or chard are the most usual with courgettes sometimes added too. It can be served hot or cold. If you're having it hot, try it with crunchy roast potatoes, tomato sauce and a colourful vegetable such as carrots. Cold it's nice with some garlic mayonnaise, tomato salad and hot French bread.

175 g (6 oz) long-grain
  brown rice
Just under 575 ml (1 pint)
  water
Sea salt
450 g (1 lb) spinach
2 tablespoons olive oil
2–3 garlic cloves, peeled and
  crushed

1 tablespoon chopped fresh
  parsley
125 g (4 oz) grated cheese
2 eggs
Freshly ground black pepper
2–3 tablespoons dried crumbs
2–3 tablespoons grated
  Parmesan cheese
2 tablespoons olive oil

Serves 4

Wash the rice then put it into the saucepan with the water and a teaspoonful of salt, bring it up to the boil then turn the heat down and leave the rice to cook very slowly, with a lid on the saucepan, for 40–45 minutes, until it's tender and all the liquid has been absorbed. (If there's still some water left in the saucepan just leave it to stand off the heat but with the lid on for 10–15 minutes, after which you should find it has been absorbed.)

Set the oven to 200 C (400 F), gas mark 6. Wash the spinach thoroughly in three changes of water, then chop it up – you can use the stalks too. Heat the olive oil in a large saucepan and put in the spinach; turn it in the hot oil for 2–3 minutes until it has softened slightly and is all glossy-looking from the oil. Take it off the heat and add the rice, garlic, parsley and grated cheese. Beat in the eggs and mix everything together, seasoning it with salt and a good grinding of pepper. Spoon the mixture into a shallow oven-proof dish and sprinkle the crumbs, Parmesan and olive oil on top. Bake without a lid for 30–40 minutes until it's puffed up and golden brown and crispy on top.

YELLOW SPLIT PEA PURÉE WITH VEGETABLES

GERMANY

In Germany this would probably be served as an accompaniment to meat, like the British pease pudding, but I think it makes a good main dish with jacket potatoes.

350 g (12 oz) yellow split peas
1 litre (1¾ pints) water
3 onions, sliced
2 carrots, sliced
1 leek, sliced
2 celery stalks, sliced

½ teaspoonful mint or
  marjoram
4 teaspoons lemon juice
Sea salt and freshly ground
  black pepper
50 g (2 oz) butter

Serves 4

Soak the split peas in cold water for an hour or two or overnight, then rinse them and put them into a pan with the water, half the sliced onion and all the other vegetables and the herbs and let it simmer gently until the split peas are soft and the vegetables tender – this takes 30–40 minutes – then sieve or liquidize. Add the lemon juice, season with salt and pepper and turn the mixture into a shallow heatproof dish. Set the oven to 180°C (350°F), gas mark 4 or preheat the grill, set fairly high. Fry the remaining onion in the butter until it's beginning to soften, then pour the onion and butter over the top of the split pea purée and put it into the oven for about 20–30 minutes or under the grill until the top is slightly crusted looking and the onion crisp and brown.

Stuffed Vegetables

I love stuffed vegetable dishes because they always look festive and special and I think they're ideal for entertaining. Some of them, particularly the aubergines *à la duxelles*, the stuffed aubergines in Béchamel sauce, the red cabbage stuffed with chestnuts, the stuffed courgette bake and the stuffed onions make good main courses. Others are more suitable for serving as a first course – I think the stuffed tomatoes and stuffed vine leaves are particularly good for this.

Some of these stuffed vegetables contain a fair amount of protein but others don't, so you need to look at the recipe and plan the meal accordingly. If you want to serve one of the low-protein stuffed vegetables you can add nourishment to the meal very simply by serving the vegetables with a well-flavoured cheese sauce or with the green salad with Gruyère cheese. Or of course you can have a protein-rich starter or pudding – *hummus* or the Middle Eastern bean pâté are particularly good with the Grecian recipes, with ground rice and rosewater pudding, yoghurt tart or honey cheese cake as suggestions for pudding; or for the French recipes, *coeurs à la crème* or little coffee custards; and coffee *ricotta* or ice cream after the Italian ones.

With the exception of the red cabbage, which needs a good deep saucepan or flameproof dish big enough to hold the whole cabbage, the stuffed vegetables need to be cooked in a large shallow ovenproof dish. I find one measuring about 28 cm × 18 cm (11 in × 7 in) is just right for recipes serving 4 people, while when I'm doing them for 6 people I use an oval Pyrex one measuring about 39 cm × 27 cm (15$\frac{1}{2}$ in × 10$\frac{1}{2}$ in). It looks vast and institutional when it's empty but it's just right and looks super when it's filled with delicious vegetables bursting with tasty stuffing. I've also seen some lovely large shallow French ovenproof dishes in deep muted shades and one of these would look even better.

STUFFED AUBERGINES IN BÉCHAMEL SAUCE   GREECE

Really, minced meat should be used for this recipe and you might feel that the lentils I've suggested are rather a corruption. But as lentils are used so much in Middle Eastern cookery I don't think they're too far-fetched, and they do make a tasty and satisfying dish.

3 medium aubergines – about
   700 g (1½ lb) in all
Kitchen salt
3–4 tablespoons oil
2 medium onions, peeled and
   chopped
3 tablespoons tomato purée
3 garlic cloves, peeled and
   crushed in a little salt
175 g (6 oz) split red lentils
225 ml (8 fl oz) water
2 tablespoons chopped fresh
   parsley

Serves 6

75 g (3 oz) grated cheese
Sea salt
Freshly ground black pepper
50 g (2 oz) grated cheese
A little sugar

For the sauce:
25 g (1 oz) butter
25 g (1 oz) flour
400 ml (¾ pint) milk
1 egg
Nutmeg

Cut the aubergines in half lengthwise then scoop out the centres to leave space for the stuffing and chop up the scooped-out flesh. Sprinkle the aubergine flesh and the inside of the skins with kitchen salt; leave for half an hour, then squeeze out the bitter brown juice, rinse the aubergine flesh and skins under the tap and dry. Heat 3 tablespoons of oil in a frying pan and fry the aubergine skins for about 5 minutes on each side to soften them; drain them and put into a shallow ovenproof dish. Set the oven to 180°C (350°F), gas mark 4. Fry the onion in the same saucepan, adding a little more oil if necessary; when it is soft but not brown – about 10 minutes – add the aubergine flesh, tomato purée, garlic, lentils and water and cook for about 20–30

157

minutes until the lentils are done. Remove from the heat, add the parsley and grated cheese and season carefully to taste. Divide the filling between the aubergine skins, piling it up well.

Make the Béchamel sauce: melt the butter in a saucepan and stir in the flour then add a third of the milk and stir over a high heat until the mixture is smooth and thick; repeat the process twice more using the rest of the milk. Remove from the heat and beat in the egg and salt, pepper and grated nutmeg to taste. Pour the sauce over and round the aubergines, sprinkle with the grated cheese and bake them in the oven for 35 minutes until they're tender and the sauce is bubbly and golden brown.

These aubergines are nice with a crisp herby green salad or a cooked green vegetable.

AUBERGINES STUFFED WITH CHEESE
YUGOSLAVIA

This is a simple but delicious way of serving aubergines. I think a tomato sauce goes well with them and also something crisp – triangles of toast or fried bread, for instance, or crunchy roast potatoes.

4 small/medium aubergines –
  about 700 g (1½ lb) in all
Sea salt
25 g (1 oz) butter
1 onion, peeled and finely
  chopped

175 g (6 oz) grated cheese
1 egg
1 tablespoon chopped fresh
  parsley
Freshly ground black pepper

Serves 4

Set the oven to 200°C (400°F), gas mark 6. Wash the aubergines and remove the stalk ends. Half fill a good-sized saucepan with cold water, add a teaspoonful of salt and bring up to the boil.

Cook the aubergines in the water for about 5 minutes, until they feel just barely tender when pierced with the point of a knife. Drain and cool the aubergines, then split them in half lengthways and scoop the flesh out into a bowl, leaving the skins intact.

Arrange the skins in a lightly greased shallow ovenproof dish. Mash the aubergine flesh with a fork, then stir in the onion, grated cheese, egg, parsley and salt and pepper to taste. Bake the aubergines for 30–40 minutes until they're golden brown.

STUFFED AUBERGINES À LA DUXELLES

FRANCE

If you chop up an onion and some mushrooms and cook them in a little butter until they make a thick, dry purée you have what the French call *duxelles*. It will keep in a screw top jar ready for flavouring soups and sauces, but in this recipe the whole batch is used to give the aubergines a rich mushroomy flavour.

This dish is nice served with a wine or tomato sauce, new potatoes or *gratin dauphinoise* and another vegetable. There isn't much protein in the aubergine mixture, though, so you really need to serve a protein-rich starter such as individual cheese soufflés, or round off the meal with a nourishing pudding like *coeurs à la crème* or little coffee custards.

450 g (1 lb) mushrooms
1 onion
25 g (1 oz) butter
2 medium aubergines
Sea salt
Oil
2 tablespoons chopped fresh
  parsley

225 g (8 oz) cottage cheese or
  low-fat quark
Freshly ground black pepper
50 g (2 oz) grated cheese,
  preferably Parmesan or a
  mixture of Parmesan and
  cheaper cooking cheese
50 g (2 oz) fine breadcrumbs

Serves 4

First prepare the *duxelles:* wash the mushrooms then chop them finely: peel and finely chop the onion. Put the chopped mushrooms and onion into a cloth and squeeze firmly to extract excess liquid – this can be saved and added to a soup or a sauce. Melt the butter in a large saucepan, then stir in the chopped mushroom and onion and fry, without a lid on the saucepan, until the mixture is thick, dry and purée-like – 15–20 minutes. Remove from the heat.

While the *duxelles* is cooking start preparing the aubergines: cut them in half lengthwise and scoop out the centres to form cavities for stuffing. Sprinkle the scooped-out aubergine and the insides of the skins with salt and leave them on one side for the bitter juices to be extracted. After about 30 minutes squeeze the liquid out of the aubergine, rinse it under cold water and pat dry.

Set the oven to 180°C (350°F), gas mark 4. Fry the aubergine skins on both sides in hot oil, then drain them and put them into a shallow ovenproof dish, ready for stuffing. Fry the scooped-out aubergine flesh in a couple of tablespoons of oil for about 5 minutes, then add the *duxelles*, chopped parsley, cottage cheese or quark and most of the cheese. Taste the mixture and season as necessary, then pile it into the prepared aubergine skins and sprinkle the tops with breadcrumbs and remaining grated cheese. Cover the dish with foil and bake for about 40 minutes, removing the foil for the last 10 minutes so that the crumbs get crisp.

STUFFED COURGETTE BAKE   SPAIN

In this dish courgettes are filled with a mixture of tomatoes, onion and garlic then baked in a well-flavoured cheese sauce. It's best to use fairly large courgettes as these hold the filling well.

4 medium/large courgettes –
  about 700 g (1½ lb) in all
2 large onions
25 g (1 oz) butter
450 g (1 lb) tomatoes, skinned,
  or a 425 g (15 oz) can
2 garlic cloves
Sea salt
Freshly ground black pepper

Serves 4

50 g (2 oz) grated cheese

For the sauce:
50 g (2 oz) butter
50 g (2 oz) flour
575 ml (1 pint) milk
50 g (2 oz) grated Parmesan or
  strong tasting cheese

Set the oven to 190°C (375°F), gas mark 5. Peel the courgettes then cut them in half lengthways and scoop out the seeds – a teaspoon is good for this. Cook the courgettes in 1 cm (½ in) of boiling salted water for 5–10 minutes until they're just tender, but don't let them get soggy. Drain the courgettes very well and dry them lightly with kitchen paper or a clean cloth. Leave them on one side while you prepare the filling and make the sauce.

To make the filling, peel and chop the onions and fry them in the butter in a medium-sized saucepan for 10 minutes. Remove the seeds from the tomatoes and chop the flesh. If you're using canned tomatoes drain off the juice – you won't need it for this recipe. Peel the garlic and crush it in a little salt. Add the garlic to the onions, together with the tomatoes, and cook the mixture for a further 10–15 minutes until it is fairly thick and will hold its shape. Season with salt and pepper.

While the tomato mixture is cooking make the sauce. Melt the butter in a medium-sized saucepan and stir in the flour, cook for a moment or two, then pour in a third of the milk. Stir over a high heat until the milk is incorporated and the mixture has become very thick and smooth, then repeat with the rest of the milk, adding it in two instalments. When you have added all the milk and have a smooth sauce, take the saucepan off the heat and stir in the grated Parmesan cheese and salt and pepper to taste.

Pour half the sauce into a shallow ovenproof dish and arrange

161

the courgette halves on top. Spoon the tomato mixture into the cavities in the courgettes, piling it up as necessary. Pour the remaining sauce over the courgettes, sprinkle the grated cheese on top and bake them just above the centre of the oven for about 40–45 minutes, until the mixture is bubbly and golden brown on top. Serve at once. They're nice with buttery new potatoes, rice or noodles and a green vegetable such as spinach, with a fresh fruity pudding to follow.

COURGETTES STUFFED WITH CHEESE AND ONION CARIBBEAN

This is a simple dish that's quickly made but the combination of the tender courgettes and crisp cheese topping is delicious. It's a good recipe for slimmers if you cook the onions in the minimum of fat in a non-stick saucepan and use Edam cheese. On the other hand for a special occasion it's delicious with a couple of tablespoons of white wine added.

4 good-sized courgettes – about 175 g (6 oz) each
50 g (2 oz) butter
2 large onions, peeled and chopped
1 garlic clove, peeled and crushed

350 g (12 oz) grated cheese
½ teaspoon dried thyme
Sea salt
Freshly ground black pepper

Serves 4

Set the oven to 190°C (375°F), gas mark 5. Wash the courgettes thoroughly, then cut them in half lengthwise. Heat 5 cm (2 in) of water in a large saucepan and when it boils add the courgette halves and simmer them gently for about 3 minutes, just to soften them a little, then drain them well. Using a teaspoon, scoop out the centre of the courgettes to leave a cavity for stuffing. Chop up the scooped-out courgette centre.

Melt the butter in a medium-sized saucepan and fry the onion for 5 minutes; then add the garlic and chopped courgette flesh and cook for a further 4–5 minutes. Remove the saucepan from the heat and stir in the grated cheese, thyme and seasoning to taste. Grease a shallow oblong dish and arrange the courgette halves in it. Divide the onion and cheese mixture between the courgette halves, arranging it in the cavities. Bake in the pre-heated oven for 20–30 minutes, until the courgettes are tender and the filling is golden and brown.

Serve with fresh tomato sauce. New potatoes and spinach or French beans go well with it.

STUFFED ONIONS   ITALY

Onions, macaroons, cheese and sultanas sound a very strange mixture but the combination of sweet and savoury really works well, like cheese and chutney or curry and banana. I like to use those big Spanish onions to make this when they come into the shops early in September.

4 large Spanish onions
4 macaroons
75 g (3 oz) soft wholewheat
   breadcrumbs
¼ teaspoon ground cinnamon
¼ teaspoon ground cloves
¼ teaspoon grated nutmeg
2 eggs, beaten

50 g (2 oz) grated Parmesan
   cheese – or use strong cooking
   cheese
25–50 g (1–2 oz) sultanas
Sea salt
Freshly ground black pepper
15 g (½ oz) butter

Serves 4

Rinse the onions but don't peel them. Put them into a large saucepan of water and simmer them for about 20 minutes, until they feel tender when pierced with the point of a knife. (They should not be completely cooked through at this stage.) Drain the onions and let them get cool enough to handle, then remove the skins and root ends and cut the onions in half horizontally. Scoop out the centre of each half making a nice cavity for the stuffing and leaving three or four layers of onion. Arrange the onion halves in a greased shallow ovenproof dish.

Set the oven to 180°C (350°F), gas mark 4. Now make the stuffing. Chop the scooped-out onion fairly finely and put it into a bowl. Crush the macaroons – press them with a rolling pin or pop them into the liquidizer and blend for a moment or two. Add them to the onions, also the breadcrumbs, spices, eggs, cheese and sultanas and stir until everything is well mixed to a softish consistency. You might need to add a drop or two of milk but I usually find the natural juiciness of the onions together with the eggs sufficient. Season with salt and a good grinding of pepper then spoon the mixture into the onion cavities, piling them up. Put a piece of butter on top of each and bake them, uncovered, for 30 minutes.

Stuffed onions are good with a sharply flavoured cheese sauce, mashed potatoes and a cooked green vegetable.

STUFFED PEPPERS   SPAIN

In this recipe rice, mushrooms, onions and grated cheese are used to stuff peppers and then they're baked in a simple fresh tomato sauce. They're nice as a main course, served with a cooked vegetable and some buttery new potatoes.

125 g (4 oz) long-grain brown
  rice
275 ml ($\frac{1}{2}$ pint) water
Sea salt
2 medium green peppers
1 large onion, peeled and
  chopped
1 garlic clove, peeled and
  crushed in a little salt
4 tablespoons olive oil

125 g (4 oz) button
  mushrooms washed and
  finely sliced
1 teaspoon dried thyme
$\frac{1}{2}$ teaspoon mustard powder
2 teaspoons lemon juice
125 g (4 oz) grated cheese
Freshly ground black pepper
450 g (1 lb) tomatoes, peeled
  and chopped – or use a 425
  (15 oz) can

Serves 4

First cook the rice: put it into a heavy-based saucepan with
the water and a pinch of salt. Bring it up to the boil then turn
the heat down and let it cook very gently, with a lid on the
saucepan, for about 40 minutes, until the rice is tender and
has absorbed all the liquid. (The rice can be cooked well in
advance because it will keep for several days in the fridge.)

Set the oven to 180°C (350°F), gas mark 4. Halve the peppers
and remove the centre and seeds; rinse them under the cold tap.
Put the peppers into a saucepan half full of cold water and bring
them up to the boil, then take them off the heat, drain them and
leave on one side.

Fry the onion and garlic in the oil for 10 minutes. Mix half the
onion and garlic with the cooked rice and add the mushrooms,
thyme, mustard, lemon juice, grated cheese and a good seasoning
of salt and pepper.

Mix the tomatoes with the remaining onion and garlic in the
pan and add salt and pepper to taste. Pour the tomato mixture
into a shallow ovenproof dish and place the peppers on top.
Spoon the rice mixture into the peppers, piling it up well. Bake
the peppers, uncovered, for about 40 minutes, until the stuffing is
golden brown and the peppers tender.

RED CABBAGE STUFFED WITH CHESTNUTS

The sweetness of chestnuts goes particularly well with red cabbage and if you add butter and red wine too you get a really rich-tasting, warming dish, just right for the winter when the chestnuts and cabbage are in season. There's not much protein in the dish, though, so it's a good idea to follow it with a protein pudding like biscuits and cheese, *crème brûlée* or rice and almond pudding.

700 g (1½ lb) fresh chestnuts or 225 g (8 oz) dried chestnuts
1 small/medium red cabbage, about 1·4 kilos (3 lb)
125 g (4 oz) butter
2 large onions, peeled and chopped

1 tablespoon lemon juice
Sea salt
Freshly ground black pepper
2 carrots, peeled and sliced
1 tablespoon redcurrant jelly
275 ml (½ pint) red wine

Serves 6

First prepare the chestnuts. If you're using fresh ones slash each one with a sharp knife then simmer them in boiling water for about 10 minutes until the cuts open and you can remove the skins using a small, sharp pointed knife. Keep the rest of the chestnuts in the boiling water as you work because the skins get hard again as they cool. If you've decided to save time by using dried chestnuts, as I must admit I usually do, let them soak in some cold water for a while if possible – this isn't essential but it helps as they can be very hard sometimes – then simmer them gently in plenty of water for at least an hour, until they're tender, then drain them.

Now wash and trim the cabbage, removing any tough or damaged leaves and cutting the stalk end level. Slice a lid from the top of the cabbage and using a small sharp knife and a spoon scoop out as much of the inside of the cabbage as possible, leaving a neat, good-sized cavity for stuffing. Chop the cabbage which you've scooped out fairly finely. Heat half the butter in a largish saucepan and fry half the onion for about 5 minutes, without browning, then stir in the chopped-up cabbage and cook for a further 5 minutes, with a lid on the saucepan, stirring occasionally. Add the chestnuts and half the lemon juice and season with salt and pepper. Leave on one side. Put the whole cabbage into a large saucepan half filled with cold water. Bring to the boil and simmer for 2 minutes with a lid on the saucepan. Drain and rinse the cabbage under cold water.

Melt the remaining butter in a saucepan that's large enough to hold the cabbage and fry the remaining onion and the carrots for 5 minutes. Mix the redcurrant jelly and the rest of the lemon juice with the onion and carrots, add some salt and pepper, then place the cabbage on top and carefully fill the cavity with the chestnut mixture, piling it up high. Pour the wine around the sides of the cabbage, put the saucepan over a low heat and cover with a lid. Leave it to cook very gently for about 3 hours or until the cabbage feels beautifully tender when pierced with the point of a knife.

It's easiest to serve this straight from the cooking pot and it's delicious with really light mashed potatoes.

TOMATOES STUFFED WITH CHEESE   PORTUGAL

These juicy tomatoes with their cheesy breadcrumb stuffing make a delicious hot starter or light supper dish for late summer when tomatoes are plentiful, and they're quick and easy to do.

8 large or 4 very large tomatoes – about 700 g (1½ lb) in all	225 g (8 oz) grated cheese
Sea salt	1 garlic clove, peeled and crushed
125 g (4 oz) wholewheat breadcrumbs	Freshly ground black pepper
	1 tablespoon olive oil

Serves 4–5

Set the oven to 190 °C (375 °F), gas mark 5. Halve the tomatoes and scoop out the centres. Sprinkle a little salt inside each tomato and put them upside down on a plate to drain off any excess liquid while you make the filling. Chop the tomato centres and mix them with the breadcrumbs, grated cheese and garlic. Season with salt and pepper to taste. Arrange the tomato halves in a shallow greased dish. Pile the stuffing mixture into the tomato halves and sprinkle the olive oil on top. Bake the tomatoes for 20–30 minutes until they're tender and the filling is golden brown.

They're nice served with creamy mashed potatoes, buttered noodles or brown rice and a cooked green vegetable or crisp green salad.

STUFFED TOMATOES À LA PROVENÇALE
FRANCE

These tomatoes, with their herby, garlicky stuffing, make a very good first course but if you serve them with some buttery noodles or rice and a sharp-flavoured cheese sauce they also make an excellent lunch or supper, with a crisp green salad to accompany them.

8 large tomatoes – about 700 g (1½ lb) in all
Sea salt
1 large onion
150 ml (¼ pint) olive oil
4 garlic cloves, peeled and crushed

75 g (3 oz) fine fresh wholewheat breadcrumbs
4 tablespoons chopped fresh parsley
½ teaspoon dried thyme
Freshly ground black pepper

Serves 4

Cut a thin slice off the top of each tomato and leave these slices on one side to use as lids later. Using a teaspoon scoop out the tomato pulp to leave a cavity for stuffing (you won't need the pulp for this recipe but it can be used to flavour sauces and soups). Sprinkle the inside of each tomato with a little salt then turn them upside down on a large plate and leave them while you prepare the filling.

Peel and finely chop the onion. Heat the olive oil in a large saucepan and fry the onion until it's golden, then take it off the heat and add the garlic, breadcrumbs, herbs and a good seasoning of salt and pepper.

Set the oven to 200°C (400°F), gas mark 6. Place the tomatoes in a lightly greased baking dish; fill each with some of the stuffing mixture and arrange the reserved lids on top.

Bake them in the oven for 15–20 minutes, to heat them right through, then serve them at once.

TOMATOES STUFFED WITH RICE   GREECE

Like the stuffed tomatoes in the previous recipe these can be served either as a starter or as a main course. If you're making a meal of them I think it's a good idea to start off with a first course like *hummus* and finish with the yoghurt tart or special ground rice, all of which add protein to the meal and continue the Middle Eastern theme.

125 g (4 oz) long-grain brown
   rice
275 ml (½ pint) water
Sea salt
8 large tomatoes – about 700 g
   (1½ lb) in all
2 tablespoons olive oil
1 medium onion, peeled and
   chopped
2 cloves of garlic, peeled and
   crushed

6 tablespoons tomato purée
6 tablespoons chopped fresh
   parsley
2 tablespoons chopped fresh
   mint
Pinch of oregano
Freshly ground black pepper
150 ml (¼ pint) stock – or red
   wine is delicious

Serves 4

Put the rice into a heavy-based saucepan with the water and half a teaspoonful of salt; bring it up to the boil then turn the heat right down, put a lid on the saucepan and cook the rice very gently for about 40 minutes until it's tender and all the water has been absorbed.

While the rice is cooking prepare the tomatoes. Cut a small piece off the top of each and hollow out the centre, using a teaspoon – keep the sliced-off tomato tops to use as lids later. Sprinkle some salt inside each tomato then leave them upside down to drain.

Set the oven to 180°C (350°F), gas mark 4. Next make the stuffing. Heat the oil in a fairly large saucepan and fry the onion until beginning to soften – about 5 minutes – then add the garlic, rice, scooped-out tomato pulp, half the purée, the herbs and seasoning. Cook over a highish heat until the mixture is fairly dry. Arrange the tomatoes in a greased ovenproof dish, fill with the stuffing and put the slices back as lids. Mix the remaining tomato purée with the stock or red wine and a little salt and pepper and pour it round the tomatoes, then bake them for about 20 minutes until they're tender.

A cheesy sauce goes well with these, and a crisp green salad.

STUFFED VINE OR CABBAGE LEAVES   GREECE

These *dolmades*, or little leafy parcels of rosemary-flavoured rice with nuts and raisins can be served hot or cold. If you're serving them cold – as is frequently done in Greece – you can omit the sauce and just bake them in some seasoned tomato juice or a mixture of tomato purée and stock. This is really a more authentic way of doing them but I'm giving my version which has a flour-thickened sauce because I've found this is the most popular. I also like to finish them off with a crunchy topping of crumbs and grated cheese but this isn't very Grecian either, so you might prefer just to sprinkle them with chopped parsley after cooking.

I think the *dolmades* are very much better served hot, with a

crisp green salad and some dry white wine. The green salad with
Gruyère cheese goes well with them and supplies some extra
protein; or you could of course serve a protein-rich starter or
pudding. The *dolmades* also make rather a nice unusual hot
starter themselves if you bake them in individual ovenproof
dishes.

36 fresh vine leaves, if
available, or a small can; or
about 18 cabbage leaves –
Savoy, January King and
Primo are all fine
1 large onion
2 tablespoons olive oil
225 g (8 oz) cooked long-grain
brown rice (about 75 g (3 oz)
uncooked)
1 teaspoon fresh rosemary,
chopped, or ½ teaspoon dried
50 g (2 oz) chopped mixed nuts

50 g (2 oz) raisins
Sea salt
Freshly ground black pepper
50 g (2 oz) soft fresh brown
breadcrumbs and
50 g (2 oz) grated cheese; or
A little fresh parsley

For the sauce:
50 g (2 oz) butter
50 g (2 oz) flour
575 ml (1 pint) water or stock
2 tablespoons tomato purée

Serves 3–4 as a main meal, 4–6 as a starter

If you're using fresh vine leaves or cabbage leaves, first of all half
fill a large saucepan with water and bring it to the boil. Trim the
leaves, removing the tough cabbage stalks with a 'V' shaped cut,
then put them into the boiling water, cover and simmer for 2
minutes. Then drain them and run them under the cold tap to
refresh them; drain well. With canned vine leaves just drain
them and rinse them well under the cold tap.

Set the oven to 180°C (350°F), gas mark 4. Make the filling
by peeling and chopping the onion and frying it in the olive oil for
10 minutes – don't let it brown – then stir in the rice, rosemary, nuts,
raisins and salt and pepper to taste. Mix well, then put a spoonful
of this filling on each leaf, fold over the edges and place the little
bundles side by side in a shallow ovenproof dish. If there are some
leaves over use them to fill in any gaps.

Make the sauce: melt the butter in a saucepan and stir in the flour, cook it for a minute or two, then mix in a little of the water, stirring vigorously over a high heat until the mixture is thick and smooth; then add a bit more water and continue like this until all the water has been used and you have a smooth, thick sauce. Then stir in the tomato purée and salt and pepper to taste. Pour this sauce over the stuffed leaves, making sure they are completely covered, then sprinkle them with the crumbs and grated cheese, if you're using them, and bake in the oven for 30 minutes. If you haven't used the crumb topping sprinkle the top of the dish with chopped parsley before serving.

Note: Pine kernels are really the correct nut to use for this dish but they are so expensive that I use this more economical mixture of chopped mixed nuts (which you can get at any super-market) and pine-flavoured rosemary.

Cereals, Rice and Curry Dishes

These dishes are satisfying to make because the cereal gives a good basis to which you can add all sorts of colourful and tasty ingredients. The red bean rice from the Caribbean, the vegetarian paella from Spain and the Indian *biriani* are all examples of this, and they're very good to eat.

I use brown rice for all these recipes and I find it perfectly satisfactory but it does vary considerably from batch to batch and so it's not always easy to be sure it's going to behave in exactly the same way each time. In particular I've found that rice varies in its ability to absorb water, sometimes needing 2 cups of water to 1 cup of rice and sometimes only $1\frac{3}{4}$ cups of water, so a little experimentation is probably advisable when you buy a new type. Start with the larger amount of water and if you find there is some over at the end of the cooking time let the rice stand, off the heat, but with the lid still in place, for 10–15 minutes. Then if there is still some water left, try using less next time. My favourite long-grain brown rice for all these savoury recipes is the type with the slenderest, most pointed grains; Harmony foods do a good one which cooks up beautifully and takes between 40 and 45 minutes. You can either cook it gently with just the right amount of water and the lid on the saucepan, or boil it in lots of water in a large saucepan so that the rice moves around as it cooks. I've given instructions in the individual recipes.

The other cereals used in this section are bulgur wheat, couscous and semolina. Bulgur is a delightful grain to use. In the packet it looks rather like a very granular semolina but when you soak it in boiling water for a few minutes it quickly absorbs the water and puffs up to become light and fluffy and you then simply heat it through. As it's quick I find it more useful for emergency meals than rice and in fact it can take the place of boiled rice for serving with vegetable stews and casseroles.

Couscous is a form of coarse-grained semolina and rather like bulgur to look at. You have to sprinkle couscous with cold salted water and allow it time to absorb the water, then steam it for 20–30 minutes. It's nice for a change, served with a spicy sauce. If you can't get couscous you could use bulgur wheat instead.

Semolina is used in one of the recipes, the tasty cheese *gnocchi* from Italy (and also in one of the dishes in the fritter section). I know people don't always like the idea of serving semolina as a savoury dish, but *gnocchi* is cheap and tasty and well worth trying. If you can get wholewheat semolina from the health shop that is ideal – you use it in exactly the same way as ordinary semolina and it isn't too dark-looking when it's cooked.

You will notice that I suggest using *ghee* in the Indian recipes. This does give a lovely nutty flavour and makes the food taste that much more Indian, but if you haven't got any don't worry, just use butter or vegetable oil instead. If you like Indian food and make it a lot, though, you might like to make your own *ghee* which is quite easy to do and keeps for 2 or 3 months at room temperature or for months in the fridge.

To make the *ghee*, cut 225 g (8 oz) unsalted butter into rough pieces and melt it very gently, in a heavy-based saucepan. Don't let the butter brown. When it has melted stir it then let it simmer, without a lid on the saucepan, over a very low heat, for about 45 minutes or until the solids at the bottom of the melted butter turn golden brown, and the butter on top becomes transparent. Strain the *ghee* through a sieve lined with 4 layers of damp muslin. If any of the solids come through, strain the *ghee* again; it must be perfectly clear otherwise it won't keep properly.

If you store the *ghee* in the fridge, it will solidify and you will need either to stand the container in a warm place before using the *ghee*, or to melt the *ghee* in a saucepan before use, but it will taste just as good.

BIRIANI

This deliciously spicy Indian rice dish is popular in our family. I usually serve it with lots of little bowls of extras for people to add at the table and the children love helping themselves to these. Favourites include chopped apple, mango chutney, diced cucumber, roasted peanuts, raisins, desiccated coconut, sliced onion, quarters of tomato and chopped hardboiled egg.

450 g (1 lb) long-grain brown rice
4 teaspoons turmeric
2 teaspoons sea salt
1·2 litres (2 pints) water
4 onions
3 tablespoons *ghee* or 75 g (3 oz) butter
2 teaspoons garam masala

2 teaspoons ground coriander
2 teaspoons poppy seed
2 teaspoons mustard seed
½ teaspoon chilli powder
225 g (8 oz) can tomatoes
125 g (4 oz) frozen green beans or canned okra
Freshly ground black pepper

Serves 4

Put the rice, turmeric, sea salt and water into a heavy-based saucepan and bring to the boil, then turn down the heat, put a lid on the saucepan and leave the rice to simmer gently for 40 minutes.

While the rice is cooking peel and chop the onions and fry them in the *ghee* or butter for 10 minutes until they're soft and golden but not browned. Stir in the garam masala, coriander, poppy seed, mustard seed and chilli powder and cook for 2 minutes, then add the tomatoes and cook gently for 10 minutes. Set the oven to 180°C (350°F), gas mark 4.

When the rice has cooked for 40 minutes add the tomato mixture to the saucepan and also the green beans or okra; mix lightly with a fork. Season with salt and pepper. Transfer the mixture to an ovenproof dish and bake the *biriani*, covered, for 20–30 minutes.

Biriani is nice served with curry sauce, a moist side salad and some crunchy golden poppadums. A cool, yoghurty or milky pudding goes well with it and supplies some extra protein.

BULGUR WHEAT PILAF   MIDDLE EAST

You can get bulgur wheat from health shops. It looks like a very large-grain semolina and is a pre-cooked cracked wheat. It makes a delicious pilaf and is quick and easy to use. I like it very much as a change from rice and you can make this pilaf the basis of a lovely Middle Eastern-style meal, starting with *hummus* or chilled cucumber soup and ending with the special ground rice pudding.

225 g (8 oz) bulgur wheat
575 ml (1 pint) boiling water
2 large onions
1–2 garlic cloves
1 red pepper
50 g (2 oz) butter

50 g (2 oz) raisins
Sea salt
Freshly ground black pepper
50–100 g (2–4 oz) roasted
 cashew nuts, almonds or
 pine kernels

Serves 3–4

Put the bulgur wheat into a large bowl and cover it with boiling water. Leave it on one side for 15–30 minutes; it will absorb most of the water and swell up.

While the bulgur is soaking peel and chop the onions, peel and crush the garlic and chop the pepper, discarding the seeds. Heat the butter in a large saucepan and fry the onions for 5 minutes, without browning them, then put in the garlic and pepper and fry gently for another 5 minutes. Drain the bulgur and add it to the onion mixture together with the raisins, stirring over the heat until the bulgur is well coated with butter. Season with salt and pepper to taste. Let the bulgur cook gently for 5–10 minutes until it's hot.

You can serve it at this point, but I think it's even better if you put a lid on the saucepan and let the pilaf stand for another 10–15 minutes, gently cooking in its own heat. Serve it sprinkled with the nuts. A juicy salad goes well with this dish.

Note: I find you can make the bulgur pilaf in advance and heat it through in a covered casserole in a moderate oven for about 30 minutes but it's best to add the nuts just before serving so that they retain their crispness.

BULGUR WHEAT AND CHEESE PILAF
MIDDLE EAST

The mixture of chewy garlic-flavoured bulgur wheat and soft melted cheese is very good. You don't have to add the raisins but I think this touch of sweetness is pleasant. The pilaf can be made in advance and reheated in a covered casserole in a moderate oven but don't add the cheese until just before serving.

225 g (8 oz) bulgur wheat
575 ml (1 pint) boiling water
2 large onions
50 g (2 oz) butter
1–2 cloves of garlic
1 green pepper

50 g (2 oz) raisins
Sea salt
Freshly ground black pepper
175–225 (6–8 oz) Lancashire
   cheese, cut into small dice

Serves 3–4

Put the wheat into a large bowl and pour in the boiling water; leave for 15–20 minutes to give the wheat a chance to expand. While this is happening peel and chop the onions and fry them for about 5 minutes in the butter in a large saucepan. Peel and crush the garlic; chop the pepper, discarding the seeds. Add the pepper and garlic to the onion and cook for a further 3–4 minutes.

Drain the wheat and stir this into the onion mixture, turning it over several times so that it all gets coated with the butter. Add the raisins and some salt and pepper then let the pilaf cook gently over a low heat for 5–10 minutes, until it's heated through. If you can then let it stand for 10 minutes, with a lid over the pan, steaming in its own heat, it will be even better. Heat it up again gently, then just before serving, when the pilaf is piping hot, stir in the pieces of cheese. Serve at once.

A tomato salad goes well with this followed by a fresh, fruity pudding.

CHEESE CURRY INDIA

In India the cheese for this curry would probably be made at home from yoghurt. As this is rather a laborious process I use white Lancashire cheese instead. You may feel my method is cheating a bit but I think you'll agree the spicy sauce and melting, creamy cheese make a delicious combination.

1 large onion
2 tablespoons oil, butter or *ghee*
1–2 cloves of garlic, peeled and crushed
225 g (8 oz) can tomatoes
½ teaspoon ground ginger
1 teaspoon ground cumin
2 teaspoons ground coriander

1 bay leaf
275 ml (½ pint) water
225 g (8 oz) frozen peas
Sea salt
Freshly ground black pepper
175–225 g (6–8 oz) Lancashire cheese
Hot cooked rice and mango chutney to serve

Serves 3–4

Peel or chop the onion then fry it in the butter, oil or *ghee* in a large saucepan for 10 minutes, until it's tender but not browned. Add the garlic, tomatoes, spices and bay leaf to the onions, mixing them around so that they all get coated with the fat. Pour in the water and bring up to the boil, then turn the heat down, partially cover the saucepan and leave the mixture to simmer for about 20 minutes. Then add the peas and cook for a further 3–4 minutes, just to heat them through. Season with salt and pepper. Cut the cheese into smallish dice – about 6 mm (¼ in) – and stir them into the curry just as you are about to serve it. Don't add

178

them too soon or they will melt too much and spoil the curry.
Serve with hot cooked rice and mango chutney.

COUSCOUS
MOROCCO

Couscous looks rather like tiny grains of rice but it's actually
made from semolina formed into little pellets. You sprinkle the
pellets with salted water then steam them and serve them with a
spicy vegetable stew. In Morocco couscous is cooked in a steamer
called a *couscousier* but you don't really need any special equip-
ment – I cook mine in a steamer with the vegetable stew cooking
in the saucepan below. You could equally well put the couscous
into a metal colander, put it on top of the saucepan of vegetables
and cover with a lid or some foil.

225 g (8 oz) couscous
½ teaspoon sea salt dissolved
   in a cupful of warm water
A little butter or olive oil

For the vegetable stew:
1 large or 2 medium onions
3 tablespoons oil
2 large carrots
2 tomatoes, skinned and
   chopped
125 g (4 oz) chick peas,

soaked, cooked until tender
   and drained
1 teaspoon cinnamon
1 teaspoon ground cumin
1 teaspoon ground coriander
2 tablespoons tomato purée
75 g (3 oz) raisins
400 ml (¾ pint) water
1 tablespoon chopped parsley
2 teaspoons lemon juice
Sea salt
Freshly ground black pepper

Serves 3–4

First of all start preparing the couscous: spread it out on a large
plate and sprinkle it with about a third of the salted water then
rub the grains gently between your fingers – rather like rubbing
fat into flour for pastry – to help separate the grains. Leave the

couscous for 10 minutes then repeat the process twice more, using the rest of the water.

While you're waiting for the couscous you can begin the stew. Peel and chop the onions and fry them in the oil in a large saucepan for 10 minutes until they're tender. Peel and dice the carrots and add them to the onions together with the tomatoes, chick peas, spices, tomato purée, raisins and water. Bring the mixture to the boil.

Line a steamer or metal colander with a piece of clean muslin or a double layer of kitchen paper and put in the couscous. Set the steamer over the saucepan containing the stew and cover with a lid or a piece of foil. Let it simmer gently for about 30 minutes, until the vegetables are cooked and the couscous is tender. Add some more water to the vegetable mixture if it is too thick and stir in the parsley, lemon juice and salt and pepper to taste.

Stir the couscous gently with a fork to make sure the grains are separate and fluffy and mix in a little butter or olive oil just to add flavour and make the couscous look shiny and appetizing.

To serve, spoon the couscous on to a large, warmed dish and pour the stew in the centre. Couscous makes a pleasant change from curry and rice. It shouldn't be too hot-tasting, just warmly and fragrantly spiced.

GNOCCHI ALLA ROMANA   ITALY

When this is brought from the oven, sizzling and golden brown, people find it difficult to believe it's made from semolina which they associate with dull school puddings. It's delicious and though you've got to allow time for the semolina mixture to get completely cold, it's not a difficult dish to make and one which you can do in stages and get ready in advance. It also freezes well.

Gnocchi should really be made with Parmesan cheese which of course gives it a lovely flavour, but when I'm making it for the family I use Cheddar spiced up with plenty of mustard powder and a pinch of cayenne pepper. For more flavour you can add some crushed garlic and/or grated onion to the basic mixture too.

This dish is lovely baked in little individual dishes and served as a first course. Or as a main dish I like to serve it with a tasty tomato sauce and either a lightly cooked green vegetable or a well-flavoured green salad. Another variation which is totally un-Italian is gnocchi with chips and parsley sauce!

Many people add semolina to milk by sprinkling it over the top of the boiling milk and stirring. I find it's all too easy to get lumps this way, so as you will see I use a different method which I find works well.

175 g (6 oz) semolina – you can buy the wholewheat variety from health shops
1½ teaspoons sea salt
A good grinding of black pepper and nutmeg
850 ml (1½ pints) milk

175 g (6 oz) grated cheese – including some Parmesan or Cheddar with 1½ teaspoons mustard powder and a pinch of cayenne
2 eggs
Oil

Serves 4 as a main dish, 6–8 as a starter

Put the semolina into a large bowl with the salt, pepper and nutmeg and mix it to a cream with some of the milk. Bring the rest of the milk to the boil, then pour it into the semolina mixture, stirring all the time. Tip the semolina and milk mixture back into the saucepan and stir over a fairly high heat until it thickens. Then let the mixture simmer gently until it's very thick and has lost its very granular appearance, stirring from time to time. In Italy they say that the mixture is ready when a spoon will stand up in it unsupported. In practice I find you can only achieve this if you've happened to use a small, deep saucepan, and that 10 minutes of simmering is about right. Remove the saucepan from the heat and stir in two-thirds of the cheese (and the mustard and cayenne if you're using them) and the eggs which will cook in the heat of the mixture. Taste and add more seasoning if necessary.

Lightly oil a large plate, tray or other suitable flat surface and turn out the semolina mixture on to this, spreading it to a thickness of about 6 mm ($\frac{1}{4}$ in). Leave it to get completely cold – overnight if possible.

When the mixture is cold it should be firm enough to cut into shapes. Traditionally it should be cut into circles with a pastry cutter which makes the finished dish look very attractive and doesn't really take a moment, but squares will do if you're in a hurry. Brush a large flat ovenproof dish with oil – I use one of those big white pizza plates which is ideal – and arrange the *gnocchi* in slightly overlapping circles, like roof tiles. Brush the top of the *gnocchi* with some oil and sprinkle with the remaining grated cheese, then either bake for about 15 minutes in a fairly hot oven 200°C (400°F), gas mark 6, or put the whole dish under a hot grill for about 20 minutes, if you have a grill which is big enough. Get the *gnocchi* really crisp and golden, then serve at once.

KHITCHARI INDIA

This is the dish from which the English kedgeree is derived. Although modern kedgeree is usually a fishy dish, the original *khitchari* was a spicy mixture of rice and lentils, ideal for vegetarians.

The usual way of making this, and the method I used to use, is to cook the lentils and rice together. But it's difficult to judge the amount of water and the timing and recently I've been cooking them separately then mixing them together and find that this gives a better result – light and slightly dry. I like *khitchari* with a juicy tomato salad and some mango chutney or lime pickle, but some people like to have some curry sauce with it too – there's a recipe for this in the sauces section of this book.

225 g (8 oz) split red lentils	1 garlic clove, peeled and
700 ml (1¼ pints) water	crushed
1 bay leaf	2 teaspoons curry powder
225 g (8 oz) long-grain brown	1 teaspoon cumin seeds
rice	(optional – from health
Sea salt	shops)
2 large onions	Freshly ground black pepper
2 tablespoons butter or *ghee*	1–2 teaspoons lemon juice

Serves 4

Put the lentils into a saucepan with the water and bay leaf and simmer them gently until the lentils are tender and have absorbed most of the water to make a thickish purée when you mix them. Take out the bay leaf. Keep the lentils warm.

While the lentils are cooking boil the rice in plenty of salted water until it's just tender – this will take 40–45 minutes – then drain and rinse it.

Peel and chop the onion and fry it in the butter or *ghee* in a small saucepan for 5 minutes, then stir in the garlic, curry powder and cumin seeds and cook for a further 5 minutes, until the onion is softened but not browned.

To assemble the dish, gently mix together the rice and lentils – use a fork for this to avoid damaging the grains of rice – then gently stir in the onion mixture. Season with salt and pepper and add a little lemon juice to taste.

You can vary *khitchari* in a number of ways. It's good with some sliced skinned tomato, chopped hardboiled eggs or fried mushrooms or green pepper stirred in just before serving.

PAELLA   SPAIN

Paella usually consists of saffron-flavoured rice with onions, tomatoes, fish and sausages, but the composition varies enormously depending on the whim of the cook and the contents of the store cupboard so I hope you won't think my vegetarian version too far-fetched. Anyway, people seem to enjoy this mixture of pale yellow saffron rice and tomatoes or green peas with its crunchy topping of golden brown flaked almonds. We like it with a fresh-tasting tomato sauce and a Spanish green salad. A chilled protein-rich pudding goes well with it – *crème brûlée* or little coffee custards, or chocolate and orange mousse if you want to continue the Spanish theme.

2 large onions
6 tablespoons olive oil
350 g (12 oz) long-grain
   brown rice
850 ml (1½ pints) water
1 packet of saffron – or 2
   packets give a more intense
   colour and flavour for a
   special occasion
2 teaspoons sea salt

Freshly ground black pepper
2 large garlic cloves, crushed
4 large carrots
1 large red pepper
4 tomatoes, skinned
125 g (4 oz) frozen peas
125 g (4 oz) flaked almonds
   toasted on a dry baking
   sheet in a moderate oven
   for 10–15 minutes

Serves 4

Peel and slice the onions. Heat the oil in a large saucepan and fry the onions for 10 minutes until they're soft but not browned. Wash and pick over the rice then add it to the onion together with the water, saffron, salt, a good grinding of pepper and the garlic. Bring the water up to the boil then turn the heat down, put a lid on the saucepan and leave the rice to cook very gently for 40 minutes. While the rice is cooking scrape the carrots and cut them into chunky dice. Cut the pepper into rings, discarding the seeds, and quarter the tomatoes. After the rice has been cooking for 20 minutes add the carrot – just put it in on top of the rice then put the lid back on the saucepan.

Ten minutes later add the pepper in the same way. After the rice has cooked for its 40 minutes put the tomatoes and peas into the saucepan. Put the lid back on and leave the rice, off the heat, for a further 15 minutes, to finish cooking slowly in its own heat. Then gently reheat the mixture, stirring with a fork to mix the rice with all the other vegetables. Sprinkle the nuts on top of the paella just before you serve it, so that they keep nice and crisp.

RED BEAN RICE   CARIBBEAN

This rice dish is a lovely medley of reds: tomato-coloured rice, with pieces of bright red pepper and deep crimson kidney beans – warming fare indeed and with a spicy taste to match! Serve it with pumpkin soup as a starter, a well-dressed green salad as an accompaniment and exotic fruit salad for dessert for a delicious Caribbean meal.

125 g (4 oz) red kidney beans, soaked, cooked (see p. 22), rinsed and simmered for 1 hour or so until tender
2 large onions, peeled and chopped
3 tablespoons vegetable oil
2 large garlic cloves, peeled and crushed

2 large red peppers, de-seeded and sliced
425 g (15 oz) can tomatoes
150 ml ($\frac{1}{4}$ pint) water or stock
225 g (8 oz) long-grain rice
Sea salt
3 teaspoons ground coriander
$\frac{1}{2}$–1 teaspoon chilli powder
Freshly ground black pepper

Serves 4

Drain the kidney beans; leave on one side. Peel and chop the onions and fry them for 10 minutes until they're tender. Stir in the garlic and red pepper and fry for a further minute or two, stirring so that everything gets coated with the oil. Add the can of tomatoes and the water or stock. Rinse the rice in cold water then put this into a saucepan together with a teaspoonful of salt, the spices and a grinding of pepper. Bring the mixture up to the boil then turn the heat right down and leave it to cook very gently for 40–45 minutes, until the rice is tender. Take the saucepan off the heat and leave it to stand, with the lid still on, for 10–15 minutes. Add the red beans, mixing them in gently with a fork. Check the seasoning then reheat.

FRIED RICE

This is a basic recipe for a spicy rice to eat with curries. It comes out a pretty bright yellow colour because of the turmeric. You can vary it by stirring in some nuts, sesame seeds or poppy seeds at the end to make it more crunchy and nutritious or you can add raisins or currants for sweetness, or chopped red or green peppers for extra colour.

225 g (8 oz) long-grain brown rice	1 teaspoon turmeric
1 tablespoon *ghee*	3 cloves
575 ml (1 pint) boiling water	1 bay leaf
	Salt and pepper

Serves 4

Wash the rice thoroughly, then drain it and, if possible, leave it for half an hour or so to dry off a little.

Heat the *ghee* in a heavy-based saucepan and add the drained rice. Fry the rice over a gentle heat until it has become opaque – this will take about 5 minutes and it's best to stir the rice all the time so that it doesn't brown – then put in the boiling water, turmeric, cloves and bay leaf and a seasoning of salt and pepper. When the mixture is boiling vigorously, turn down the heat and put a lid on the saucepan. Leave the rice to cook very gently for about 45 minutes, after which it should be tender and have absorbed all the liquid. Take out the cloves and bay leaf before serving the rice. (If there is still a little water left in the saucepan let the rice stand, still covered with the lid, for a further 10–15 minutes, after which you should find all is well.)

RICE AND PEAS   ITALY

This Italian dish, *risi e bisi*, is really halfway between a risotto and a soup, with a lovely creamy consistency. It's easy to make and good served with a tomato salad and some triangles of crisp toast.

2 large onions	350 g (12 oz) frozen peas
25 g (1 oz) butter	175 g (6 oz) finely grated
350 g (12 oz) long-grain	cheese
brown rice	1 teaspoon dry mustard
1·2 litres (2 pints) water	Freshly ground black pepper
Sea salt	Grated nutmeg

Serves 4

Peel and chop the onions. Melt the butter in a large saucepan and add the onions; fry them gently for about 10 minutes until they're soft and buttery but not browned. Wash the rice and put it into the saucepan with the onion; stir in the water and a rounded tea-spoonful of salt. Bring the mixture up to the boil then put a lid on the saucepan, turn the heat down and leave the rice to cook gently for 40 minutes.

If the peas are very icy put them into a sieve and rinse them under hot water, then put them into the saucepan on top of the rice 5 minutes before it's cooked. At the end of the cooking time take the rice off the heat and leave it, with a lid on the saucepan, for 10 minutes, to finish cooking in its own heat. After this you should find that the rice and peas are both cooked but that there is still some liquid left in the saucepan.

Stir the mixture with a fork, mixing in the cheese, dry mustard and salt, pepper and nutmeg to taste. Reheat very gently then serve at once.

RICE AND PEAS WITH TOMATO SAUCE

GERMANY

This German dish, *Schoten*, is made from ingredients similar to those used for the Italian *risi e bisi* but the result is different. The rice and pea mixture is drier, more like a pilaf, and it's served with a tomato sauce which provides moisture and colour.

350 g (12 oz) long-grain
   brown rice
850 ml (1½ pints) water
Sea salt
350 g (12 oz) frozen peas

50 g (2 oz) butter
1 onion, peeled and chopped
425 g (15 oz) can tomatoes
Freshly ground black pepper

Serves 4

Wash the rice and put it into a heavy-based saucepan with the water and a rounded teaspoonful of salt. Bring it up to the boil then turn the heat down, put a lid on the saucepan and let the rice cook very gently for 40 minutes. If the peas are very frozen tip them into a sieve and put them under the hot tap for a minute, then put them on top of the rice 5 minutes before it's ready.

When the rice is cooked take it off the heat and leave it, with the lid still on the saucepan, for 10 minutes to finish steaming in its own heat. While this is happening make the sauce. Melt half the butter in a medium-sized saucepan and fry the onion for 10 minutes until it's tender. Stir in the tomatoes and cook for 2–3 minutes, then liquidize the mixture. Season with salt and pepper and reheat gently.

To finish the dish add the remaining butter to the peas and rice and stir gently with a fork. Season carefully and serve with the tomato sauce.

RISOTTO BIANCO   ITALY

The proper way to make risotto is to add the liquid a little at a time, pouring in some more as each batch is absorbed. This means that you have to stand over the saucepan and with brown rice, which takes a long time to cook, it's very time-consuming. So I make risotto by cooking the rice slowly with a lid on the saucepan in the usual way, then beating it to make it creamy. You could leave out the fried mushrooms or red pepper if you want to but I think they make the risotto more interesting.

You might think that the quantity of rice I've given is rather large, but as you won't be serving potatoes and will probably just have a salad with the risotto, I think this is the right quantity. But if there's any left over it makes lovely little croquettes, rolled in crumbs and fried until crisp and golden.

2 large onions
75 g (3 oz) butter
450 g (1 lb) long-grain brown
  rice, washed
1·5 litres (2½ pints) water,
  stock or, for special
  occasions, replace 150 ml
  (¼ pint) of the liquid
  with white wine

Sea salt
125 g (4 oz) grated Parmesan
  cheese
225 oz (8 oz) mushrooms,
  lightly fried in a little
  butter; or 225 g (8 oz) red
  pepper, chopped and fried
  in oil
Freshly ground black pepper

Serves 4–6

Peel and chop the onions. Melt the butter in a heavy-based saucepan and fry the onions for 5 minutes, but don't let them brown. Add the rice and stir for a minute or two until it is well mixed with the buttery onion. Pour in the liquid and add some salt. Bring the mixture up to the boil, then put a lid on the saucepan, turn the heat right down and leave the rice to cook gently for 45 minutes. There will still be a little liquid left in the saucepan after the rice is done. Now beat the mixture with a wooden spoon to break up the grains of rice a bit and give a creamy texture.

Just before you serve the rice stir in the grated cheese and mushrooms or red peppers if you're using them. Check the seasoning, then take the rice to the table while it's still beautifully hot and the melting cheese all soft and creamy. Risotto is delicious with a tomato salad or a well-dressed green salad.

VEGETABLE CURRY INDIA

This vegetable curry is spicy but not 'hot'. If you want to you can make it 'hotter' by increasing the amount of chilli powder. It's lovely with plain boiled rice, or the spicy fried rice, some mango chutney and crunchy golden poppadums or chapatis. I usually serve it with a juicy side salad, too, which is cooling and refreshing.

50 g (2 oz) *ghee* or butter
1 large onion, peeled and chopped
2 garlic cloves, peeled and crushed
1 bay leaf
3 teaspoons ground coriander
3 teaspoons ground cumin
1 teaspoon ground ginger

$\frac{1}{4}$ teaspoon chilli powder
225 g (8 oz) canned tomatoes
1 teaspoon sea salt
Freshly ground black pepper
575 ml (1 pint) water
350 g (12 oz) carrots
350 g (12 oz) potatoes
125 g (4 oz) peas

Serves 4

Heat the *ghee* or butter in a large saucepan and fry the onion for 7–8 minutes, then add the garlic, bay leaf and spices and stir over the heat for 2–3 minutes. Mix in the tomatoes, salt, a grinding of pepper and the water. Simmer for 5–10 minutes while you prepare the vegetables. Scrape and slice the carrots, peel the potatoes and cut them into even-sized chunks. Add the potatoes and carrots to the tomato mixture and simmer gently for 15–25 minutes, until the vegetables are almost tender, then put in the peas and simmer for a further 5 minutes. Check the seasoning before serving.

Cheese and Egg Dishes

This section contains perhaps the most classic recipes of the vegetarian repertoire, with its omelettes and soufflés from France and cheese fondue from Switzerland, all delicious and surprisingly easy to make. There are also a couple of quick bread and cheese dishes, two interesting stuffed egg bakes and two beautiful savoury choux pastry rings which make an impressive centrepiece to a special meal.

Although I know it's a straightforward chemical process that makes a soufflé rise in the oven I still feel a thrill of pride and delight when I open the oven and see a puffed up golden soufflé! And despite its simplicity a soufflé always seems to impress people and convince them you're a wonderful cook – but really if you've got the proportions right in the mixture all you need are punctual guests, good nerves and the right-sized dish. Actually regarding the first two requirements, although a soufflé really is best if you eat it as soon as it's done I have found that as long as it is fairly well cooked it will stay risen in the oven for a few extra minutes if I turn off the heat. As far as the dish is concerned you need one of the correct capacity, which I've given in the recipes, and as long as the dish is big enough it doesn't really matter, from the flavour point of view, what shape it is. But if you want to produce a flamboyant, well-risen soufflé you need a narrow, fairly tall dish and the mixture should come just level with the rim when you put it into the oven. Don't pile it up any higher, as I rather foolishly did once, or you will find half your soufflé on the floor of the oven. If you're buying a soufflé dish look out for French ones made of metal with little handles at each side at the top. They may be called by their French name of *charlotte* and the ones I've seen are not very expensive.

Of course all the dishes in this section are rich in protein so menu planning is easy and straightforward. When I'm serving eggs or cheese for the main course I try to plan for a low-fat or non-dairy starter and pudding; perhaps a vegetable purée soup or mushrooms *à la Grecque*, for instance, and a simple fruity pudding.

BAKED STUFFED EGGS

RUSSIA

Usually stuffed eggs are served cold as a first course or part of a salad so this hot version from Russia is a pleasant variation. They're good as a first course baked in individual dishes and served with hot toast or as a main course, with fluffy boiled rice and perhaps a buttery spinach purée.

8 hardboiled eggs	Sea salt
2 large onions	Freshly ground black pepper
50 g (2 oz) butter	
1 tablespoon chopped fresh parsley	

Serves 4 as a main course, 8 as a starter

Set the oven to 180°C (350°F), gas mark 4. Cut the hardboiled eggs in half and take out the yolks; put the whites on one side. Peel and finely chop the onions. Melt the butter in a medium-sized saucepan and use some of it to brush a shallow oblong ovenproof dish which is big enough to hold all the egg whites in a single layer. Add the onion to the rest of the butter in the saucepan and fry it gently for 10 minutes, without letting it brown. Take the saucepan off the heat and add the egg yolks, mashing them into the onions until they're fairly creamy and smooth then stir in the parsley, salt and pepper. Spoon the mixture into the egg white cavities, piling it up neatly, then put the egg whites into the greased dish. Cover the dish with foil and bake in the oven for about 30 minutes, until the eggs are heated through.

These are also good with ½–1 teaspoon of dried dill, fennel or caraway seeds added to the mixture, if you like the taste.

BREAD AND CHEESE PUDDING WALES

This is rather like a Welsh rabbit baked in one dish in the oven. It's useful if you want to make a toasted cheese dish that you can prepare in advance for cooking later. You could use cider or beer instead of the milk for a more heady result, rather like a baked fondue.

8–10 slices of wholewheat bread
Butter
350 g (12 oz) grated Caerphilly
   or double Gloucester cheese
275 ml ($\frac{1}{2}$ pint) milk

Serves 4

You need enough slices of bread to line the base of a shallow ovenproof dish, and the same again to make a bread topping for the cheese. Grease the dish lightly. Toast all the bread and butter it on one side. Lay half the toast in the dish, unbuttered side down, then put most of the cheese and the remaining toast on top, buttered side down, and sprinkle with the last of the grated cheese. Pour the milk over the pudding and leave it to soak for about 30 minutes – or longer if you want. Put a few little pieces of butter over the top of the pudding.

When you're ready to cook the pudding, preheat the oven to 190°C (375°F), gas mark 5, then bake for about 40 minutes, until the pudding is crusty and brown on top. This is quite rich so it's nice served fairly simply with a tomato or watercress salad.

CHEESE FONDUE SWITZERLAND

Although fondue is very quick and easy to prepare I always think there's something rather festive and special about it – perhaps it's because everyone is dipping their bread into the communal pot of bubbling golden cheese. If you haven't got a fondue burner you can improvise with nightlights in a shallow dish with a couple of supports or a grill rack across to hold the saucepan of fondue.

Although fondue is at its best when made with dry white wine, Gruyère and Emmenthal cheeses and kirsch, I've found you can make an excellent, much cheaper version with Edam cheese and dry cider.

1 garlic clove	Sea salt
275 ml ($\frac{1}{2}$ pint) dry white wine or cider	Freshly ground black pepper
	Grated nutmeg
225 g (8 oz) Gruyère cheese and 225 g (8 oz) Emmenthal cheese, grated; or use 450 g (1 lb) grated Edam cheese	1 large French loaf or crusty wholewheat loaf – or half of each – cut into bite-sized pieces and warmed in the oven
1 tablespoon cornflour	
1–2 tablespoons kirsch (optional)	

Serves 4–6

Halve the garlic and rub the cut surfaces over the inside of a medium-sized saucepan (or special fondue pan). Put the wine or cider and cheese into the saucepan and heat gently, stirring all the time until the cheese has melted. Mix the cornflour to a paste with the kirsch if you're using it, or use a drop more wine or cider; pour this paste into the cheese mixture, stirring all the time until you have a lovely smooth creamy consistency. Occasionally the cheese goes all lumpy and stringy at this point. Don't despair; if you beat it vigorously for a moment or two with a rotary whisk all will be well. Season the fondue then place the saucepan over the lighted burner and let everyone start dipping their bread into the delicious mixture.

Fondue is rich so the menu planning needs some care. If you have a starter, keep this light and salady; follow the fondue with something refreshing and non-creamy like fresh peaches or pineapple sorbet.

CURRIED STUFFED EGGS INDIA

This is a tasty dish, hardboiled eggs stuffed with a curry mixture and baked in a spicy sauce. They're lovely served with hot boiled rice, some mango chutney and crisp poppadums.

8 hardboiled eggs
1 large onion
3 tablespoons *ghee*, oil or butter
1 garlic clove
225 g (8 oz) can tomatoes
1 teaspoon ground cumin

1 teaspoon ground coriander
1 teaspoon ground ginger
½ teaspoon turmeric
275 ml (½ pint) water
Sea salt
Freshly ground black pepper

Serves 4

Halve the eggs, take out the yolks and put them into a bowl. Leave the whites on one side for the moment. Peel and finely chop the onion and fry it gently in the *ghee* for 10 minutes. Peel and crush the garlic and add it to the onion, together with the tomatoes, spices, water and some salt and pepper. Let the mixture simmer, with a lid on the saucepan, for 20 minutes, then sieve or liquidize this sauce. Check the seasoning. Set oven to 180°C (350°F), gas mark 4. Mash the egg yolks and stir in 2 or 3 tablespoons of sauce, enough to make a soft but not sloppy mixture.

Spoon the yolk mixture into the egg whites. Pour the curry sauce into a shallow ovenproof dish that's big enough to hold all the eggs in one layer, then put the eggs in on top of the sauce. Cover with foil and bake for 30 minutes just to heat the eggs through.

GOUGÈRE WITH MUSHROOMS, ONIONS AND RED WINE SAUCE

This is an impressive and delicious dish, a big puffed-up ring of golden choux pastry, the centre filled with button mushrooms and onions in red wine sauce. It's lovely served with baby Brussels sprouts and creamy mashed potatoes. *Gougère* is not difficult to make but it's best eaten as soon as it's ready, so you need to be able to get everyone to the table on time. Don't be put off by the long list of ingredients for the sauce; it's really quite easy to do.

For the gougère:
125 g (4 oz) butter or margarine
275 ml (½ pint) water
150 g (5 oz) plain wholewheat flour – or half wholewheat and half unbleached white flour
1 teaspoon sea salt
4 eggs, beaten
175 g (6 oz) grated cheese
A good pinch of cayenne pepper

For the filling:
3 onions, peeled and sliced
15 g (½ oz) butter
225 g (8 oz) baby button mushrooms, washed and left whole

Serves 6

For the sauce:
400 ml (¾ pint) stock – or water and a good teaspoon of vegetarian stock powder
400 ml (¾ pint) red wine
1 bay leaf
1 piece of onion, peeled
1 garlic clove, peeled and sliced
A good pinch of thyme
½ teaspoon black peppercorns
1–2 parsley stalks if available
1 tablespoon redcurrant jelly
Sea salt
Freshly ground black pepper
Sugar
40 g (1½ oz) soft butter
20 g (¾ oz) flour

You can make the main preparations for the various parts of this dish in advance if that is most convenient for you. To make the *gougère*, put the butter or margarine and water into a medium-sized saucepan and heat gently until the butter has melted, then turn up the heat and bring the mixture to the boil. Mix the flour with the salt and quickly pour into the saucepan all at once. Stir over the heat with a wooden spoon for 1 minute, by which time the mixture will have formed a glossy ball of dough, then take the saucepan off the heat and tip the dough into a clean bowl.

Add about a quarter of the beaten egg and beat vigorously with a wooden spoon until the dough has absorbed the egg and become smooth and glossy again, then add another quarter and beat again. Repeat until all the egg has been used. I sometimes find when I'm using all wholewheat flour that the mixture will only take three-quarters of the egg; by then it is quite soft and any more would make it sloppy – it must hold its shape softly. If this happens to you don't worry; just use the extra to glaze the top before sprinkling on the cheese and baking. The reason is that wholewheat flour is not as absorbent as white and varies quite a bit from batch to batch. Stir in about two-thirds of the grated cheese, and the cayenne pepper. You can cover the mixture with a plate and leave it at this point for several hours if you wish.

To make the filling, fry the onions in the 15 g ($\frac{1}{2}$ oz) butter for 10 minutes until they're soft, then put in the mushrooms and fry for a further 3–4 minutes until they too are tender. Season with salt and pepper and leave on one side. If the mushrooms produce a great deal of liquid drain it off and use it as part of the stock for the sauce.

For the sauce put the stock and red wine into a good-sized saucepan with the bay leaf, onion, garlic, thyme, peppercorns and parsley stalks if you've got them and bring up to the boil. Let the mixture bubble away furiously without a lid for 10–15 minutes until it has reduced by half and you're left with 400 ml ($\frac{3}{4}$ pint) of liquid. Strain this liquid into a clean saucepan and stir in the redcurrant jelly and salt, pepper and sugar to taste. Make a *beurre manié*: put half the butter on a plate with the flour and mash them together with the back of a spoon to make a paste. Add this *beurre manié* to the wine mixture in several pieces, beating well after each, then put the sauce back on the heat and stir it for a minute or two until it's slightly thickened. Let it simmer for a further 4–5 minutes to cook the flour, then take the saucepan off the heat and dot the remaining butter over the surface of the sauce to prevent a skin forming. Leave on one side until you're ready to serve the *gougère*.

To finish the *gougère* preheat the oven to 200˚C (400˚F), gas mark 6. Oil a large ovenproof dish – one of those big white pizza plates is ideal if you have one but any large shallow ovenproof dish will do – and spoon the *gougère* mixture all round the edge, heaping it up into as neat a ring as possible but leaving the centre free. Sprinkle the top of the ring with the rest of the grated cheese then bake the *gougère* for 40 minutes until it is puffed up and golden brown. When the *gougère* is nearly done reheat the onions and mushrooms gently, also the sauce.

Take the *gougère* out of the oven, spoon the mushroom mixture into the centre and pour a little sauce over the mushrooms and onions – serve the rest of the sauce separately in a jug. Serve the *gougère* immediately.

You can put other things into the centre of the *gougère*; it's nice with a buttery purée of spinach in the middle and cheese sauce served separately.

COLD GOUGÈRE WITH CREAM CHEESE FILLING
FRANCE

If you make a *gougère* as in the previous recipe and bake it for longer so that it's really firm, you can split it round the middle and serve it cold, sandwiched with soft white cheese and its centre filled with crisp lettuce, tomato, watercress and spring onion salad. It makes an attractive buffet dish.

Gougère mixture as in the previous recipe.

For the filling:	*To garnish:*
700 g (1½ lb) low-fat quark or cream cheese	1 crisp lettuce
	½ bunch watercress
Sea salt	4 tomatoes, sliced
Freshly ground black pepper	6 spring onions, trimmed

Serves 8–12

Make the *gougère* as described in the preceding recipe but bake it for a good hour until it is well-risen and very firm – all 'sizzling' should have ceased in the choux pastry. If it's not really firm it will collapse and be soggy inside.

Take the *gougère* out of the oven, slit it horizontally with a sharp knife and leave it on the dish to get completely cold.

It's best not to fill the *gougère* until just before you're going to serve it so that it stays as crisp as possible. Put the cheese into a bowl and mash it with a fork to break it up, then beat it until it's soft and light. Season the cheese with salt and pepper – a touch of garlic is nice too, if you like it. Carefully remove the top half of the *gougère* and spread the cheese over the bottom layer, then replace the top half. Arrange the salad in the middle of the circle. An alternative is to put the salad inside the *gougère* on top of the cheese.

OMELETTE
FRANCE

I think a well-made omelette, light and golden brown on the outside, creamy and moist within, is still one of the best and quickest convenience foods of all. It's versatile, too, because you can serve it with all sorts of different fillings. The important thing is to have the filling all ready to pop into the omelette and everyone sitting at the table before you start to cook the omelette because it's speed that's the essence of success.

For the filling:
Any of the following:
50 g (2 oz) finely grated cheese
50 g (2 oz) button mushrooms, sliced and lightly fried
50 g (2 oz) canned cut green asparagus, heated in its own liquid and drained just before using
50 g (2 oz) canned artichoke hearts, sliced, heated and drained just before using
1 tablespoon chopped fresh green herbs – parsley, chives, chervil, tarragon – whatever is available

For the omelette:
2 eggs
2 teaspoons cold water
Sea salt

Freshly ground black pepper
1 teaspoon oil
15 g ($\frac{1}{2}$ oz) butter

Serves 1

Beat the eggs in a bowl with the water, a pinch of salt and a grinding of pepper. Put the frying pan – a 15–18 cm (6–7 in) one is best if you've got one as it makes a nice thick omelette – over a high heat for about one minute, then turn the heat down and put in first the oil and then the butter. When the butter has melted turn up the heat again and put in the beaten egg. Immediately start moving the egg using a palette knife to push the edges of the omelette towards the centre, tipping the pan as you do so to make the liquid egg in the middle run to the edges – keep the heat up high. All this happens very quickly – the omelette should be done in under a minute. Loosen the edges of the omelette quickly with the palette knife, spoon the filling on top then tip the pan away from you so that the omelette folds over itself, then gently tip it on to a warmed plate. Serve immediately.

PIPÉRADE   FRANCE

This tasty mixture of tomatoes, peppers and onions in creamy lightly-set scrambled egg makes a good quick supper dish. It's lovely served with warm crisp French bread or wholewheat rolls.

2 onions
2 garlic cloves
1 green pepper
1 red pepper
4 tomatoes

50 g (2 oz) butter
6 eggs
Sea salt
Freshly ground black pepper
Chopped fresh parsley

Serves 4

Peel and chop the onions, peel and crush the garlic; wash, de-seed and chop the peppers, skin and chop the tomatoes. Melt the butter in a large saucepan, put in the onion and fry it for about 5 minutes without letting it brown, then mix in the garlic, peppers and tomatoes and cook for a further 5 minutes over a low heat with the lid on the saucepan.

Meanwhile beat the eggs in a small bowl with some salt and pepper. When the vegetables are tender pour the egg into the saucepan and stir gently over a low heat until the egg is lightly scrambled, but don't let it get too dry – it's best to keep the heat low all the time and take the *pipérade* off the stove while it's still runny. Check seasoning, then serve at once, sprinkled with chopped parsley and accompanied by the warm bread. Follow with fresh fruit or a fruity type of pudding.

CHEESE SOUFFLÉ   FRANCE

I think this is perhaps the best soufflé of all with its satisfying savoury flavour and lovely golden colour. The classic cheese to use is Gruyère but I find Cheddar is fine for everyday cooking whilst a red cheese such as Leicestershire or double Gloucester makes the soufflé a beautiful rich golden colour which looks very appetizing.

40 g (1½ oz) butter	1 teaspoon mustard powder
40 g (1½ oz) flour	Sea salt
275 ml (½ pint) milk	Freshly ground black pepper
125 g (4 oz) grated cheese	5 egg whites
4 egg yolks	

Serves 4

Grease a 1¾ litre (3 pint) soufflé dish or tin with a little butter or oil. Melt the butter in a large saucepan and stir in the flour; cook for a few seconds than add a third of the milk. Stir the mixture over a high heat until it first goes lumpy then smooth and very thick, then add another third of the milk and repeat until you've used all the milk. Stir for a minute or two then draw the saucepan off the heat and pour the sauce into a large bowl. Let the mixture cool slightly then mix in the grated cheese, egg yolks, mustard and a good seasoning of salt and pepper. (You can cover the mixture and leave it for several hours at this stage if necessary.)

Set the oven to 190°C (375°F), gas mark 5. If you have a baking sheet place this on the shelf above the centre – it will get hot and when you put your soufflé dish on it there will be a nice blast of heat from the base to get things off to a good start. Whisk the egg whites. They should be stiff enough for you to be able to turn the bowl over without them coming out, but not so stiff that you could almost slice them with a knife, so stop in time. Mix a rounded tablespoonful of egg white into the cheese mixture to soften it then tip the rest of the egg white on top of the mixture and using the side of a flattish metal spoon cut and fold the egg whites into the cheese mixture until the egg white has all been incorporated and you have a very light airy mixture. Pour the soufflé gently into the prepared dish – ideally the mixture should come up level with the rim; it doesn't matter if it's lower but don't pile it up above the rim. Bake the soufflé for 30–35 minutes until it looks firm when you shake it slightly – you can test it if you like with a fine skewer which should come out clean.

Cheese soufflé is lovely with a green salad or simply cooked vegetables such as new potatoes and French beans; it also makes an excellent first course, followed by a vegetable-based main course such as ratatouille and garlic bread or stuffed tomatoes à la Provençale and courgettes, with a fruity pudding to follow.

If you want to make a soufflé feed 6 people, use a 2 litre (3½–4 pint) dish and increase the quantities like this: 50 g (2 oz) each of butter and flour; 400 ml (¾ pint) milk; 175 g (6 oz) grated cheese; 5 egg yolks and 6 egg whites. You will need to cook it for just a little longer, too.

INDIVIDUAL CHEESE SOUFFLÉS

FRANCE

Puffy golden individual cheese soufflés look impressive and make a lovely first course or lunch dish. They're also very practical because they only take 15–20 minutes to cook so you can get the initial preparation done in advance, receive your visitors or round up the family, then add the egg whites and put the soufflés to cook 15 or 20 minutes before you want to eat. As a starter these soufflés are ideal before one of the low-protein vegetable dishes. Or for a special lunch serve them after avocados, with a tasty green salad and fruity pudding.

25 g (1 oz) butter or margarine
25 g (1 oz) flour
150 ml (¼ pint) milk
Pinch each of mustard powder
  and cayenne pepper

125 g (4 oz) grated cheese
2 eggs, separated

Makes 3 individual soufflés

Prepare 3 individual soufflé dishes – those little white porcelain ones are ideal – by greasing lightly with oil or butter. Place a baking sheet in the centre of the oven.

Melt the butter or margarine in a medium-sized saucepan and stir in the flour; when it froths add the milk mixing well over a gentle heat for a few minutes until smooth and thick. Remove from the heat, cool slightly then add the seasoning, grated cheese and the egg yolks. (The mixture can be prepared in advance up to this stage.)

Set the oven to 190°C (375°F), gas mark 5. Whisk the egg whites until they are very stiff and able to hold their shape but not dry. Mix a heaped tablespoonful of egg white into the cheese mixture to loosen it, then add the rest and carefully incorporate it by folding the cheese mixture gently over it with a metal spoon, so that you don't flatten the egg white. Divide the mixture between the little dishes and place them in the oven on the baking sheet.

Bake for 15–20 minutes until risen and golden brown. Serve immediately; they will keep in the oven for a further few minutes if you turn off the heat but the sooner they are served the better they are.

These quantities will double satisfactorily to serve 6. To serve 4 use the basic mixture with an extra egg.

LEEK SOUFFLÉ

FRANCE

The chunky pieces of leek in this soufflé give it a lovely delicate flavour and interesting texture. Try to find really thin leeks if you can then they can be sliced into nice neat pieces which will stay firm when they're cooked.

3–4 thin leeks, weighing 350 g	275 ml ($\frac{1}{2}$ pint) milk
(12 oz) before you trim them	4 egg yolks
Sea salt	Freshly ground black pepper
40 g ($1\frac{1}{2}$ oz) butter	Nutmeg
40 g ($1\frac{1}{2}$ oz) flour	5 egg whites

Serves 4

First of all prepare a $1\frac{3}{4}$ litre (3 pint) soufflé dish or tin by greasing generously. Then cut the roots and leafy green part off the leeks. Slit the leeks down one side and wash them carefully under running water, then cut them into 2·5 cm (1 in) lengths. Cook the leeks in 1 cm ($\frac{1}{2}$ in) boiling salted water until they're just tender – about 7–10 minutes. Drain the leeks well and keep them on one side.

Melt the butter in a medium-sized saucepan and put in the flour; cook for a few moments then add about a third of the milk. Stir all the time over a high heat until the mixture has thickened, then add another third of the milk and repeat the process until all the milk has been added and you've got a nice smooth thickish sauce. Transfer the sauce to a large bowl – this cools it slightly ready for adding the egg yolks and is more convenient later when you want to fold in the egg white. Beat in the egg yolks one by one then gently stir in the leeks. Season the mixture with salt, pepper and nutmeg – be fairly generous because the egg whites will 'dilute' the mixture. Now you can leave this mixture until just before you want to cook the soufflé – I have kept it for several hours in the fridge and it has been perfect.

When you're ready to cook the soufflé place a baking sheet on the middle shelf of the oven. Set the oven to 190°C (375°F), gas mark 5. Whisk the egg whites until they're thick and standing in soft peaks but don't let them get hard and dry. Stir a generous heaped tablespoonful of egg white into the leek sauce mixture to loosen it then tip all the egg white on top of it and gently fold it in with a metal spoon. When it has all been incorporated pour the mixture gently into your prepared dish – it should come just up to the rim. If it is lower it will still taste good even though it won't look so impressively high and puffy but if it is piled up above the rim it will overflow.

Put the soufflé on the baking sheet and bake for 30–35 minutes until it looks firm when you move the dish slightly and a skewer pushed gently down into the soufflé comes out clean. If it's done before you're quite ready turn off the oven and the soufflé will keep for 4–5 minutes longer although it won't be quite so puffy. I think this soufflé is nicest served with just one well-cooked vegetable such as buttered baby carrots, sprouts or peas.

If you want to make this soufflé serve 6 people grease a 2 litre (3½–4 pint) dish and use 50 g (2 oz) butter and flour and 400 ml (¾ pint) milk for the sauce with 5 egg yolks and 6 egg whites – cook the soufflé for a little longer.

MUSHROOM SOUFFLÉ   FRANCE

This is a delicious soufflé – when you cut it open the chunks of mushroom look most appetizing. It's nicest made with those firm white button mushrooms.

175 g (6 oz) firm white button mushrooms

275 ml ($\frac{1}{2}$ pint) milk

50 g (2 oz) butter

4 egg yolks

1 garlic clove, peeled and crushed

Sea salt

40 g ($1\frac{1}{2}$ oz) flour

Freshly ground black pepper

5 egg whites

Serves 4

Prepare a $1\frac{3}{4}$ litre (3 pint) soufflé dish or tin by greasing with a little butter. Wash the mushrooms then cut them into halves or quarters so that the pieces are all roughly the same size. Melt a quarter of the butter in a medium-sized saucepan and put in the mushrooms. Cook them gently without a lid on the saucepan for about 5 minutes, then stir in the garlic.

Melt the rest of the butter in another medium-sized saucepan and stir in the flour, then add about a third of the milk, stirring over a high heat until the mixture has thickened, then add another third and continue like this until it has all been added. Take the saucepan off the heat and pour the sauce into a large bowl. Let it cool a bit then mix in the mushrooms (drain off any excess liquid), egg yolks and seasoning to taste. Leave on one side (for several hours or overnight in the fridge if necessary) until you're ready to cook the soufflé.

Put a baking sheet on the shelf above the centre of the oven and heat to 190°C (375°F), gas mark 5. Whisk the egg whites until they're stiff but not dry and fold them carefully into the mushroom mixture. Spoon the soufflé into the prepared dish – ideally it should come to the top but no higher – and bake it for 30–35 minutes, until it's golden brown, well risen and it looks firm when moved slightly. A skewer inserted should come out clean. Serve at once. This soufflé is nice with some green beans, baked tomatoes and creamy mashed potatoes.

If you want to expand this soufflé to serve 6 people, here are the quantities. Use a 2 litre ($3\frac{1}{2}$–4 pint) dish and 60 g ($2\frac{1}{2}$ oz) butter, 225 g (8 oz) mushrooms, 50 g (2 oz) flour, 400 ml ($\frac{3}{4}$ pint) milk, 5 egg yolks and 6 egg whites. You will need to allow a few minutes longer for the soufflé to cook.

POTATO AND WATERCRESS SOUFFLÉ

I have to admit that I've allowed myself a bit of licence here because the addition of the watercress is my own idea and you could omit it if you want to be more authentic. But I found the plain potato soufflé rather dull and so I added the watercress which I think gives the soufflé a more interesting flavour and colour. It makes a good light main dish and it's nice served as a protein-rich accompanying vegetable dish.

700 g (1½ lb) potatoes
Sea salt
50 g (2 oz) butter
150 ml (5 fl oz) milk or single cream

2 bunches watercress
4 egg yolks
Freshly ground black pepper
5 egg whites

Serves 4–6

Peel the potatoes, cut them into even-sized pieces and cook them in boiling salted water until they're tender, then drain and mash them with the butter and milk or cream. Wash the watercress carefully and remove the coarse stems, then chop the leaves fairly finely and stir them into the potato mixture together with the egg yolks and plenty of salt and pepper to taste.

You can prepare the soufflé up to this point in advance. When you're ready to cook it set the oven to 190°C (375°F), gas mark 5; grease a 1¾ litre (3 pint) soufflé dish or tin. Whisk the egg whites until they're very stiff but not dry, then fold them into the potato mixture. Spoon the soufflé into the dish and bake for 45 minutes, until it's puffed up and golden and looks firm when you move the dish slightly. Serve the soufflé at once – or within 5 minutes at the most. It's nice with home-made tomato sauce and a lightly cooked colourful vegetable such as carrots.

WELSH RABBIT

Some people say that this dish derives its name from the fact that it was served instead of rabbit when times were hard; anyway, it's one of our favourite quick supper dishes.

4 large slices wholewheat bread
225 g (8 oz) grated Cheddar or
  Caerphilly cheese

3 tablespoons milk or beer
Cayenne pepper
Freshly ground black pepper

Serves 2–4

Toast the bread; arrange the slices in a grill pan or on a baking sheet which will fit under the grill. Put the grated cheese and milk or beer into a saucepan and heat them together, stirring all the time until the cheese has melted. Remove from the heat and add a pinch of cayenne pepper and a grating of black pepper. Pour the cheese mixture over the toast and pop it under a moderately hot grill for about 5 minutes, until the cheese is bubbly and lightly browned. Serve immediately.

This goes well with a tomato and onion salad or a nice crisp lettuce salad with fresh green herbs in it; alternatively serve the Welsh rabbit on its own and follow with some fresh fruit.

Fritters and Rissoles

It's surprising what a variety of dishes come into this section. There are delicious, crisp little cheesy fritters – the fried *gnocchi* and rice croquettes from Italy and the Glamorgan sausage from Wales; there are spicy lentil fritters from the Middle East and fritters made from wheat protein from China. Then from Germany and Switzerland there are potato fritters which are crisp and delicious but need to be served with some extra protein, and sweetcorn fritters from the USA.

Perhaps the most unusual recipes are the *gnocchi* which are a kind of savoury dumpling. They don't sound at all exciting but when they're served all hot and puffed up and oozing with melted butter and cheese they're delicious, excellent as either a first course or a main course.

Some of the fritters need to be dipped in crisp crumbs. I make these by cutting up a wheatmeal loaf and baking the slices in a low oven until they're really dry and crisp, then crushing them with a rolling pin, popping them into a liquidizer or putting them through an electric grater. They keep very well in an airtight jar. When it comes to coating the fritters with the crumbs, which I think is a horrid, messy job, I find the task of clearing up is greatly eased if you put the dry crumbs on a large piece of grease-proof paper and work on this. Afterwards you can simply roll up the paper with any left over crumbs and sticky eggy bits and pieces and throw it away.

GLAMORGAN SAUSAGE
WALES

These little cheesy sausages are delicious and an excellent source of protein. They're good with salad and some chutney or with a parsley or tomato sauce and cooked vegetables. If you make the sausages tiny they're lovely as a nibble with drinks.

350 g (12 oz) Caerphilly cheese, grated
125 g (4 oz) soft wholewheat breadcrumbs
1 teaspoon mustard powder
6 tablespoons cold water

Freshly ground black pepper
A little flour
1 egg, beaten with 1 table-spoonful of cold water
Dried crumbs for cooking
Oil for shallow frying

Serves 4

Mix together the cheese, soft breadcrumbs, mustard, cold water and some pepper to taste. Gather the mixture into a ball then divide it into 8 pieces and roll each into a sausage shape on a floured board. Dip each little sausage into the beaten egg and then into dried crumbs. Heat a little oil in a frying pan and fry the sausages quickly until they're crisp, then drain them and serve immediately.

I've found that you can also make a delicious nut version of this recipe which I'm sure a Welshman wouldn't own but which we prefer. Use 225 g (8 oz) grated cheese and 125 g (4 oz) grated cashew nuts or hazel nuts with the breadcrumbs and water as above. It's nice flavoured with a little chopped rosemary.

Both this mixture and the proper version are good baked instead of fried – press the mixture into a greased ovenproof dish and bake it at 200°C (400°F), gas mark 6 for about 45 minutes. The result is rather a crisp savoury cake which can be cut up and served with a parsley or tomato sauce; it's also nice cold with chutney and salad.

FRIED GNOCCHI
ITALY

This is my version of the fried *gnocchi* or *bombolini* sold in the market in Verona. People sometimes hesitate to try them because they associate semolina with school puddings, but it's completely different and delicious in this crisp, savoury form.

125 g (4 oz) semolina –
 ordinary semolina or the
 wholewheat variety from
 health shops
575 ml (1 pint) milk
1 bay leaf
1 small onion, peeled
1½ teaspoons mustard powder
125 g (4 oz) grated Cheddar
 cheese

1 teaspoon sea salt
A good grinding of black
 pepper
1 egg, beaten with a
 tablespoonful of water
Dried crumbs
Oil for deep or shallow frying

Serves 4

Put the semolina into a medium-sized bowl and mix to a paste with a little of the milk. Heat the remaining milk with the bay leaf and onion; bring just to the boil then cover the saucepan and leave it on one side, off the heat, for 10 minutes or so for the flavours to infuse the milk. Remove the bay leaf and onion and reheat the milk. When it boils pour it over the semolina cream in the bowl, then return the mixture to the saucepan and bring to the boil, stirring all the time. Let the mixture cook for a few minutes until it's thick and has lost its granular appearance – about 10 minutes. Take the saucepan off the heat and stir in the mustard, grated cheese, salt and pepper. Taste the mixture and add more seasoning if necessary to give a tangy savoury flavour.

Turn the mixture on to a lightly oiled plate, spread it out to a thickness of about 1 cm (½ in) and leave it to get completely cold. As it cools it will firm up and you will be able to cut it into small squares or other shapes. Dip the shapes first into the beaten egg then into the dry crumbs and deep or shallow fry them until

214

they're golden brown and crisp. Drain the *gnocchi* on kitchen paper.

These are very popular with my children who like them best with chips, lemon slices and parsley sauce. They freeze very well; I open-freeze them after coating them with egg and bread-crumbs, then store them in a polythene bag. They can be shallow-fried straight from the freezer.

GNOCCHI IN MUSHROOM SAUCE   AUSTRIA

Although in Italy *gnocchi* are usually served with grated cheese on top, in France and Austria it's more common to find them covered in a sauce, as in this version.

75 g (3 oz) flour –
  wholewheat is fine
50 g (2 oz) butter
125 g (4 oz) grated
  Cheddar cheese
½ teaspoon sea salt
½ teaspoon mustard powder
2 eggs
Dried breadcrumbs
A little grated cheese

For the sauce:
50 g (2 oz) butter
50 g (2 oz) flour
1 bay leaf
575 ml (1 pint) milk
125 g (4 oz) mushrooms,
  washed and chopped
Freshly ground black pepper
Grated nutmeg

Serves 4

To make the *gnocchi* mix together the flour, butter, cheese, salt and mustard; when they're combined break in the eggs one by one and blend well with a fork to make a dough. Form the dough into walnut-sized balls on a lightly floured board. Heat half a saucepanful of salted water; when it boils drop in the little *gnocchi* and let them simmer gently for about 7 minutes, until they puff up, rise to the surface of the water and look firm. (Cut one in half to see if it's cooked and set inside.) Take the *gnocchi* out of the water with a draining spoon and put them into a lightly greased shallow ovenproof dish.

For the sauce melt the butter in a large saucepan and add the flour and bay leaf; stir for a moment or two, then add a quarter of the milk, stirring all the time over a high heat until the mixture is smooth. Then add another quarter of the milk, repeating the process until all the milk has been added and you have a smooth sauce. Take the saucepan off the heat and mix in the mushrooms and plenty of salt, pepper and nutmeg to taste. Pour the sauce over the *gnocchi* and sprinkle with dried crumbs and a little grated cheese.

When you're ready to finish the *gnocchi* set the oven to 190°C (375°F), gas mark 5 and bake them for 30–40 minutes, until they're heated through and the topping is crisp and golden.

This is good served with either a salad or a cooked green vegetable. It also makes an excellent first course if you bake small portions in individual ovenproof dishes.

RICOTTA GNOCCHI ITALY

These little savoury dumplings are quick and easy to do and make a delicious light meal or first course with their golden cheesy topping. If it's more convenient you can make them in advance and just put them into a fairly hot oven for about 20 minutes to heat them through and brown the topping before you serve them. A green salad with a tasty dressing goes best with them I think.

75 g (3 oz) flour – wholewheat is fine	125 g (4 oz) *ricotta* or cottage cheese
50 g (2 oz) butter	½ teaspoon sea salt
125 g (4 oz) grated Cheddar cheese – if you can include a little Parmesan it gives a lovely flavour	½ teaspoon mustard powder
	2 eggs

216

To finish:	1 garlic clove, peeled and
A little extra flour	crushed in a little salt
25 g (1 oz) butter	75 g (3 oz) grated cheese

Serves 4 for supper, 6 as a first course

Put the flour into a bowl and mix in the butter, Cheddar cheese, *ricotta* cheese, salt and mustard, then break in the eggs, one by one, and mix well with a fork until everything is blended to a dough. Put walnut-sized pieces of the dough on to a lightly floured board and with your fingers form them into smooth balls, using more flour to coat them as necessary.

Half fill a large saucepan with water, add a teaspoon of salt and bring to the boil. Drop the *gnocchi* into the gently boiling water – you'll probably have to do them in 2 batches – and let them simmer gently for about 7 minutes. They will swell and rise to the surface of the water as they cook. When I think they're done I find it best to test one by cutting it in half to make sure it's cooked inside. Take the *gnocchi* out of the water with a draining spoon and put them into a lightly greased shallow ovenproof dish. When all the *gnocchi* are done melt the butter and mix it with the garlic; pour this over the *gnocchi* and sprinkle the grated cheese on top.

When you're ready to bake the *gnocchi* set the oven to 200°C (400°F), gas mark 6. Put the *gnocchi* in the oven for about 20 minutes until they're golden brown on top, then serve at once.

A variation of this recipe which I make sometimes is to fry some chopped walnuts or flaked almonds in the butter and pour them over the *gnocchi* instead of the grated cheese.

SPINACH GNOCCHI   ITALY

Spinach *gnocchi* are light and tender and when served with a topping of melted butter and cheese I think they're one of the most delicious dishes. The secret of success when making them is to let the spinach get completely cold before mixing everything together.

450 g (1 lb) spinach or 225 g (8 oz) frozen chopped spinach
75 g (3 oz) wholewheat flour
50 g (2 oz) butter
125 g (4 oz) grated cheese
2 eggs

Serves 4

½ teaspoon sea salt
½ teaspoon mustard powder
Grated nutmeg
Freshly ground black pepper

To finish
25 g (1 oz) melted butter
Grated cheese

Wash the spinach thoroughly then cook it without any additional water until it's tender – about 10 minutes. Drain, cool and chop the spinach. If you're using frozen spinach just let it thaw then put it into a sieve and press out as much liquid as possible.

Mix the cold spinach with the flour, butter, cheese, eggs and seasonings – it's easiest to use a fork. Form the mixture into about 20 walnut-sized balls and roll them in flour. Bring half a saucepan of salted water to the boil and drop in the *gnocchi* – you will probably have to do them in more than one batch. Let them simmer for 7–8 minutes. They will puff up and rise to the surface of the water; I think the best way to tell if they're done is to cut one in half and taste some of the middle to make sure there is no raw flavour. Put the *gnocchi* into a lightly greased ovenproof dish, dot with butter and sprinkle with grated cheese. Before you serve the *gnocchi* heat them through in a moderate oven – 180°C (350°F), gas mark 4 – for 25–30 minutes until they're piping hot and bathed in a buttery cheesy glaze.

Like the other *gnocchi* they make an excellent starter or supper dish. If you're serving them for supper some hot noodles or crusty garlic bread will go well with them – bake the garlic bread in the oven with the *gnocchi* – and a tomato salad.

SWISS FRIED POTATO CAKE   SWITZERLAND

Swiss potato cake, *rösti,* is different from the German potato
pancakes because it uses cooked potato and it's made into one
large cake which fills the whole frying pan. This makes a good
basis for a cooked supper; protein can be introduced into the
meal by serving a protein-rich side salad or by having something
like yoghurt, cheese cake or biscuits and cheese for pudding.

900 g (2 lb) cooked potatoes   4 tablespoons vegetable oil
Sea salt

Serves 4

Grate the potatoes coarsely – this is easiest to do if you chill them
beforehand for a while in the fridge. Season them with salt.
Heat half the oil in a large frying pan and put in all the potato,
pressing it down gently with the back of a spoon. Fry the potato
over a moderate heat until the underside is golden brown,
then turn the cake over and cook the other side, adding the
remaining oil if necessary. You may be able to turn the cake
with a fish slice; alternatively you can turn it out on to a plate
then tip it back into the frying pan again, crispy side uppermost.
When the second side is cooked turn the potato cake out on to
a hot plate and serve it in big chunky wedges.

   You can vary the basic potato cake in a number of ways –
it's nice with chopped herbs or spring onions added; sunflower
seeds, sesame seeds and chopped hazel nuts are also good.

POTATO PANCAKES   GERMANY

These crispy little pancakes make a good quick supper dish or
children's tea. It's typically German – and I think delicious –
to serve them with a sharp-tasting apple or cranberry sauce, but
children usually prefer them with tomato ketchup.

219

450 g (1 lb) potatoes, scrubbed
1 onion, peeled
Sea salt
Freshly ground black pepper

2 eggs
3 tablespoons flour
Oil for shallow frying
Cranberry or apple sauce

Serves 4

Grate the potatoes coarsely, peeled or unpeeled according to taste. Grate the onion. Mix potatoes and onion with salt and pepper, eggs and flour and stir to make a batter. Heat a little oil in a frying pan and fry tablespoonfuls of the mixture until golden and crispy, turning them over so that both sides are cooked. Drain on kitchen paper and serve immediately with the sauce and a crunchy salad.

RICE CROQUETTES

ITALY

These crisp croquettes are good for a first course if you serve them on small plates with a tomato or mushroom sauce; or, with vegetables and potato, they make a tasty supper. They're an excellent way of using up leftover risotto and I sometimes make an extra large batch specially with this in mind – you simply form the risotto into little rounds and coat them in beaten egg and dried crumbs. But if you're making the croquettes from scratch, this is the way to do them.

225 g (8 oz) long-grain
  brown rice
1 teaspoon sea salt
400 ml ($\frac{3}{4}$ pint) water
1 large onion, peeled and finely
  chopped
25 g (1 oz) butter
125 g (4 oz) grated cheese
$\frac{1}{2}$–1 teaspoon mustard powder

1 egg
Freshly ground black pepper

To finish:
1 egg, beaten with 1 tablespoon
  of cold water
Dried crumbs
Oil for deep or shallow frying

Serves 4

Wash the rice and put it into a saucepan with the salt and water. Bring up to the boil, then turn the heat down low, put a lid on the saucepan and leave it to simmer for 40 minutes until the rice is cooked. Then take it off the heat and leave it to stand, with the lid still on the saucepan, for a further 10 minutes.

While the rice is cooking fry the onion gently in butter for 10 minutes until it's golden and soft. Stir the onion into the cooked rice together with the grated cheese, mustard and egg. Mix well and season to taste with salt and plenty of pepper. It's easier to shape the mixture into croquettes if it's cool and better still if there's time to chill it in the fridge. Dip tablespoonfuls of the mixture first into the beaten egg then into the dried crumbs, shaping them into rounds with your hands. Fry the croquettes in deep or shallow oil until they're crisp all over. Drain them on kitchen paper and serve them as soon as possible.

SPICY FRITTERS   MIDDLE EAST

This is a cheating recipe for these spicy chick pea fritters, or *felafel*, as they're called, because they're really supposed to be made from chick peas. I've given the proper chick pea version in *The Bean Book* but if, like me, you find the long cooking then the sieving of the chick peas rather time-consuming, I thought you might like to try this red lentil recipe which is just as tasty but easier to do.

350 g (12 oz) split red lentils
700 ml (1¼ pints) water
25 g (1 oz) butter or margarine
1 medium onion, peeled and
    grated
1½ teaspoons ground cumin
1½ teaspoons ground coriander

1 tablespoon chopped fresh
    parsley
1 egg
Sea salt
Freshly ground black pepper
A little wholewheat flour
Oil for shallow frying

Serves 4

Put the lentils and water in a medium-sized saucepan and bring to the boil, then let them simmer gently until the lentils are soft and golden and all the water has been absorbed. Mash the lentils with the butter or margarine and mix in the onion, cumin, coriander, parsley and egg. Season the mixture with plenty of salt and pepper.

Form the lentil mixture into small flat cakes on a lightly floured board – it's easier to handle if there's time to chill it in the fridge for a while first. Fry the little cakes in hot shallow oil and drain them well.

Served with pitta bread and a bowl of salad – lettuce, tomatoes, cucumber and spring onion tossed in vinaigrette – these little fritters make a tasty and filling lunch. They're also nice with garlic mayonnaise, chilled yoghurt or mango chutney; or with gravy, potatoes and a cooked vegetable they make a simple cooked meal that usually appeals to children.

SWEETCORN FRITTERS · USA

Although these fritters are usually served as an accompaniment to meat they are quite filling and make a good supper or lunch dish, with tomato sauce, mashed potato and a green vegetable. They also make an interesting first course.

330 g (11½ oz) can sweetcorn   Sea salt
1 egg, separated   Freshly ground black pepper
25 g (1 oz) wholewheat flour   Oil for shallow frying

Serves 3

Drain the sweetcorn, put it into a bowl with the egg yolk, flour and some salt and pepper and mix well. Whisk the egg white until it's standing in soft peaks, then gently fold it into the sweetcorn mixture. Heat a little oil in a frying pan and fry the sweetcorn mixture, a tablespoonful at a time, on both sides, until crisp.

(Stand back as you do so because the corn tends to 'pop'.) As soon as they're ready drain the fritters on kitchen paper. Keep the first ones warm while you fry the remainder, then serve them straight away.

FRIED WHEAT PROTEIN WITH SWEET AND SOUR SAUCE

CHINA

We talk about 'knitted soya steaks' and textured vegetable proteins as though they were something very new and unusual, but the inventive Chinese have been using wheat protein for centuries and it's an entirely natural product which you can make from strong flour in your own home if you want to. You just make a dough with flour, a little salt and water, soak it in a bowl of cold water for 1 hour then pummel and knead it under cold running water. As you do this the white starch washes away and you're left with a firm, pliable piece of dough which you can then simmer in well-flavoured stock and use in stews and casseroles – or in this recipe.

It's quite easy to do but a bit laborious so I usually buy it in a can: you can get it at Chinese shops or from health shops where it's called meatless savoury cuts. The wheat contains good protein and I think it's delicious fried like this and served in a sweet and sour sauce. The ingredients and proportions for the sauce are those recommended by the distinguished Chinese cook and author, Kenneth Lo.

For the sauce:
2½ tablespoons soft brown sugar
2 tablespoons red wine vinegar
1½ tablespoons cornflour
1½ tablespoons tomato purée or tomato ketchup
1½ tablespoons soy sauce
1 tablespoon cheap sherry
1 tablespoon orange juice
4 tablespoons cold water

For the fried wheat protein:
425 g (15 oz) can and 225 g
  (8 oz) can wheat protein
1 garlic clove
Sea salt
1 egg, beaten
1 piece of fresh root ginger,

about 2·5 cm (1 in) long;
  or ½ teaspoon ordinary
  ground ginger
Dry crumbs
Oil for shallow frying –
  sesame oil if possible

Serves 4

First prepare the sauce. Put all the ingredients into a small saucepan and mix to a smooth paste. Leave on one side while you prepare the wheat protein.

If the wheat protein has been prepared with liquid, drain this off and keep it on one side. Cut the wheat protein into chunky bite-sized pieces. Peel the garlic, crush it with a knife then mix it to a creamy paste with a little salt and put it into a smallish bowl with the beaten egg. Peel the ginger and grate it finely into the bowl with the garlic and egg, or add the ground ginger. Mix it all together. Dip the pieces of wheat protein into the egg mixture then coat them with dry crumbs. Fry the little fritters in hot shallow oil, turning them so that they're crisp all over. Drain them well on kitchen paper and keep them warm.

Now quickly finish the sauce by putting the small saucepan over a moderate heat and stirring the mixture for a couple of minutes until it has thickened. If you think it's too thick, thin it down with a little extra orange juice, water or the liquid from the canned wheat protein. Pour the sauce over the hot fritters and serve at once.

This is nice served with hot cooked rice and some Chinese vegetables – the Chinese cabbage or chop suey go well with it and so does some Chinese plum sauce which you can get at Chinese shops – or you can use ordinary chutney.

Pasta and Pancakes

Pasta and pancake dishes are warming and filling and some of them are also very quick and easy to make. They are perfect served with just a simple salad, which helps to cut down on preparation time.

For all the pasta recipes I use the wholewheat variety. It's very easy to get these days and although it looks rather dauntingly dark in the packet it cooks up much lighter and is just as quick to use as ordinary white pasta. One of the secrets of cooking wholewheat pasta successfully is to use a big saucepan and plenty of water so that the pasta can move around as it cooks. It's also helpful to add a couple of tablespoons of cooking oil to the water as this prevents the pasta from sticking together and also stops the water frothing up and boiling over. When the pasta is cooked so that it's just tender I find it best to drain it then put it back into the still hot saucepan with a knob of butter or a little olive oil. There's no need to rinse the pasta in either hot or cold water.

Although stuffed pancake dishes, which I've also included in this section, are not particularly quick to make, I do think they're quite convenient when you're busy because each part – the pancakes, the filling and the sauce – can be quickly made on its own when you can fit it in and then the whole dish can be assembled at the last minute. Actually stuffed pancakes are one of my favourite dishes for entertaining; I can make the pancakes, filling and sauce gradually during the week before and freeze them, then it doesn't take long to assemble them on the day. Also they don't spoil if they're kept covered with foil in a cool oven (150°C (300°F), gas mark 2) for quite a long time which gives me a chance to relax and enjoy myself without worrying what's going on in the oven. I take the foil off the top of the dish and turn the oven up when we start the meal to brown the top of the pancakes.

You can make excellent nutty-tasting pancakes with wholewheat flour. If you want them very light use half wholewheat flour and half white – if these are successful you might like to try them with all wholewheat which is fine as long as you take care to make the pancakes really thin.

When you're making pancakes the important thing is to have the right-sized frying pan. I have a small non-stick pan measuring 17–18 cm (6–7 in) and it's ideal because the pancakes are just the right size, and the fact that the frying pan is non-stick means I only have to add the very minimum of fat to cook the pancakes which makes them easier to control in the pan and of course less fatty when they're finished.

A large shallow ovenproof dish is best for baking the stuffed pancakes in because they are nicest if you can arrange them in one layer. I put them in the same big Pyrex dish that I use for stuffed vegetables – it measures about 39 cm × 27 cm ($15\frac{1}{2}$ in × $10\frac{1}{2}$ in). A similar-sized porcelain or earthenware dish would be even better.

BLINI

RUSSIA

These buckwheat yeast pancakes from Russia have a character all their own. They come out light and delectable; the buckwheat gives them a dark, nutty flavour. I think they're nicest served hot from the pan with melted butter or soured cream, accompanied by a big bowl of crunchy salad; hearty chunks of lettuce, celery, spring onions, tomatoes and fingers of carrot.

400 ml (¾ pint) milk
1 teaspoon sugar
15 g (½ oz) dried yeast
225 g (8 oz) flour
75 g (3 oz) buckwheat flour
25 g (1 oz) butter

½ teaspoon salt
2 tablespoons soured cream
3 eggs, separated
Oil for shallow frying
Soured cream or melted
  butter to serve

Serves 4

Heat two-thirds of the milk to lukewarm; add the sugar and yeast and leave in a warm place for 5 minutes to froth up. Put the flour and half the buckwheat flour into a bowl and add the yeast mixture. Beat hard until smooth then cover and put in a warm place until doubled in bulk – about 1½ hours. Add the rest of the buckwheat flour and beat the mixture again. Put back into a warm place for another 2 hours.

Melt the butter in a small pan and add the remaining milk; heat the mixture to lukewarm. Add this to the flour mixture together with the salt, soured cream and egg yolks. Beat well. Whisk the egg whites until they're standing in peaks, then fold them gently into the mixture with a metal spoon. Cover the bowl and leave for a further 30 minutes.

Heat a little oil in a frying pan; put 2 tablespoonsful of the *blini* mixture into the hot fat and fry until crisp on one side; flip the little pancake over with a spatula and cook the other side.

These pancakes can also be served as a pudding, with soured cream and/or jam, syrup or sugar.

CHICK PEAS AND VERMICELLI ITALY

At first glance this seems a strange mixture but it works well, the firm golden chick peas contrasting with the soft creamy-coloured vermicelli, and both shiny with olive oil and pungent with garlic and Parmesan cheese. Incidentally, if you use canned chick peas for this recipe it brings it into the quick-to-make emergency meal category.

225 g (8 oz) chick peas
Sea salt
6 tablespoons olive oil
175 g (6 oz) vermicelli or fine
   wholewheat spaghetti

1–2 garlic cloves, peeled and
   crushed
Freshly ground black pepper
25–50 g (1–2 oz) grated
   Parmesan cheese

Serves 4

Cover the chick peas with cold water and leave them to soak for several hours, then drain and rinse them, put them into a saucepan with plenty of fresh water and simmer them gently until they're tender. Keep them hot. Half fill a large saucepan with cold water; add a teaspoon of salt and 2 tablespoons of the olive oil and bring to the boil. Cook the pasta in the water until it's just tender. Drain the pasta and return it to the hot saucepan with the rest of the olive oil, the garlic and salt and pepper. Drain the hot chick peas and add them to the pasta, turning the mixture gently so that everything gets coated with the oil. Serve immediately, sprinkled with grated Parmesan cheese.

This dish is rich in protein and is lovely served with a simple tomato or green salad.

LASAGNE WITH SPINACH AND CHEESE ITALY

An easy-to-make dish that's very tasty and filling. The exact amount of lasagne needed will depend on the brand you're using and the shape of your dish. I think it's best to try the pieces of lasagne in the dish before you cook them – arrange the pieces in a shallow square or oblong ovenproof dish so that they make a complete layer but don't overlap, and then allow the same amount again so that you will have 2 layers in the finished dish. This will probably be about 125 g (4 oz) of lasagne – if the dish you're planning to use calls for very much more than this you'll probably have to double all the other ingredients and it will then feed 6 or 8 people.

This lasagne is lovely served with a juicy tomato salad.

About 125 g (4 oz) lasagne
450 g (1 lb) spinach or 350 g (12 oz) chopped frozen spinach
Sea salt
Freshly ground black pepper

450 g (1 lb) *ricotta* or curd cheese or low-fat quark
25 g (1 oz) Parmesan cheese
2 eggs
175 g (6 oz) grated Edam cheese

Serves 3–4

Set the oven to 200°C (400°F), gas mark 6. Half fill a large saucepan with salted water. When the water is boiling put in the strips of lasagne – stand them in the water and as the ends soften gradually ease the rest of the lasagne down until it's all submerged. Simmer the lasagne gently for about 15 minutes, until it's tender, then drain it in a colander.

While the lasagne is cooking wash and pick over the spinach then put it into a large saucepan; don't add water, as that still clinging to the spinach should be sufficient. Put a lid on the saucepan and cook the spinach for about 7–10 minutes until it's tender. Drain the spinach, then chop it in the saucepan using the end of a fish slice. Season with salt and pepper. Mix the *ricotta* or curd cheese or quark with the Parmesan, eggs and salt and pepper.

Lightly grease your selected ovenproof dish and put half the spinach in the base, followed by half the cheese mixture. Spread a layer of lasagne evenly over the top, then repeat the layers. Sprinkle the grated cheese over the top. Bake the lasagne for 45 minutes, until it's golden brown on top, hot and bubbly within. Serve at once.

MACARONI CHEESE   ENGLAND

People usually laugh when I tell them I like macaroni cheese but I think it's delicious if it's well made, quite as good as some of the Italian pasta dishes which people rave about. I think the secret with macaroni cheese is to make the sauce quite thin so that you get a light, moist result. It's lovely with a juicy tomato salad or a crisp green salad. You can cook macaroni cheese in the oven or under the grill, whichever is more convenient.

125 g (4 oz) wholewheat short macaroni
Sea salt
40 g (1½ oz) butter
40 g (1½ oz) flour
850 ml (1½ pints) milk
175 g (6 oz) grated cheese, preferably double Gloucester which gives a lovely colour
1 teaspoon mustard powder
Freshly ground black pepper
Dried crumbs
A little extra grated cheese

Serves 4

If you're going to bake the macaroni cheese set the oven to 200 C (400°F), gas mark 6. Half fill a large saucepan with water and add a teaspoonful of salt. Bring the water to the boil, put in the macaroni and let it simmer until it's just tender – this will be in about 10 minutes; the time given on the packet will be a guide but keep your eye on it and bite a piece when you think it's nearly done to check it. Drain the macaroni.

While the macaroni is cooking make the sauce. Melt the butter in a large saucepan and stir in the flour; let it cook over the heat for a few moments, then mix in about a fifth of the milk. Keep the heat up high and stir vigorously until the mixture is smooth, then add some more milk as before and repeat until it's all in and you have a smooth, rather thin sauce. (You may think it's *too* thin, but don't worry, it will be all right.) Take the saucepan off the heat and mix in the grated cheese, mustard powder and salt and pepper to taste.

Stir the macaroni into the sauce then pour the mixture into a lightly greased shallow ovenproof dish. Cover the top all over with the crumbs and a little grated cheese. Bake the macaroni cheese in the oven for about 40 minutes or put it under a hot grill for about 15–20 minutes until it's bubbling and golden and crisp on top.

PANCAKES STUFFED WITH ASPARAGUS

FRANCE

I'm afraid this is rather an extravagant dish, using four cans of asparagus, but for a special occasion it really makes a lovely main course that's no more expensive than good meat or fish would be.

For the pancakes:
125 g (4 oz) plain flour – I use wholewheat but you could also use a mixture of wholewheat and white
A pinch of sea salt
2 eggs
2 tablespoons vegetable oil
200 ml (7 fl oz) milk
Extra oil for frying

For the filling:
Four 300 g (10½ oz) cans cut asparagus
2 tablespoons chopped parsley

Serves 6

For the sauce:
75 g (3 oz) butter
75 g (3 oz) flour
850 ml (1½ pints) milk
1 bay leaf
1–1½ teaspoons mustard powder
175 g (6 oz) grated cheese, preferably double Gloucester
Sea salt
Freshly ground black pepper

To finish:
50g (2oz) grated cheese

First make the pancake batter: the easiest way to do this is to put all the ingredients into the liquidizer and blend until you have a smooth creamy mixture. If you do this I have found that it doesn't matter if you don't let the batter stand for 30 minutes as in the traditional method. If you haven't a liquidizer, put the flour and salt into a bowl, break in the eggs and beat, then gradually mix in the oil and milk until you've got a creamy mixture. Beat well, then leave the batter to stand for 30 minutes and beat again.

To make the pancakes brush a small frying pan with oil and set it over a moderate heat. When it is hot pour in enough pancake batter to coat the base of the pan thinly. Tip and swirl the pan so that the mixture runs all over the base. Then put the pan over the heat for 20–30 seconds until the top of the pancake is set and the underside is flecked golden brown. Flip the pancake over using a small palette knife and your fingers if necessary. Cook the other side of the pancake, then lift it out on to a plate. Brush the frying pan with more oil if necessary (I find with a non-stick frying pan I only have to do this after about every three pancakes) and make another pancake in the same way, putting it on top of the first pancake when it's done. Continue until you've finished the mixture and have a nice pile of 12 or 15 pancakes. (You can do all this well in advance if you want to.)

To make the filling drain the asparagus and mix it with the chopped parsley. This may seem a rather simple filling but it's delicious when put with the pancakes and sauce.

For the sauce, melt the butter in a large saucepan and stir in the flour, cook for a moment or two then add about a fifth of the milk and the bay leaf and stir over a good heat until the mixture is smooth and very thick. Then add another lot of milk and repeat the process until it has all been incorporated and you've got a smooth sauce. Take the saucepan off the heat, stir in the mustard and grated cheese and season the sauce carefully. If you're having some white wine with the meal a couple of tablespoons of it will make a delicious addition.

To assemble the dish put a heaped tablespoonful of asparagus on each pancake, roll the pancake neatly and place it in a large shallow greased casserole. These pancakes look best arranged in a single layer but you will need a big dish to accommodate them. When the pancakes are all in the dish pour the sauce evenly over them, removing the bay leaf when it comes to light. Sprinkle the grated cheese over the top and cover the dish with a piece of foil.

When you're ready to bake the pancakes set the oven to 180°C (350°F), gas mark 4. Bake them for about 1 hour, removing the foil about 15 minutes before the end of the cooking time to brown the cheese on top.

These pancakes are good served with *gratin dauphinoise* and either a green salad or a cooked vegetable.

PANCAKES STUFFED WITH CHEESE AND BAKED IN SPICY TOMATO SAUCE

MEXICO

When you put the spoon into this dish the creamy white filling oozes out and looks very appetizing against the golden pancakes and tomato sauce. The 'pancakes' are actually tortillas, which are very easy to make; they're not as light as pancakes but very good and very filling – you could use ordinary wholewheat pancakes instead if you prefer.

12 tortillas as described on page 332

For the filling:
700 g (1½ lb) cottage cheese, curd cheese or quark
350 g (12 oz) grated cheese
1½ teaspoons mustard powder
2 garlic cloves, peeled and crushed
Sea salt
Freshly ground black pepper

For the sauce:
1 large onion, peeled and chopped
1 tablespoon oil
1 garlic clove, peeled and crushed
792 g (1 lb 12 oz) can tomatoes
½–1 teaspoon chilli powder

To finish:
125 g (4 oz) grated cheese

Serves 6–8

Make the filling by mixing together the cottage cheese, curd cheese or quark, the grated cheese, mustard powder and garlic; add salt and pepper to taste.

Fry the onion in the oil for 10 minutes, then stir in the garlic, tomatoes, chilli powder and salt and pepper to taste. Sieve or liquidize the sauce.

Heat the oven to 190°C (375°F), gas mark 5. Grease a large shallow ovenproof dish. Spoon the filling on to the tortillas, rolling them neatly round and dividing the mixture evenly between them. Place the plump rolls side by side in the dish and pour the tomato sauce over them. Sprinkle the grated cheese on top.

Cover the dish with foil and bake the pancakes, or *enchiladas*, as they're called in Mexico, for 45 minutes, then take off the foil and leave them in the oven for a further 15 minutes or so to brown the top. They're lovely with just a lightly cooked green vegetable like sprouts, or with a green salad.

PANCAKES STUFFED WITH MUSHROOMS AND ARTICHOKE HEARTS

FRANCE

I think small open mushrooms are the best to use for this recipe because they have a lovely rich flavour when they're cooked, but you could use button mushrooms. Like the pancakes stuffed with asparagus this dish is a bit extravagant but it's a delicious mixture of tender pancakes, tasty filling and light cheesy sauce.

For the pancakes:
125 g (4 oz) plain flour – all wholewheat or half wholewheat and half white
Pinch of sea salt
2 eggs
2 tablespoons vegetable oil
200 ml (7 fl oz) milk
Extra oil for frying

For the filling:
1 onion

50 g (2 oz) butter
700 g (1½ lb) mushrooms
2 large garlic cloves, peeled and crushed
400 g (14 oz) can artichoke hearts, drained and sliced
2 tablespoons chopped parsley
4 tablespoons cream
2–3 teaspoons lemon juice
Freshly ground black pepper

For the sauce:
75 g (3 oz) butter
75 g (3 oz) flour
1 bay leaf
850 ml (1½ pints) milk
175 g (6 oz) grated cheese,
    preferably double
    Gloucester

1–1½ teaspoons mustard
    powder

To finish:
50 g (2 oz) grated cheese

Serves 4

Mix the batter as explained in the recipe for pancakes stuffed with asparagus, page 231 and make 12 or 15 small thin pancakes. This can be done several days in advance if convenient.

For the filling peel and finely chop the onion and fry it in the butter for 10 minutes but don't let it brown. Wash the mushrooms and pat them dry in a cloth, then halve or quarter them and add them to the butter; let them cook for 5 minutes or so until they're tender. If the mushrooms produce much water let them boil vigorously until the mixture is fairly dry. Take the saucepan off the heat and stir in the garlic, artichoke hearts, parsley and cream. Sharpen the mixture with a little lemon juice and add salt and pepper to taste.

To make the sauce melt the butter in a largish saucepan and add the flour. Cook for a moment or two then add the bay leaf and about a fifth of the milk and stir vigorously over a high heat until you have a smooth, very thick mixture. Repeat, stirring in another fifth of the milk and continue in this way until all the milk has been added and you have a smooth sauce. Take the saucepan off the heat and mix in the grated cheese, salt and pepper and enough mustard to give the mixture a nice tang. This, like the pancakes and the filling, can be made in advance.

When you're ready to assemble the dish divide the filling between the pancakes, rolling them up neatly and placing them side by side in a shallow ovenproof dish. Take the bay leaf out of the cheese sauce and pour the sauce evenly over the pancakes; sprinkle with the grated cheese. Cover the dish with foil and bake the pancakes at 180°C (350°F), gas mark 4 for about an hour, taking the foil off for about the last 15 minutes to brown the top of the dish.

The pancakes are equally good served with a cooked vegetable or a green salad, with or without potatoes.

PANCAKES STUFFED WITH SPICY RED BEANS MEXICO

If you don't like making ordinary pancakes you might like to try this recipe which uses tortillas instead. The tortillas are very easy to make from a wholewheat flour and maize flour (or just wholewheat flour) dough; I've given the recipe and method in the bread, scones and sandwiches section.

12 tortillas, see page 332

For the filling:
1 large onion, peeled and chopped
1 tablespoon oil
2 garlic cloves, peeled and
   crushed
780 g (1 lb 11½ oz) can tomatoes
225 g (8 oz) red beans, soaked,
   cooked (see p. 22) and
   drained
½–1 teaspoon chilli powder
Sea salt
Freshly ground black pepper

Serves 6–8

For the sauce:
75 g (3 oz) butter
75 g (3 oz) flour
850 ml (1½ pints) milk
175 g (6 oz) grated cheese
1½ teaspoons mustard powder

To finish:
125 g (4 oz) grated cheese

First make the filling. Fry the onion in the oil in a large saucepan for 10 minutes, until it's soft but not browned, then stir in the garlic, tomatoes, red beans and enough chilli powder, salt and pepper to give a good flavour. Mash the beans and tomatoes a bit with the spoon to break them up.

Next make the sauce. Melt the butter in a medium-sized saucepan and stir in the flour. Cook for a moment or two then pour in about a fifth of the milk. Stir over a high heat until you have a smooth, very thick mixture, then put in some more milk and continue in this way until all the milk has been added and you have a smooth sauce. Take the saucepan off the heat and mix in the grated cheese, mustard and a good seasoning of salt and pepper.

When you're ready to assemble the dish set the oven to 190°C (375°F), gas mark 5. Grease a large shallow ovenproof dish. Put some of the bean mixture on to each tortilla and roll the tortilla up neatly. Place the tortillas side by side in the dish and cover them evenly with the sauce. Sprinkle the grated cheese over the top and cover the dish with a piece of foil. Bake for 45 minutes, then remove the foil and leave the pancakes in the oven for a further 15 minutes or so to brown the top. Serve with a crisp green salad or cooked green vegetable.

PASTA AND BEANS   ITALY

You can serve this mixture as soon as it's ready or you can spoon it into a shallow ovenproof dish, sprinkle the top with bread-crumbs and grated cheese and bake until it's crisp and golden. Whichever you do I think you'll agree it's a tasty, satisfying and economical dish.

125 g (4 oz) red kidney beans
125 g (4 oz) split red lentils
1 large onion
2 tablespoons olive oil
1 garlic clove, crushed
2 tomatoes, skinned
1 litre (1¾ pints) water
125 g (4 oz) cut wholewheat
    macaroni
1 tablespoon tomato ketchup

2 tablespoons chopped parsley
1 teaspoon cinnamon powder
1 teaspoon lemon juice
Sea salt
Freshly ground black pepper

Optional topping:
Dry crumbs
50 g (2 oz) grated cheese

Serves 3–4

Put the beans and lentils into a big bowl, cover with plenty of cold water and leave for several hours if possible, then drain and rinse them. Peel and chop the onion and fry it in a large saucepan in the oil for 10 minutes. Add the garlic, tomatoes, beans and lentils and the water. Bring up to the boil, put a lid on the saucepan and leave it to simmer for 1–1¼ hours until the beans are tender. At this stage the mixture will look more like soup than anything else, but don't worry. Add the macaroni, tomato ketchup and parsley to the saucepan and let it simmer for about 10 minutes until the macaroni is tender. The mixture should still be quite moist – add a little liquid if necessary (red wine if you've got any). Then stir in the cinnamon, lemon juice and salt and pepper to taste. Serve immediately or spoon the mixture into a lightly greased shallow casserole, sprinkle with the crumbs and grated cheese and bake in a moderate oven for 30–40 minutes until golden brown.

This is lovely served with a fresh juicy salad with a good dressing.

PASTA WITH CREAM CHEESE AND WALNUTS

ITALY

Although it's quick and easy to do this dish is rich and luxurious tasting. I think it's nicest made with wholewheat pasta rings but you could use other types of pasta. Hazel nuts can be used instead of walnuts – bake them first for about 20 minutes in a moderate oven until the skins will rub off easily and the nuts underneath are golden brown.

Sea salt
1 tablespoon oil
225 g (8 oz) wholewheat pasta
  rings
15 g (½ oz) butter
350 g (12 oz) low-fat quark:
  you could use real cream

cheese but I think this
  makes the dish rather
  too rich
1 garlic clove, crushed
Freshly ground black pepper
125–175 g (4–6 oz) fresh walnuts,
  roughly chopped

Serves 4

Half fill a large saucepan with water; add a teaspoon of salt and the oil. Bring to the boil then put in the pasta rings and simmer them gently until they're just tender.

While the pasta rings are cooking make the cheese sauce. Melt the butter in a medium-sized saucepan over a gentle heat then add the quark or cream cheese and garlic. Stir all the time, over the heat, until the cheese has heated through and is very smooth and creamy. Season with salt and pepper.

Spoon the pasta into a hot serving dish, pour the sauce over the top and scatter with the chopped nuts. Serve with a green salad but don't put too much dressing on it as the pasta dish is rather rich.

PASTA WITH LENTILS   MIDDLE EAST

In the Middle East this would probably be made with noodles but I generally use fine wholewheat spaghetti instead. You can use either the little red split lentils or continental lentils.

For the lentils:
225 g (8 oz) split red lentils or
    continental lentils
1 large onion
2 tablespoons oil
2 garlic cloves
1 small green pepper or 125 g
    (4 oz) mushrooms
575 ml (1 pint) water
1 tablespoon tomato ketchup

1 tablespoon chopped parsley
½ teaspoon cinnamon
Sea salt
Freshly ground black pepper

For the pasta:
225 g (8 oz) noodles or
    wholewheat spaghetti
2 tablespoons oil

Serves 4

Wash the lentils. Peel and chop the onion and fry it in the oil in a large saucepan for 5 minutes. While this is happening peel and crush the garlic and wash, de-seed and chop the pepper or wash and chop the mushrooms. Add the garlic and pepper or mushrooms to the saucepan and cook for a further 2–3 minutes, then put in the lentils and stir them so that they get coated with the oil. Mix in the water, tomato ketchup, parsley and cinnamon; bring up to the boil then cover the saucepan and leave it to simmer gently until the lentils are cooked – from 30 minutes to an hour, depending on the type. Season with salt and pepper.

When the lentils are nearly done cook the noodles or spaghetti in plenty of boiling salted water for about 10 minutes. Drain the pasta and turn it in the oil. Serve the pasta with the lentils. A green salad goes well with this.

SPAGHETTI WITH PESTO   ITALY

Pesto looks a curious thick green mixture when it's first made, but when it's added to the hot, cooked spaghetti it really transforms it into something special with a delicious, rich flavour. You should really use fresh basil for this recipe but it's not easy to get and I find that a bunch of fresh parsley plus a good seasoning of dried basil makes a very good alternative.

225 g (8 oz) wholewheat spaghetti
Sea salt
2 tablespoons vegetable oil
2 garlic cloves, peeled and crushed
1 large bunch of fresh basil or
  a large bunch of fresh parsley
and 2–3 teaspoons dried
  basil
40 g (1½ oz) pine kernels
40 g (1½ oz) grated Parmesan
  cheese
8 tablespoons olive oil

Serves 4

Half fill a large saucepan with water and add a teaspoon of salt and the vegetable oil. Bring to the boil then gently ease in the spaghetti, pushing it down into the water as it softens. Let the spaghetti simmer gently until it's just tender – about 10 minutes. Drain the spaghetti and return it to the hot saucepan.

While the spaghetti is cooking make the *pesto*. Take the stalks off the fresh basil or parsley and put the leaves into the liquidizer goblet, together with the dried basil if you're using it and the garlic, pine kernels, Parmesan and olive oil. Blend at medium speed until you have a thick purée the consistency of softly whipped cream.

Put the pasta on to a hot serving dish and spoon the *pesto* on top; or serve the *pesto* separately and let everyone help themselves.

You'll need to serve a protein starter or pudding with this for a balanced meal – or you could offer a protein-rich salad.

Savoury Pastries, Pizzas and Pies

Savoury pastries and pies are always popular and there are some lovely vegetarian ones: light and delicious flans from France, flaky golden pies from the Middle East and cheesy pizzas from Italy which fill the kitchen with their warm fragrance as they cook and make your mouth water.

These are useful dishes for the cook because they're so adaptable. Most of them can be served either hot or cold, with salad or with cooked vegetables, for lunch or for supper. They make good starters as well as main courses and are also splendid picnic food.

The pies and flans in this section are made from three basic types of pastry. For the pies there's a light crumbly shortcrust pastry made from wholewheat flour, and a quick flaky pastry which uses half wholewheat and half white flour; and for the flans I use a wholewheat shortcrust which cooks crisply.

One of the main problems when making savoury flans is to get the pastry crisp while keeping the filling light and moist. Over the years I've tried all sorts of different ways of achieving this but the best method and the one which I always use now was discovered by a friend, a super cook, who very kindly let me into the secret of her very crisp flans. All you do is simply to brush the flan case all over with a little very hot oil as soon as you take it out of the oven; and if there's time it helps if you pre-cook the custard part of the flan before pouring it into the flan case – I've explained this is in the recipes where applicable. It also helps if you use a metal flan dish, although the method I've described works well even with a porcelain one. And in my experience there's no need to fiddle around with pieces of greaseproof paper and baking beans. Pricking the base of the flan with a fork before baking is all I ever do and seems to be completely adequate. I do think it helps, though, if you put a baking sheet on the oven shelf and heat it up with the oven, then stand the flan dish on this to get it off to a good start.

These are filling dishes and most of them contain a good quantity of protein so a vegetable starter and a fruity pudding go well with them.

INDIVIDUAL ASPARAGUS TARTS FRANCE

These light creamy little tarts make a very good starter for a dinner party; they're also nice with salad for lunch. They would be lovely made in individual flan dishes if you've got them. Otherwise use patty tins or any small ovenproof containers.

For the pastry:
150 g (6 oz) plain wholewheat
   flour
1 teaspoon baking powder
Pinch of salt
75 g (3 oz) butter
5–6 teaspoons cold water
2 tablespoons oil

For the filling:
1 onion, peeled and finely
   chopped

1 small garlic clove, peeled
   and crushed
25 g (1 oz) butter
4 egg yolks or 2 whole eggs
275 ml ($\frac{1}{2}$ pint) milk or single
   cream
Sea salt
Freshly ground black pepper
Grated nutmeg
300 g ($10\frac{1}{2}$ oz) can cut
   asparagus, drained

Serves 6

Place a baking sheet in the centre of the oven and set the temperature to 200°C (400°F), gas mark 6. To make the pastry sift the flour, baking powder and salt into a bowl, including also the bran left in the sieve. Rub in the butter with your fingertips until the mixture looks like breadcrumbs, then stir in enough water to make a dough. Roll out the pastry on a lightly floured board and use it to line 6 individual patty tins. Prick the bases all over and place the tins on the baking sheet in the oven. Bake for 10–15 minutes until crisp and golden brown. Have the 2 tablespoons of oil very hot and brush this over the tarts as soon as you take them out of the oven. Turn the oven setting down to 180°C (350°F), gas mark 4.

Fry the onion and garlic in the butter over a gentle heat for 10 minutes, but don't let them brown. Take the saucepan off the heat. Whisk together the eggs and milk or cream then add these to the onion and garlic and cook very gently, stirring all the time until the mixture thickens. Season with salt and pepper and add some grated nutmeg to taste. Arrange the asparagus in the flans and then pour in the egg mixture, dividing it equally between them.

Bake the flans in the preheated oven for about 20 minutes until the filling is set. Serve them hot or warm.

CHEESE PIE   GREECE

This is a beautiful flaky golden pie with a creamy mild-tasting cheese filling. In Greece the crust would be made from phyllo pastry and the filling from feta and mitzithra cheeses but as these ingredients are not easy to get I make it with a quick flaky pastry, and a mixture of cottage cheese, curd cheese or quark and Lancashire cheese for the filling. I also sometimes add some lightly fried onion which gives extra flavour. You might think all this is very unauthentic but it still makes a lovely pie! It's nice as a hot starter or as a main meal with a cooked vegetable, such as the cauliflower in tomato sauce. If you want to try making the pie with phyllo pastry see page 260.

For tne pastry:
250 g (9 oz) plain flour – I use half wholewheat and half white flour
225 g (8 oz) butter, hard from the fridge
Cold water to mix

For the filling:
450 g (1 lb) cottage cheese, curd cheese or quark
225 g (8 oz) Lancashire cheese, grated
50 g (2 oz) flour
150 ml (5 fl oz) natural yoghurt
3 eggs
Sea salt
Freshly ground black pepper

Serves 6

First make the pastry – you need to do this an hour or so in advance to give it a chance to chill before you use it. Sift the flours into a bowl adding also any residue of bran left in the sieve, then grate in the hard butter using a coarse grater. Very lightly mix the butter with the flour using a fork and making sure that there are no large lumps of butter clinging together. Stir in enough cold water to make a soft manageable dough – it should be the same consistency as scone dough. Wrap the dough in a piece of greaseproof paper and put it into the fridge to chill for at least an hour.

Meanwhile you can make the filling for the pie. Put the cottage cheese, curd cheese or quark into a large bowl and stir in all the other ingredients, beating them together until you've got a nice creamy mixture. Season with salt and pepper. (If you want to add some onion to the pie chop 1 or 2 onions, fry them in a little butter and add them to the mixture when they're tender.)

Set the oven to 200°C (400°F), gas mark 6. Roll out two-thirds of the pastry and use it to line a pie dish. Dampen the edges with cold water. Fill with the cheese mixture then roll out the remaining pastry and put that on top, pressing the edges together. Trim and decorate the pie, making two or three holes in the top to allow the steam to escape. Bake the pie for 35 minutes, until it's golden brown. Serve it while it's all hot and light and flaky.

If you want to freeze this pie I think it's best to do so after cooking. To serve, remove the coverings and let the pie defrost for about 3 hours. Heat the pie through before serving it.

LITTLE CHEESE TARTLETS   RUSSIA

In Russia these little tartlets, *vatrushki*, are usually served either on their own as a first course or as an accompaniment to beetroot soup. I think they make a lovely first course if you serve them hot from the oven and offer a bowl of soured cream and chopped dill for people to spoon over the tartlets. They are also very good with the beetroot soup, turning it into a meal, but it's quite an unusual combination, best saved for those with adventurous palates!

For the filling:
225 g (8 oz) cottage cheese,
   curd cheese or quark
1 egg
Sea salt
Freshly ground black pepper

For the pastry:
200 g (8 oz) plain
   wholewheat flour

2 teaspoons baking powder
100 g (4 oz) butter or
   margarine and white
   vegetable fat mixed
2 tablespoons cold water

For the glaze:
1 egg beaten with ½ teaspoon
   salt

Serves 4 for lunch or supper, 4–6 as a starter

Set the oven to 220°C (425°F), gas mark 7. Make the filling by mixing the cottage cheese, curd cheese or quark with the egg and seasoning with salt and pepper.

Sift the flour, baking powder and a pinch of salt into a bowl and rub in the fat until the mixture resembles fine breadcrumbs, then add the water and mix to a dough. Roll the pastry out fairly thinly on a lightly floured board and cut into 16 or 18 7·5 cm (3 in) rounds. Put a heaped teaspoonful of the cheese mixture on to each round. Press the edges of the rounds up towards the centre to make a rim. Brush the tartlets over with the beaten egg glaze then bake them for about 20 minutes until set, puffed up and golden brown. They're nicest served immediately.

CHEESE AND ONION TART   SWITZERLAND

This is a good tart and the layer of little cubes of cheese seems to help keep the pastry nice and crisp. The proper cheeses, Gruyère and Emmenthal, are expensive and I generally use Edam instead – it gives a very similar result.

100 g (4 oz) plain flour – I
  generally use all
  wholewheat but you could
  use half wholewheat and
  half white
Pinch of salt
50 g (2 oz) butter
1 tablespoon cold water
1 tablespoon oil

For the filling:
1 medium onion
25 g (1 oz) butter
75 g (3 oz) Gruyère cheese and
  75 g (3 oz) Emmenthal
  cheese; or use all Edam cheese
2 eggs
150 ml ($\frac{1}{4}$ pint) single cream
  or top of the milk
Sea salt
Freshly ground black pepper
Grated nutmeg

Serves 4–5

Put a baking sheet in the centre of the oven, then set the temperature to 200°C (400°F), gas mark 6. Sift the flour and salt into a bowl; rub in the butter until the mixture resembles fine breadcrumbs, then add the cold water and mix to a dough. On a lightly floured board roll the pastry out to fit a 20–23 cm (8–9 in) flan dish or tin. Press the pastry gently into place, trim the edges and prick the base. Cook the flan case on the baking sheet in the preheated oven for 15 minutes until it's crisp, then take the flan out of the oven. Have the tablespoon of oil smoking hot in a saucepan and as soon as you take the flan out of the oven brush it all over with the very hot oil – this will help to keep the pastry crisp.

  While the flan case is cooking make the filling. Peel and chop the onion and fry it gently in the butter for 10 minutes until it's soft but not browned. Cut the cheeses into 6 mm ($\frac{1}{4}$ in) dice. In a small bowl beat together the eggs and cream and season them with salt, pepper and nutmeg. Scatter half the cheese over the base of the cooked flan, put the onions on top and then the rest of the cheese; finally gently pour in the egg mixture. Bake the flan for 30–35 minutes until it's puffed up and golden. Serve hot.

  This makes a good lunch with a juicy tomato salad and some fresh fruit to follow.

LEEK FLAN

FRANCE

Leeks make a delicious flan, delicate in flavour and colour, and there are many versions of this dish. I like to use soured cream or yoghurt because I think its sharp creaminess contrasts well with the slight sweetness of the leeks.

For the flan:
100 g (4 oz) plain wholewheat
   flour
Pinch of salt
50 g (2 oz) butter
1 tablespoon cold water
1 tablespoon oil

For the filling:
900 g (2 lb) leeks
25 g (1 oz) butter
150 ml (5 fl oz) soured cream
   or natural yoghurt
4 egg yolks or 2 whole eggs
Sea salt
Freshly ground black pepper

Serves 4

Put a baking sheet in the centre of the oven then set the temperature to 200°C (400°F), gas mark 6. Sift the flour and salt into a bowl, adding also the residue of bran left in the sieve, and rub in the butter until the mixture looks like breadcrumbs. Then add the water and mix to a dough. Roll out the pastry on a lightly floured board and use it to line a 20–23 cm (8–9 in) lightly greased flan tin. Prick the base of the flan with a fork, then put the flan case on the baking sheet in the oven and bake it for about 15 minutes until set and golden. Just before the flan is ready heat the tablespoon of oil in a small saucepan then take the flan out of the oven and immediately brush the surface over with the oil. Reduce the oven heat to 180°C (350°F), gas mark 4.

To make the filling cut the roots and most of the green leaves off the leeks; then slit them down the side and open up the layers under cold running water to wash away the grit. Slice the leeks fairly finely. Melt the butter in a large saucepan and put in the leeks; let them cook over a gentle heat for 10–15 minutes, with a lid on the saucepan, until they're tender. Stir them often and don't let them brown or it will spoil the flavour.

When the leeks are ready take them off the heat and stir in the soured cream. Whisk the eggs and add them to the creamy leek mixture together with seasoning to taste. Pour the mixture into the flan case and bake in the preheated oven for about 30 minutes, until the filling is set.

Serve the flan hot or warm with some cooked vegetables such as baby carrots, French beans and perhaps a good home-made tomato sauce, or serve it with a juicy tomato salad. It's also nice cold but I think it's at its best when warm.

LEEK PIE   ENGLAND

This pie from Cornwall is rather similar to the French *flamiche*. Both these pies usually contain small quantities of crumbled bacon but you can also make a very good vegetarian version, rich and creamy tasting. You could use a little of the bacon-flavoured soya protein, 'smoky snaps' with the leeks if you like, or sprinkle them with Parmesan cheese to add extra flavour.

My method of making the pie differs a little from the traditional one. Instead of baking the leeks under the pie crust then carefully removing it and pouring in the cream, which is very tricky if the pastry is light and crumbly, I find it best to boil the leeks first then mix them with the cream, cover with pastry and bake for about 20–25 minutes until the pastry is golden and the filling set.

For the filling:
1 kilo (2¼ lb) leeks
25 g (1 oz) grated Parmesan cheese; or 25–50 g (1–2 oz) 'smoky snaps'
150 ml (¼ pint) Cornish cream (or use double cream) or low-fat quark if you want a less rich, healthier dish
2 eggs, beaten
Sea salt
Freshly ground black pepper

For the pastry:
175 g (6 oz) plain wholewheat flour
1½ teaspoons baking powder
125 g (4 oz) white fat and margarine, mixed
1 tablespoon cold water
A little beaten egg (optional)

Serves 4

251

Wash the leeks and cut them into 2·5 cm (1 in) pieces. Put them into a large saucepan, cover them with cold water and bring to the boil. Simmer the leeks gently for 10–15 minutes, until they're tender, then drain them very well in a colander, using a spoon to press out all the water.

While the leeks are cooking make the pastry. Sift the flour and baking powder into a bowl adding also the residue of bran left in the sieve. Rub in the fat until the mixture resembles fine breadcrumbs then add the water and form the mixture into a dough. On a lightly floured board roll the pastry out big enough to fit your pie dish. Set the oven to 200°C (400°F), gas mark 6.

Mix the leeks with the Parmesan cheese or 'smoky snaps', the cream or low-fat quark, eggs, and salt and pepper to taste. Put the mixture into the pie dish and cover with the pastry, trimming it to fit and decorating it as you fancy. Brush it over with a little beaten egg if you want a shiny finish. Bake the pie for 20–25 minutes until the pastry is golden brown and cooked. Serve it immediately with cooked vegetables. The cream makes this a rich dish so I think it's best to serve a fresh salady starter or simple vegetable purée soup and fruity pudding.

MUSHROOM FLAN   FRANCE

Creamy, light and delicately flavoured, I think this is my favourite flan. It is delicious for a special lunch or supper. As it is rich I try to plan the rest of the meal accordingly: a simple cooked vegetable or salad to accompany the flan and a fresh-tasting fruity pudding to follow it.

For the pastry:
100 g (4 oz) plain wholewheat
   flour
Pinch of salt

50 g (2 oz) butter
1 tablespoon cold water
1 tablespoon oil

For the filling:

1 onion

1 garlic clove

50 g (2 oz) butter

225 g (8 oz) button
   mushrooms

1 heaped tablespoon
   chopped parsley

4 egg yolks or 2 whole eggs

150 ml ($\frac{1}{4}$ pint) single cream
   or milk for everyday

Sea salt

Freshly ground black pepper

Grated nutmeg

Serves 4–6

Place a baking sheet in the centre of the oven and set the temperature to 200°C (400°F), gas mark 6. Next make the pastry. Sift the flour and salt into a bowl and add the residue of bran left in the sieve. Rub the butter into the flour until the mixture looks like breadcrumbs then add the water and mix to a dough. Roll out the pastry and use to line a 20–23 cm (8–9 in) flan tin. Prick the base then put the flan into the oven on the baking sheet and bake for about 15 minutes, until it's cooked and golden. Heat the oil in a saucepan and immediately brush the surface of the flan with very hot oil. Reduce the oven heat to 180°C (350°F), gas mark 4.

While the flan is cooking make the filling. Peel and chop the onion, peel and crush the garlic and cook them together in the butter for 10 minutes, until the onion is soft but not browned. Meanwhile wash and slice the mushrooms; add these to the onion and garlic and fry for a further 3 minutes or so without a lid on the saucepan, then stir in the chopped parsley. Put the egg yolks into a medium-sized bowl and whisk them with the cream or milk. Add this to the mushroom mixture and season with salt and pepper to taste. Heat the mixture gently, stirring all the time, until it begins to thicken. This will happen quickly but don't worry even if it gets really very thick because it will be all right once it's baked.

Pour the mushroom mixture into the cooked flan case – it doesn't matter if the pastry is still hot – and bake in the oven for about 30 minutes, until the creamy mixture is set. Serve hot or warm.

ONION FLAN   FRANCE

This is a good flan with a creamy onion filling and crisp pastry base. I usually make it with milk but of course for special occasions it's lovely made with single cream instead – or a mixture.

For the pastry:
100 g (4 oz) plain wholewheat
   flour
Pinch of salt
50 g (2 oz) butter
1 tablespoon cold water
1 tablespoon oil

For the filling:
450 g (1 lb) onions, peeled
   and thinly sliced

Serves 4–6

25 g (1 oz) butter
4 egg yolks or 2 whole eggs
150 ml ($\frac{1}{4}$ pint) milk or
   single cream
50 g (2 oz) grated cheese
$\frac{1}{2}$ teaspoon mustard powder
Sea salt
Freshly ground black pepper
1 tomato, sliced, to decorate
   the top

Put a baking sheet in the centre of the oven and set the temperature to 200°C (400°F), gas mark 6. Sieve the flour and salt into a bowl, adding also the residue of bran left in the sieve. Cut the butter into small pieces and rub these into the flour with your fingertips so that the mixture looks like fine breadcrumbs; then mix in the water. Press the mixture lightly together to make a dough. Roll the pastry out on a lightly floured board and use it to line a 20–23 cm (8–9 in) flan tin. Trim the edges neatly and prick the base thoroughly all over. Put the flan on the baking sheet in the oven and bake it for 15 minutes, until it's crisp and golden brown. Just before you take the flan out of the oven heat the oil until it's smoking hot, then brush the surface of the flan all over with oil as soon as you take it out of the oven. Turn the oven down to 180°C (350°F), gas mark 4.

To make the filling fry the onions lightly in the butter until they're soft and golden – about 10 minutes. Whisk together the eggs or egg yolks and the milk or cream then add these to the onions in the saucepan and stir over a gentle heat until the mixture thickens. Take the saucepan off the heat and mix in the grated cheese, mustard and salt and pepper to taste. Pour this mixture into the flan case. Arrange the tomato slices on top. Put the flan into the oven on the baking sheet and bake for about 30 minutes, until the filling is set.

This flan is delicious served hot with some tender French beans or courgettes or a crisp salad. It also makes a good protein-rich starter before a vegetable-based main course.

PIZZA
ITALY

Pizza makes a very good vegetarian meal. It's filling and tasty and looks and smells so appetizing with its topping of red tomatoes, golden cheese and black olives, and its mouth-watering aroma of home-made bread. Although it sounds complicated pizza isn't really too difficult or time-consuming to make and only needs a crunchy green salad to accompany it.

The quantity given here is enough to fill two of those large white pizza dishes and feeds 4–8 people depending on how hungry they are. Instead of pizza dishes you could use two big baking sheets or four 18 cm (7 in) sandwich tins. Although mozzarella cheese is the authentic one it's expensive and not always easy to get, and I find Lancashire a very good substitute.

For the dough:
½ teaspoon sugar
2 teaspoons dried yeast
100 ml (4 fl oz) warm water
275 g (10 oz) plain wholewheat or wheatmeal flour
Pinch of salt
40 g (1½ oz) soft butter or margarine
1 egg

For the topping:
2 large onions
2 tablespoons oil
792 g (1 lb 2 oz) can tomatoes
125 g (4 oz) mozzarella or Lancashire cheese
Sea salt
Freshly ground black pepper
8–12 black olives, stoned and halved
A little olive oil

Serves 4–8

to make the dough first put the sugar, yeast and warm water into a small bowl and mix them briefly with a fork. Leave on one side for about 10 minutes for the yeast to froth up. While this is happening put the flour and salt into a bowl and rub in the butter or margarine. Add the yeast to the flour, also the egg, mixing them with your hands to make a dough. It should be soft enough to knead without effort but firm and pliable. Add a tiny bit more flour or water if necessary to adjust the consistency, then turn the dough on to a clean board or working surface and knead for about 5 minutes. Put the kneaded dough into a bowl, cover with a clean damp cloth then put the bowl under a polythene carrier bag if you have one and leave in a warm place to double in size – this takes 45–60 minutes.

While you're waiting for the dough make the topping. Peel and slice the onions and fry them gently in the oil for about 10 minutes until they're soft but not browned. Drain and chop the tomatoes, reserving the juice; cut the cheese into thin slices.

When the dough has doubled in size punch it down with your hand and turn it out on to a lightly floured board. Knead the dough briefly, then divide it into two or four pieces and roll each out to fit your plate or tin. Brush the plates or tins with oil and lay the dough on them, pressing it down and tucking in the edges to fit. Cover the top of the dough with the chopped tomatoes, adding a little of the juice as necessary to moisten, then arrange the fried onions and sliced cheese on top and decorate with the olives. Sprinkle a little oil over the top of the pizza and brush some over the edges of the dough. Season with salt and pepper.

Set the oven to 200°C (400°F), gas mark 6. Put the pizzas (uncovered) on one side to 'prove' for 15 minutes while the oven is heating up. I stand mine on top of the cooker so that they get the benefit of the heat from the oven as it warms up, but this isn't essential. Bake the pizzas for 15-20 minutes until the base is puffed up and the cheesy topping all golden brown and delicious-looking.

Pizza freezes very well. Place the uncooked pizza in the freezer and open-freeze until firm, then wrap it in foil or polythene.

To use the pizza, remove the coverings, leave for 15–30 minutes to defrost while the oven heats up and then bake as usual.

MUSHROOM PIZZA

Make this as above, but omit the olives. Instead arrange on top of the pizza 125 g (4 oz) washed and finely sliced button mushrooms, brushed lightly with olive oil.

HERBY PIZZA

Sprinkle the top of the tomato pizza with plenty of dried oregano or marjoram; drip a little extra olive oil over the top to moisten the herbs.

GREEN PEPPER PIZZA

Wash and de-seed a large green or red pepper. Cut the pepper into strips and fry these with the onions, adding them to the saucepan after 5 minutes. Arrange the slices on top of the pizza with the onions – you can make a very pretty pizza with a lattice of pepper strips on top.

ARTICHOKE PIZZA

Finely slice 3 or 4 canned artichoke hearts; arrange the slices on top of the tomato mixture. Omit the olives but keep the fried onions.

QUICK NON-YEAST PIZZA   ITALY

This pizza, *pizza al tegame,* is made from a flour and baking powder dough cooked in a frying pan in a little hot oil then finished off under the grill or in the oven. It's very useful for those emergencies when you find yourself having to rustle up food unexpectedly, because it's quick to make and uses basic store-cupboard ingredients. It's a dish I often make when we're holidaying in our caravan with more limited cooking facilities than usual but heartier appetites!

For the pizza base:
225 g (8 oz) plain wholewheat
   flour
2 teaspoons baking powder
½ teaspoon salt
2 tablespoons oil
6–8 tablespoons cold water

For the topping:
1 large onion
2 tablespoons oil
1 garlic clove, peeled and
   crushed

Two 425 g (15 oz) cans
   tomatoes
1 teaspoon marjoram
Sea salt
Freshly ground black pepper
125 g (4 oz) cheese, sliced,
   preferably white Cheshire
   or Lancashire but any firm
   cooking cheese will do in
   an emergency
Oil for shallow frying

Serves 4

Sift the flour, baking powder and salt into a bowl, adding the residue of bran from the sieve as well. Mix in the oil and enough water to make a soft but not sticky dough. Knead the dough lightly on a floured board then leave it to rest for a minute or two while you make the pizza topping.

    Peel and chop the onion and fry it in the oil in a large saucepan for 10 minutes, until it's soft but not browned, then stir in the garlic. Drain the juice from the tomatoes – you won't need it for this recipe but it's useful for soups, sauces and for the non-cream version of the potato dish on page 124. Add the tomatoes to the onion and garlic, breaking them up a bit with the spoon. Stir in the marjoram and salt and pepper to taste; then keep this mixture warm while you finish making the base.

    Divide the dough into two pieces and roll each one into a circle to fit your frying pan – probably about 20 cm (8 in). Heat a little oil in the frying pan and fry the first pizza over a moderate heat. When the underside is cooked, turn it over and fry the other side, then carefully remove the pizza and put it on to a dish or tin which will fit under the grill. Spread half the tomato mixture over the pizza, then arrange half the cheese slices on top. Put the pizza under the grill for a few minutes, just to heat up the topping and melt the cheese. Keep it warm while you make the other pizza in the same way.

A quick salad like a watercress salad or a cabbage and apple salad goes well with this and can be prepared while you're waiting for the pizzas to cook. It's also nice with frozen peas.

SAMOSAS INDIA

These little Indian pastries with their spicy vegetable filling are delicious for a main meal with some Indian curry sauce and perhaps a curried vegetable or side salad. They are also nice cold with some yoghurt or mayonnaise to dip them into and a crisp salad.

For the filling:
1 large onion
1 large garlic clove
25 g (1 oz) *ghee* or butter
1 teaspoon mustard seed
1 teaspoon ground ginger
1 teaspoon ground cumin
1 teaspoon ground coriander
900 g (2 lb) cooked mixed
   vegetables: potatoes, carrots
   and frozen peas, or whatever
   is available

Sea salt
Freshly ground black pepper

For the pastry:
200 g (8 oz) plain
   wholewheat flour
½ teaspoon sea salt
½ teaspoon baking powder
50 g (2 oz) *ghee* or butter
6–7 tablespoons cold water
Oil for deep or shallow frying

Serves 6

First make the filling. Peel and chop the onion, peel and crush

259

the garlic. Fry them gently in the fat for 10 minutes then stir in the spices. Mix well, then add the cooked vegetables and turn these gently with a spoon so that they all get coated with the spicy onion and oil. Season with salt and pepper then let the mixture cool.

To make the pastry sift the flour, salt and baking powder into a bowl, together with any residue of bran, and rub in the butter or *ghee* and enough water to make a soft but not sticky dough. Knead the dough for 5 minutes, then divide it into 16 pieces. Roll each piece into a ball then use a rolling pin to roll each into a circle about 15 cm (6 in) in diameter. Cut the circles in half to get 32 half circles. Put a heaped teaspoonful of the filling on to each half circle of pastry, dampen the edges with a pastry brush dipped in cold water and fold the corners over to make a little triangular-shaped packet, pressing the edges well together. When all the *samosas* are ready, deep or shallow fry them a few at a time until they are golden and crisp. Drain them well and serve them hot or cold.

SPINACH PIE   MIDDLE EAST

This combination of crisp golden pastry, buttery spinach and soft white cheese is very delicious. Like the cheese pie from Greece this should really be made with phyllo pastry which you can sometimes get in delicatessens and shops specializing in foreign foods. It's not always easy to obtain but if you do get some you'll need about 225 g (½ lb) for the pie. Brush the pie dish with melted butter and lay a piece of the pastry in it, then brush this with more butter and put another piece on top. Repeat this until you have used half the pastry and then put in your filling. Cover the filling with more layers of pastry and melted butter as before. Trim the pie and brush more melted butter over the top. Bake the pie as for the flaky pastry version given below. You need to work fairly fast with phyllo pastry as it hardens as the air gets to it – it's a good idea to keep the pieces you're not actually using in a polythene bag until required.

If you're using the flaky pastry version you need to get organized in advance to allow time for the pastry to chill and rest.

For the pastry:
250 g (9 oz) plain flour – I use half wholewheat, half white for this pastry or an 81% or 85% flour from the health shop
Pinch of salt
225 g (8 oz) butter, hard from the fridge
Cold water to mix

For the filling:
900 g (2 lb) fresh spinach or 450 g (1 lb) frozen chopped spinach

1 large onion
Olive oil
1 garlic clove
Chopped mixed fresh herbs as available: parsley, chives, thyme
150 g (6 oz) Cheshire or Wensleydale cheese, crumbled
Sea salt
Freshly ground black pepper
A little beaten egg (optional)

Serves 4 as a main course, 6 as a starter

First make the pastry. Sift the flour and salt into a large bowl and grate in the butter. Add enough cold water to make a manageable dough – it should be pliable but not sticky. Roll the dough into a ball, wrap it in greaseproof paper and put it in the fridge for 2 hours.

Next make the filling – this too can be done in advance. If you're using fresh spinach wash it thoroughly and cook it in a dry saucepan until it's tender, then drain and chop it. If you're using frozen spinach, put it into a colander and leave it to defrost then drain off the excess water; press the spinach with a spoon to squeeze out as much water as possible. Peel and chop the onion and fry it in a little oil in a fairly large saucepan for about 10 minutes until it is tender, then take the saucepan off the heat and stir in the garlic, spinach, herbs, cheese and salt and pepper to taste. Leave the mixture to cool.

When you're ready to finish and cook the pie, set the oven to

230°C (450°F), gas mark 8. Roll out two-thirds of the pastry on a lightly floured board and gently lay the pastry in a deep pie dish. Spoon the filling into the pastry-lined dish. Roll out the remaining piece of pastry and use this to cover the top of the pie. Trim the pastry and crimp or fork the edge. Brush the top of the pie with some beaten egg if you want a shiny finish. Bake the pie for 20 minutes then turn the heat down to 200 C (400°F), gas mark 6 and cook for a further 20 minutes.

This pie makes a delicious main course if you serve it with creamy mashed potato and a brightly coloured vegetable such as carrots. Or serve it on its own as a warming and welcoming first course before one of the lighter main dishes.

The pie can be frozen; I think it's best to freeze it before glazing and cooking. Thaw the pie for 2–3 hours then glaze it with beaten egg, if you want to, and cook as usual.

Puddings

Most people like to finish a meal with a pudding – and most adults probably feel slightly guilty about eating them! For this reason I have included quite a number of light, fruity puddings that round things off nicely without being either too rich or fattening.

One nice thing about vegetarian cooking though is that it gives you the opportunity to plan a meal to take full advantage of the pudding course if you wish. You can have a simple first course such as a puréed vegetable soup, followed by a plain but tasty main course based on rice or vegetables, such as paella or tomatoes à la Provençale with noodles and French beans, then finish the meal with a flourish by serving something like a real trifle, luscious home-made ice cream with meringues, or gorgeous crêpes suzette. Or you could offer one of the tarts from the next section of this book if you want a more substantial pudding.

Some of these puddings are rich in protein, a point worth exploiting when you're planning a meal. Remember, protein is just as good if you eat it in the pudding course as in the main course; serving a nutritious pudding after a high protein main course means you're probably eating more protein than you need and the excess is just used for energy, like carbohydrates, which is wasteful. Vegetarian cookery gives you the flexibility to utilize protein economically if you wish.

APPLE SNOW

FINLAND.

This is a useful pudding to serve after a filling meal because it's light and refreshing, but it's also nourishing because of the egg whites.

450 g (1 lb) cooking apples
125 g (4 oz) granulated sugar
2 egg whites
A little grated lemon rind

Serves 4

Peel, core and slice the apples then put them into a heavy-based saucepan with the sugar and cook them over a gentle heat, with a lid on the saucepan, until they're soft and purée-like. If the apples have produced a great deal of liquid take the lid off the saucepan and cook them for a few minutes more to thicken them up but watch them carefully and stir them often so that they don't burn. Cool the apples then sieve or liquidize them.

Whisk the egg whites until they're stiff but not dry then fold them into the apple purée. Grate enough lemon rind into the mixture to give a refreshing tang. Divide between four individual bowls and serve chilled. It's nice with some crisp biscuits – macaroons go well with it.

APRICOT AND ALMOND PUDDING

SWEDEN

This easy-to-make dish from Sweden is actually halfway between a pudding and a cake – a light, gooey almond-flavoured sponge with apricots baked into the middle. It's best eaten warm, with pouring cream if you like; or cold, when it can be decorated with some piped whipped cream and toasted flaked almonds if you want to make it extra special. You can use either canned apricots or soaked dried apricots. If you're using the latter I think it's worth getting the best quality whole (stoned) ones if possible. It's best to use a loose-based cake tin if you have one; otherwise use an ordinary deep tin lined with foil.

125 g (4 oz) soft vegetable margarine
125 g (4 oz) caster or Barbados sugar
2 eggs
50 g (2 oz) plain wholewheat flour

125 g (4 oz) ground almonds
125 g (4 oz) dried apricots, soaked and cooked until tender, or use a 425 g (15 oz) can apricot halves
A few flaked almonds

Serves 4

Lightly grease and flour a 20 cm (8 in) loose-based cake tin; set the oven to 160°C (325°F), gas mark 3. Put the margarine and sugar into a bowl and cream them until they're light, then add the eggs and beat again. Add the flour and ground almonds and beat the mixture until it's very light and fluffy. Put half the mixture into the base of the cake tin. Drain the apricots and arrange them on top of the almond mixture, then spread remaining mixture on top and scatter with a few flaked almonds. Bake the pudding for 60–70 minutes, until it is set and golden brown. Cool in the tin, then slip a knife round the edges, ease the pudding out of the tin and serve.

BANANA FRITTERS WITH LIME   CARIBBEAN

The recipe for these puffy banana fritters was given to me by a friend in the Caribbean and they make an interesting and unusual pudding. The only snag is they really need to be fried just before you serve them, so it means getting up from the table to do them, but they don't take long if you have everything ready in advance. I've found you can even shallow fry them if you prefer and they're still puffy and good.

50 g (2 oz) plain wholewheat
 flour
Pinch of baking powder
Pinch of salt
3 firm, ripe bananas
$\frac{1}{2}$ teaspoon Angostura bitters,
 if available

4 teaspoons milk
1 egg white
Fat for deep or shallow frying
Slices of lime or lemon
Soft brown sugar

Serves 4

Sift the flour, baking powder and salt into a bowl, adding also the residue of bran left in the sieve. Peel the bananas and mash them with a fork, then add them to the flour, together with the Angostura bitters and milk. (You can do all this in advance.)

When you're ready to finish the fritters, whisk the egg white until it's standing in soft peaks and fold it into the banana mixture. Drop tablespoonfuls of the mixture into hot deep or shallow fat and fry them until they're browned on one side, then turn them over to fry the other side. Take the fritters out with a perforated spoon and drain them on kitchen paper; then transfer them to a hot dish and serve them at once, garnished with the lime or lemon slices. Serve the soft brown sugar separately for people to help themselves.

CHOCOLATE AND ORANGE MOUSSE   SPAIN

This is a wickedly delicious pudding; smooth dark chocolate flavoured with the sharp freshness of orange. It's also very easy to make.

225 g (8 oz) dark chocolate
2 tablespoons orange juice
Grated rind of 1 orange
1 tablespoon orange liqueur
 such as Curaçao – or use
 brandy

4 eggs, separated
A little whipped cream
A few toasted almonds or
 chocolate curls

Serves 6

Break up the chocolate and put it into a bowl. Set the bowl over a saucepan of boiling water, or pop it into a moderate oven for about 10 minutes until the chocolate has melted. Stir the orange juice and rind into the melted chocolate, then the liqueur or brandy and the egg yolks. Whisk the egg whites until they're standing in soft peaks then gently fold them into the chocolate mixture using a metal spoon and a cutting and folding motion. Spoon the mixture into six little dishes – it looks very nice in those little white individual soufflé dishes. Put the mousse into the fridge for at least 2 hours to chill and set. You can leave it overnight if this is convenient.

It's lovely served just as it is, or you can garnish it with some whipped cream and toasted flaked almonds or chocolate curls. To make the chocolate curls just run a potato peeler down the flat side of a bar of chocolate.

Chocolate mousse is good after Spanish vegetable rice or any cereal or vegetable-based dish.

COEURS À LA CRÈME   FRANCE

Hearts of creamy white cheese surrounded by shiny red straw-berries make a beautiful summer pudding that's rich in protein and ideal for serving after something like ratatouille and rice. You need to start making the hearts the night before you want to serve the pudding. The quantities I've given are right for five of those white heart-shaped china dishes you can get with little holes in the base. Alternatively you can make some holes in the base of cream, yoghurt or small cottage cheese cartons and use these; I've also used a colander successfully. And if you can't get muslin to line the moulds, fine net curtain makes a good substitute.

450 g (1 lb) curd cheese, quark or cottage cheese – if you're using cottage cheese push it through a sieve to make it smooth

150 ml (5 fl oz) double cream
2 tablespoons caster sugar
350 g (12 oz) strawberries.
A little extra caster sugar

Serves 5

Put the cheese into a large bowl, mix it with the cream and sugar and beat with a wooden spoon until the mixture thickens and holds its shape. Line your white china dishes, yoghurt, cream or cottage cheese pots, or colander, with muslin, then spoon in the creamy mixture and smooth the surface. Stand the containers or the colander on a plate to catch the liquid which will drain off and place them in the fridge overnight.

Next day wash and hull the strawberries, halving or quartering any larger ones as necessary. Then sprinkle them lightly with sugar and leave on one side.

To serve, turn the creamy cheese mixture out on to a large plate and carefully peel off the muslin. Arrange the strawberries round the cheese or cheeses.

Don't assemble this dish until just before you need it or the juice from the strawberries can spoil the look of it. It's a good way of making a few strawberries go further when they're expensive.

If you're slimming I've found you can make this dish equally well using natural yoghurt instead of cream. The result is very similar though not so creamy-tasting, and I find if I use 450 g (1 lb) low-fat quark or cottage cheese, 150 ml (5 fl oz) natural yoghurt and 3–4 tablespoons caster sugar, the mixture fills four white china hearts, not five as it does when made with double cream. The yoghurt version also gives off a little more liquid as it drains and settles in the fridge.

LITTLE COFFEE CUSTARDS FRANCE

These little dishes of velvety, chilled coffee custard make a lovely
pudding, simple, quick to make, yet luxurious tasting. They are
splendid for serving when you want to increase the protein
content of a meal. I've given a rather economical version of this
pudding; for a special occasion it's superb with single cream
replacing some or all of the milk. You can top the custards with a
whirl of cream or with a baby meringue, which gives a pleasant
crispness.

4 eggs
1 tablespoon good quality
  instant coffee
275 ml (½ pint) milk

50 g (2 oz) caster sugar
A little whipped cream
  or 4 baby meringues (optional)

Serves 4

Set the oven to 150°C (300°F), gas mark 2. Break the eggs into a
medium-sized bowl and whisk them until they're frothy. Put the
instant coffee, milk and sugar into a small saucepan and heat
almost to boiling point. Remove the saucepan from the heat and
gradually add the milk to the beaten eggs, stirring all the time.
Strain the mixture into a jug then pour it into four little fireproof
dishes – little white ramekins are ideal. Cover each dish with a
piece of foil. Stand the dishes in a baking tin filled with 2·5 cm
(1 in) very hot water. Place the tin in the oven and bake the
custards for 45–50 minutes, or until they are firmly set and
a knife put into the centre comes out clean. Cool the custards,
keeping the foil over them, which prevents a hard skin from
forming, then put them into the fridge. Serve the little custards
straight from the fridge so that they're beautifully cold and
refreshing; garnish them with whipped cream or baby meringues
if you like.

COFFEE RICOTTA PUDDING ITALY

A very easy to make, protein-rich pudding. It's lovely served after one of the vegetable casseroles or cereal main dishes, or after a low-protein pasta dish.

2 teaspoons best quality instant coffee, continental type
1 tablespoon water, rum or Tia Maria
450 g (1 lb) *ricotta* cheese, curd cheese, quark or cottage cheese – if you're using cottage cheese try to get the type with the softest, finest curds
50 g (2 oz) caster sugar

Serves 4

Dissolve the coffee by mixing it with the water, rum or Tia Maria. If the cheese is very lumpy it might be best to push it through a sieve, otherwise put it straight into a bowl. Add the coffee mixture and sugar to the cheese, stirring until everything is combined. Spoon into small dishes; serve chilled. It's nice with macaroons or other small crunchy biscuuts.

CRÈME BRÛLÉE ENGLAND

Although this pudding sounds French it is in fact English and originated at Trinity College, Cambridge. It's a useful pudding to serve when you want to add protein to the meal. At its richest and most luxurious it's made entirely with single cream but you can also make a less extravagant version using a mixture of single cream and milk, or even just milk. You can also use two whole eggs instead of the egg yolks, but the mixture is not as smooth tasting.

400 ml (¾ pint) milk
150 ml (5 fl oz) single cream
40 g (1½ oz) sugar
4 egg yolks or 2 whole eggs

A vanilla pod or a few drops
  of vanilla essence
A little icing sugar

Serves 6

Put the milk and cream into a saucepan and bring up to the boil, then take off the heat. In a medium-sized bowl beat together the sugar and egg yolks or eggs then add the milk, stirring. Strain the mixture back into the saucepan or into the top of a double saucepan and add the vanilla pod or a few drops of vanilla essence. Stir the mixture over a gentle heat for a few minutes until it thickens, then take it off the heat, remove the vanilla pod (this can of course be washed, dried and used again and again) and pour the custard into little individual heatproof dishes. Let the custard get completely cold. Two or three hours before you want to serve them, sift a little icing sugar over the top of each custard so that they are covered completely but not too thickly. Place the custard under a hot grill for about 5 minutes to melt and lightly brown the sugar. Cool, then chill the puddings in the fridge and serve them nice and cold.

CRÊPES SUZETTE

FRANCE

Crêpes suzette sound so complicated and people are always terribly impressed by them, but they're really not at all difficult to make and you can do all the main preparation well in advance.

For the pancakes:
125 g (4 oz) plain flour – I
  use all wholewheat or half
  wholewheat, half white
Pinch of salt

2 tablespoons vegetable oil
2 eggs
200 ml (7 fl oz) milk
Extra oil for frying

For the orange sauce:
125 g (4 oz) butter
150 g (5 oz) caster sugar
Grated rind and juice of 3
   small-medium oranges

Grated rind and juice of 1 lemon
2 tablespoons orange liqueur
   such as Curaçao if available
4 tablespoons brandy

Serves 4–6

First of all make the pancakes. If you want to you can do this a day or two in advance and keep the pancakes covered in the fridge, or even further in advance if you've got a deep freeze. To make the batter either put all the ingredients into the liquidizer goblet and blend until smooth and creamy: or sift the flour and salt into a bowl, make a well in the middle, put in the oil and eggs and gradually beat in the milk until everything is well mixed. If you've made the batter by hand let it stand for 30 minutes, then beat it again before you use it.

To cook the pancakes set a small frying pan over a moderate heat and brush the base with a thin film of oil. Pour a little batter into the hot frying pan, tilting and turning it so that the batter runs quickly all over the base and coats it thinly. When the underside of the pancake is golden brown and the top of the pancake is just set – about 20–30 seconds – turn it over using a palette knife and your fingers and cook the second side – this only takes a few seconds. Take the pancake out and put it on to a plate. Brush the frying pan with a little more oil (unless you're using a non-stick frying pan which only needs oiling after about every 3 or 4 pancakes) and make another pancake in the same way. Continue until all the batter is used and you have a pile of about 14 thin pancakes. Cover them and keep them in a cool place until needed.

You can assemble the dish an hour or so in advance. Put the butter, sugar, grated rinds and juices, and the orange liqueur if you're using it, into a large frying pan or shallow flameproof dish that you can take to the table, and heat gently to melt the butter and sugar. Turn off the heat, then dip the pancakes in this mixture, one by one, coating each side of the pancake then folding

273

it in half and in half again, so that it's a triangle shape. As each pancake is done push it to the side of the frying pan. When all the pancakes have been dipped leave them in the frying pan or dish until you're almost ready to eat them then put the frying pan over the heat to warm through the sauce and the pancakes. When they're ready, turn up the heat high for about 1 minute to make the sauce very hot, quickly pour in the brandy and set it alight with a taper or by tilting the frying pan down towards the gas flame. You can take it to the table at this point, burning away. The flame will die out in a few seconds, when all the fat has been burnt. Serve immediately.

This is a protein-rich pudding that's delicious after a light main course.

DRIED FRUIT COMPOTE   GERMANY

A dried fruit compote has an intense, intriguing flavour which comes from the slow simmering of the fruits and which I think is delicious. It's a very useful winter pudding. You can buy 250 g (9 oz) packets of mixed dried fruits or you may be able to buy them loose in a health shop. If you prefer to make up your own selection you can buy dried apricots, apple rings, peaches, pears and prunes separately and mix them as you wish. Leave out the ginger in the recipe if you don't like it; I don't think it's authentically German but it makes this recipe taste unusual and specially good.

450 g (1 lb) mixed dried fruit
2 or 3 thin strips of lemon rind
1 or 2 pieces of stem ginger, finely chopped
4 tablespoons syrup from the jar

A little softly whipped cream
Crisp shortbread or almond biscuits to serve

Serves 4

274

Wash the dried fruit then put it into a bowl, cover generously with boiling water and leave to soak for a few hours. Transfer fruit and liquid to a large saucepan and add the lemon rind, and a little extra water if necessary to bring the level of the liquid just up to the fruit. Bring to the boil then leave it to simmer very gently for 30 minutes with a lid on the saucepan. The fruit should be very tender and the liquid reduced to a glossy-looking syrup. Remove the lemon rind and add the ginger and ginger syrup. Leave to cool, then chill the mixture. Serve in individual dishes.

I like this with a spoonful of softly whipped cream on top; some pouring cream or chilled vanilla custard sauce would also be nice.

EXOTIC FRUIT SALAD   SOUTH AMERICA

I like to use a can of pink guavas as the basis of this salad because they're such a beautiful colour and they give the mixture a rather exotic appearance and flavour. Kiwi fruit, or Chinese gooseberries, are quite easy to get these days – they sometimes appear in my local supermarket and are about the size of a large egg with a brown, slightly furry-looking skin. When you cut them open they're an amazing, gorgeous green and enhance any fruit salad mixture. But if you can't get them just use extra pineapple or banana or a small can of mangoes instead – or a fresh mango if you can get it.

410 g (14½ oz) can guavas   2 large ripe bananas
1 ripe pineapple   2–3 kiwi fruit

Serves 6

Put the syrup from the guavas into a bowl. Cut the pieces of guava into halves or quarters, then add these to the bowl of syrup. Slice the leaves and prickly skin off the pineapple and dice the flesh, removing the hard centre core. Peel and slice the bananas. Using a sharp knife peel the skin off the kiwi fruit – like peeling an apple – then slice the fruit into thin rounds. Mix all the fruits together and chill the salad before serving. If you need more liquid add a little fresh orange juice.

This salad is nice served with crisp coconut biscuits.

FRESH FRUIT SALAD   ITALY

This mixture of fresh figs, with their exotic-looking purple and red flesh, oranges, peaches and plums, makes an Italian-style fruit salad reminiscent of hot sun and blue seas. If you can't get fresh figs you could use canned ones or substitute something like black grapes or strawberries instead.

4 large oranges	450 g (1 lb) ripe plums
4 large peaches	4 fresh figs

Serves 6

Cut the peel and pith from the oranges then cut out the segments of flesh, leaving the skin behind. Do this over a bowl to catch any juice. Put the orange segments into the bowl. Peel the peaches as you would tomatoes, by covering them with boiling water, leaving for 1 minute then draining; slip the point of a knife under the skin and ease it off. Cut the peaches into small pieces, discarding the stones. Halve, stone and cut up the plums, and slice the figs. Add them all to the bowl and mix everything gently together, stirring in a little extra orange juice to moisten if necessary. Chill well before serving.

VARIATIONS
A fruit salad makes one of the most delicious puddings and of course the mixture of fruits can be varied according to what's

276

available. Another summer version would be peaches, melon, oranges or strawberries; in the autumn those sweet, crisp green grapes, oranges, new-season apples and plums. In the winter, oranges, pineapples, Cox's orange pippins and black grapes are delicious; in the spring, sweet juicy pears, oranges, apples and green grapes.

You can make fruit salad more substantial if you want to by serving it with crisp biscuits or sponge fingers and some whipped cream or chilled pouring egg custard, or brandy snaps filled with cream.

FRUITY MUESLI   SWITZERLAND

Most people think of this as a breakfast dish consisting mainly of oats and other cereals. But when Dr Bircher-Benner invented it for his patients in his clinic in Zurich at the turn of the century it was really a fruit dish and as such it makes a delicious pudding, light and nourishing. If you use condensed milk, which is the type Dr Bircher-Benner used, it gives the muesli a delectable, almost jellied consistency and sweet taste.

4 tablespoons sweetened condensed milk
4 tablespoons lemon juice
4 level tablespoons rolled oats

4 large eating apples
4 tablespoons chopped or grated hazel nuts or almonds

Serves 4

Put the condensed milk and lemon juice into a large bowl and mix them until they're smooth, then stir in the oats. Wash the apples and grate them fairly coarsely then add them to the bowl. If the mixture seems rather stiff add a little cold water or orange juice. Spoon the muesli into individual bowls and sprinkle the nuts over the top.

For a less sweet version of this pudding you can use natural yoghurt instead of the condensed milk but the consistency will not be quite the same.

GOOSEBERRY FOOL ENGLAND

It's up to you whether you sieve or liquidize the gooseberries for this fool. If you sieve them you'll get a very smooth mixture; if you just liquidize them it will be more lumpy, but I think this texture is rather nice. I like it best made with half yoghurt, which gives a pleasant sharpness, and half cream, but you could use all yoghurt for a more weight-conscious version. It's nice made with other fruits, too; cooked rhubarb, apple, dried apricots or blackberries, or fresh uncooked raspberries or strawberries.

450 g (1 lb) gooseberries
2 tablespoons water
125 g (4 oz) sugar
60 ml (2½ fl oz) natural yoghurt

60 ml (2½ fl oz) double cream
A little chocolate vermicelli
or a few roasted hazel nuts

Serves 4

Wash the gooseberries then 'top and tail' them with a small sharp knife. Put the gooseberries into a medium-sized heavy-based saucepan with the water and cook them gently with a lid on the saucepan until they're tender – 10–15 minutes – then strain off the liquid which you won't need for this recipe. Sieve or liquidize the gooseberries. Stir in the sugar, then leave them on one side to cool.

Mix the yoghurt into the cooled gooseberry purée. Whisk the cream until it's standing in soft peaks, then fold it gently but thoroughly into the gooseberry mixture. Spoon the fool into individual glass dishes and chill them in the refrigerator until needed. Sprinkle a few strands of chocolate vermicelli or some chopped nuts on top just before serving. This fool is nice with macaroons.

Don't make the mistake I made while testing recipes for this book: on a hot July day I served chilled cucumber soup for a starter and gooseberry fool for a pudding – the two mixtures looked almost the same!

GROUND RICE AND ROSEWATER PUDDING TURKEY

The traditional way of making this pudding involves simmering the milk for a long time to reduce it and thicken the mixture, so my method, using evaporated milk, is a shortcut, but it gives a lovely creamy result. I know the rosewater flavouring is not to everyone's taste, but I love it. This is a useful dish because it's rich with protein.

40 g (1½ oz) ground rice
1 large can evaporated milk
50 g (2 oz) sugar
2 tablespoons rosewater
A little red vegetable colouring

A few crystallized rose petals to serve
A few pistachio nuts, shelled – or a little chopped angelica, for economy

Serves 4–6

Put the ground rice into a small bowl and mix it to a paste with a little of the milk. Put the rest of the milk into a saucepan with the sugar and bring to the boil. Pour a little of the boiling milk into the ground rice paste and mix, then tip this into the saucepan of milk. Put the saucepan over a gentle heat and stir for 4–5 minutes until it has thickened and will coat the spoon fairly heavily.

Take the saucepan off the heat and stir in the rosewater and enough red colouring to tint the mixture a pale pink, then pour it into one large bowl or 4–6 individual dishes – glass ones are nice if you've got them. Leave the pudding to cool, then chill it in the refrigerator. Just before serving decorate the top with the rose petals and pistachio nuts or angelica.

LEMON WHIP   HOLLAND

This is a very light delicious pudding, just right for serving after a substantial main course that's filled you up. It's also useful because though it tastes so airy it's rich in protein. It sounds a bit fiddly to make, but really it isn't.

2 large lemons or 3–4 smaller ones
125 g (4 oz) caster sugar
4 eggs, separated

A few flaked almonds, toasted under the grill until golden brown and cooled

Serves 4–6

To make this pudding you will need a double saucepan or a china or glass basin set over a saucepan of water. Put the water to heat while you prepare the mixture. Scrub the lemons thoroughly in hot water to get rid of any residue from sprays with which they may have been treated, then grate the rind into the top of the double saucepan or the bowl. Halve the lemons, squeeze out the juice and put it in with the rind, together with the sugar. Add the egg yolks to the lemon mixture. Put the whites into a clean bowl and leave them on one side for the moment.

Stir the egg yolks, sugar and lemon over the simmering water. Gradually they will thicken to a shiny golden sauce (like lemon curd) which will coat the back of a spoon thickly. This takes about 10 minutes. Remove from the heat. Whisk the whites until they are stiff and standing in peaks, then gradually whisk in the lemon sauce. Spoon the whip into individual glasses and put it into the fridge to chill. Serve it sprinkled with the nuts.

Crisp biscuits are nice with this pudding.

MONT BLANC

Actually this pudding is found in both France and Italy. It's very simple and I think very delicious, a 'mountain' of soft sieved chestnut topped with a snowy cap of whipped cream. You could use fresh chestnuts but I must admit I use canned chestnut purée. Get the sweetened kind if you can; if not, beat unsweetened purée with 125 g (4 oz) icing sugar, form it into a ball, wrap it in foil and put it in the fridge for several hours to chill and firm up then push it through the vegetable mill as described in the recipe.

440 g (15½ oz) can sweetened chestnut purée

150 ml (¼ pint) whipping cream
1 tablespoon kirsch or brandy

Serves 6

Put the chestnut purée into a vegetable mill (a Mouli-légumes) fitted with a fairly fine blade; hold this over the flat dish from which you intend to serve the pudding and push the chestnut purée through. The sieved chestnut purée will fall into a mountain shape; don't attempt to shape it at all, let the pudding stay as it is.

You can do this a few hours in advance and keep it carefully in a cool place. Whip the cream with the kirsch or brandy until it's in soft peaks, then spoon this gently on top of the chestnut mountain just before serving.

This is quite a rich, filling pudding; lovely after something like spinach *gnocchi*.

FRESH ORANGE SALAD

This is one of the most refreshing puddings of all and I find it very useful for serving after a more substantial main course.

6 large oranges

25 g (1 oz) sugar or honey

A little extra orange juice if necessary

Serves 4

First of all wash one of the oranges and then shave off some thin slices of peel – I find a potato peeler good for this. Then using kitchen scissors snip the peel into shreds and put them into a large bowl. Next cut the peel and pith off all the oranges. Do this with a sharp knife and a round-and-round sawing action (like peeling a whole apple when you want to make a long curl of peel) and hold the oranges over the bowl as you do so to catch every drop of juice. Again with a sharp knife cut the individual sections of orange away from the white skin and add them to the bowl. When all the sections have been removed from the white skin, squeeze this over the bowl to extract the remaining juice. Add the sugar or honey to the bowl and chill.

For a Middle-eastern style orange salad, for serving after say *hummus* followed by stuffed vine leaves or pilaf, add a tablespoonful of orange flavoured water or rosewater to the mixture and garnish with a scattering of toasted almonds.

PASHKA   RUSSIA

This traditional Easter dish from Russia makes a beautiful pudding and it's useful when you're planning a cereal or vegetable meal because it's rich in protein. In Russia it's made in a special tall pyramid-shaped mould and decorated with the initials 'XB' for 'Christ is Risen'. I use a 15 cm (6 in) clay flower pot which I scrubbed and baked in a hot oven and now keep in my kitchen cupboard. *Pashka* needs to be prepared several hours before you want to eat it to allow time for the liquid to drain away through the hole in the flower pot leaving the mixture firm enough to turn out. It's nice served with macaroons, sponge fingers or slices of Madeira cake.

2 egg yolks

75 g (3 oz) vanilla sugar; or caster sugar and a drop or two of vanilla essence

4 tablespoons single cream or creamy milk

700 g (1½ lb) curd cheese, quark or cottage cheese

125 g (4 oz) unsalted butter, softened

50 g (2 oz) chopped candied fruits

50 g (2 oz) chopped blanched almonds

A little chopped glacé fruit

Serves 6

Beat the egg yolks and sugar together until they're pale and foamy. Put the cream or creamy milk into a small saucepan and bring it just to the boil, then pour it over the egg yolks and sugar. Tip the whole lot back into the saucepan and stir over a gentle heat until it has thickened – this won't take a moment, so watch it carefully. Leave on one side to cool.

Beat together the cheese and butter; add the candied fruits and nuts and finally the cooled custard. Line your 15 cm (6 in) flower pot with a double layer of dampened muslin or fine net curtain, spoon in the *pashka* mixture and smooth the top. Fold the ends of the muslin over the top, cover with a saucer and a weight and leave in a cool place or the fridge for several hours, preferably overnight. Some moisture will seep out of the hole in the base of the flower pot so stand it on a plate.

To serve the pudding invert the flower pot on to a serving dish, turn out the *pashka* and carefully peel off the muslin or net. Decorate with the glacé fruit.

FRESH PEACH SALAD   ITALY

A luscious salad that's very refreshing after a substantial main
course. I make it with orange juice instead of a sugar syrup; this is
healthier and also adds its own delicious flavour. It's lovely
accompanied by crunchy macaroons.

8 large ripe peaches
150 ml ($\frac{1}{4}$ pint) orange juice

Serves 6

Put the peaches into a bowl and cover them with boiling water.
Leave the peaches for 1 minute, then drain and cover them with
cold water. Strip the skins off using a small, sharp pointed knife.
Cut the peaches in half, remove the stones, then slice the flesh
fairly thinly. Put the slices into a serving dish – a pretty glass bowl
is ideal – cover them with orange juice and chill until needed.

STUFFED PEACHES   ITALY

In this recipe peaches are stuffed with macaroon crumbs and
baked until tender. It's a curiously pleasant blend of flavours and
a good way of using peaches which are not quite as luscious as they
might be.

4 large peaches
75 g (3 oz) macaroons (about 3)
1 egg yolk

Serves 4

Set the oven to 180°C (350°F), gas mark 4. Cut the peaches in half
and carefully prise out the stones, then scoop out a little of the
peach flesh to make a larger cavity for the stuffing. Crush the
macaroons with a rolling pin; mix the macaroon crumbs with

the chopped, scooped-out peach flesh and the egg yolk. Spoon the mixture into the peach cavities and place the two halves of the peach together again. Put the stuffed peaches into a buttered ovenproof dish – a nice one that you can take to the table is best – and bake them for 45–60 minutes until they're tender when pierced with a knife. They're good with single cream or chilled vanilla custard.

PEARS BAKED IN WINE   FRANCE

One of the nicest things about this dish is its appearance: shapely whole pears, richly and deeply stained and flavoured with wine. A large bowl of them always goes down well. The only trouble is that they take about 4 hours to cook in a lowish oven, so they're only really worth doing if you can justify the oven heat by baking a fruit cake, casserole or even meringues at the same time.

Serve the pears with a big bowl of light, fluffy whipped cream and some home-made shortbread or macaroons for a special occasion pudding.

900 g (2 lb) small, hard pears – I   400 ml ($\frac{3}{4}$ pint) cheap red wine
 like Conference   125 g (4 oz) granulated sugar

Serves 4

Set the oven to 160°C (325°F), gas mark 3. Peel the pears, keeping them whole and leaving their stalks on. Put them into a shallow ovenproof casserole and add the wine and sugar. Place the casserole in the oven and bake (uncovered) for about 4 hours, until the pears feel very tender when pierced with the point of a knife. Turn the pears over once or twice during the cooking time so that they bake evenly.

When the pears are ready pour the liquid off into a small saucepan and bubble it over a high heat for about 10 minutes until it has reduced in quantity and looks syrupy. Arrange the pears in a serving dish and pour the syrupy liquid over them. Serve them warm or chill them in the fridge.

PINEAPPLE SORBET ITALY

If you've got a liquidizer this is very easy to make. It turns out a beautiful pale yellow and has a lovely sweet true pineapple flavour, very refreshing after a filling meal. Because the pineapple is naturally sweet you don't need to add much sugar.

1 large ripe pineapple
50 g (2 oz) sugar
2 egg whites

Serves 4–6

Turn the fridge to its coldest setting. Slice the pineapple into quarters then cut off the leafy top and all the prickly skin; also any hard core. Cut the pineapple into rough chunks, put them into the liquidizer with the sugar and blend them to a smooth creamy looking purée. Tip this purée into a container which will fit into the freezing part of your fridge and freeze until it's solid round the edges.

Whisk the egg whites until they stand in soft peaks. Break up the pineapple mixture with a fork then gradually add it to the egg whites, still whisking. Put the mixture back into the fridge and freeze until it's solid.

Turn the fridge back to its normal setting. The sorbet tastes best when it's not too cold and iced so it's a good idea to move it from the freezing part of the fridge on to one of the shelves about 30–45 minutes before you sit down for your first course. It's nice with crumbly shortbread fingers and I must admit I also like some whipped cream with it.

PRUNE DELIGHT   NORWAY

In Norway this is called *sviskeblancmange,* which means prune
blancmange but if I call it this I find it tends to put people
off and so I refer to it as prune delight which I think describes it
better. I know that to some people the thought of prunes can never
be delightful, but if you like them, as I do, then I think you will
enjoy this pudding.

350 g (12 oz) prunes   Flaked almonds
2 tablespoons cornflour   Whipped cream
Grated rind of ½ lemon   A little cinnamon powder
About 50 g (2 oz) sugar

Serves 4–6

Put the prunes into a good-sized bowl, cover them with boiling
water and leave them to soak for several hours if possible. Then
transfer them to a saucepan and simmer them gently until they're
tender. Drain the prunes but keep the liquid. Using a small sharp
knife remove the stones. Put the prunes into the liquidizer with
400 ml (¾ pint) of the liquid in which they were cooked and blend
until smooth; or put the prunes through a Mouli-légumes then mix
them with the liquid.

Put the cornflour into a small bowl and mix it to a smooth
paste with a little of the prune purée. Bring the remaining purée to
the boil in a medium-sized saucepan and then add a little of it to
the cornflour; when it is blended pour all of this cornflour mixture
in with the rest in the saucepan and stir it over a gentle heat for a
couple of minutes to cook the cornflour. Take the mixture off the
the heat and let it cool slightly then add the lemon rind and sugar
to taste. Pour into individual dishes and leave to cool, then chill in
the fridge.

Scatter the top of each pudding thickly with almonds and serve
with whipped cream, or pipe or spoon some cream on top of each
portion and sprinkle with cinnamon powder. Crumbly shortbread fingers go well with this.

I haven't tried this yet but I think this pudding would be delicious for a special occasion if you soaked the prunes in sweet white wine or cider instead of water with maybe a dash of brandy added to the mixture after cooking.

PUMPKIN IN ORANGE SYRUP SOUTH AMERICA

If you don't tell people what this is they may well think it's some exotic fruit they're eating!

1½ kilos (3½ lb) pumpkin, weighed in the shop with skin and pips	275 ml (½ pint) water 125 g (4 oz) sugar 1 orange

Serves 4

Remove the peel and seeds from the pumpkin and slice the flesh into pieces. Put the water and sugar into a medium-sized saucepan and bring to the boil over a gentle heat. Scrub the orange under hot water then cut off 3 thin ribbons of peel – a potato peeler is good for doing this. Add the peel and the pumpkin to the sugar syrup in the saucepan and let it all simmer gently for about 10 minutes, until the pumpkin is tender. Remove the pumpkin and orange peel with a draining spoon and put them into a bowl. Boil the syrup in which the pumpkin was cooked until it has reduced to just 2–3 tablespoonfuls and is very thick. This will take just a few minutes over a high heat without a lid on the saucepan. Pour the syrup over the pumpkin in the bowl and leave it to get cool.

Serve the pumpkin chilled. A tablespoonful of orange liqueur is lovely added to the syrup if you really want to be impressive. Another variation is to cover the cooked, drained pumpkin with orange juice instead of the syrup – this is a fresh-tasting, lower calorie version!

RED FRUIT PUDDING   DENMARK

I think this is one of the most delicious puddings and it makes a little fruit go a long way. My version is unusual in that I hardly cook the fruit; I think this gives a particularly fresh-tasting result. Serve the pudding in individual glass bowls if possible to show off its rich ruby red colouring.

225 g (8 oz) fresh ripe fruit –
    redcurrants, raspberries or
    strawberries, or a mixture
575 ml (1 pint) water
50 g (2 oz) cornflour

125 g (4 oz) caster sugar
A few flaked almonds
Whipped cream (optional)
Sponge fingers

Serves 4

Wash the fruit and remove any little bits of stalk. Put the fruit into the liquidizer goblet with all the other ingredients and blend to a purée. Tip this purée into a saucepan and stir over a gentle heat until it thickens. Cook for a couple of minutes, then take off the heat and pour into 1 large or 4 smaller dishes. Let the pudding cool, then chill it if you wish. Decorate the top with a sprinkling of flaked almonds and some cream if you like, and serve with sponge fingers.

RHUBARB COMPOTE   NORWAY

I think this pretty pink, slightly jellied compote is one of the nicest rhubarb puddings. It's light and refreshing, delicious with crisp crumbly shortbread biscuits or sponge fingers.

450 g (1 lb) rhubarb
275 ml (½ pint) water
125 g (4 oz) caster sugar
A vanilla pod or a few drops
  of vanilla essence
2 tablespoons cornflour or
  arrowroot

Shortbread biscuits or
  sponge fingers
Lightly whipped cream
  (optional)

Serves 4

Wash and trim the rhubarb, cutting off the leaves and scraping off tough fibres if necessary, then cut the stalks in 2·5 cm (1 in) lengths. Put the water, sugar and vanilla into a medium-sized saucepan and bring to the boil. Add the rhubarb and simmer very gently, with a lid on the saucepan, until the rhubarb is almost tender. This takes from 5–15 minutes, depending on the age and type of rhubarb. Remove the vanilla pod.

Mix the cornflour or arrowroot to a paste with a little cold water and add to the rhubarb, stirring all the time. Simmer for 2 minutes, until thickened. Pour into 4 individual serving bowls; cool, then chill. Serve with the crunchy biscuits or sponge fingers and cream.

RICE AND ALMOND PUDDING   DENMARK

This is rich and luxurious-tasting and guaranteed to appeal even
to people who think they don't like rice pudding! In Denmark
it's served at Christmas time. You will notice that I use ordinary
white 'pudding' rice for this recipe. If you're very keen on whole
foods you might not approve of this but I haven't found brown
rice satisfactory, and the amount is so small anyway.

40 g (1½ oz) white 'pudding'
  rice
575 ml (1 pint) milk
40 g (1½ oz) sugar
50 g (2 oz) flaked almonds
1 teaspoon vanilla essence

150 ml (5 fl oz) whipping
  cream
225 g (8 oz) frozen raspberries
A little caster sugar
1 tablespoon cherry brandy
  or kirsch (optional)

Serves 4–6

Wash the rice and put it into a pie dish with the milk and sugar.
Bake in a lowish oven for 2–3 hours, to make a rice pudding. The
temperature isn't crucial: 150°–160°C (300–325°F), gas mark 2–3
is best but if necessary the pudding can cook near the bottom of
a hotter oven. As the skin forms stir it into the pudding – this gives
a nice creamy result. When the rice is soft and the pudding thick
take it out of the oven and leave it to get cold, then beat it and
add the almonds and vanilla. Whip the cream until it stands in
soft peaks, then fold into the rice mixture. Chill.

Next make the raspberry sauce. Sieve the raspberries, sweeten
them with just a little caster sugar and flavour with the cherry
brandy or kirsch if using it. Serve the pudding in small bowls and
spoon the sauce attractively over the top.

TRIFLE   ENGLAND

Proper trifle, made with egg custard and topped with whipped
cream, is a delicious pudding, light, not too sweet and excellent
served after a cereal or vegetable-based main course or to round
off a salady buffet meal.

1 small sponge cake or 1
  batch of sponge fingers
  (page 313)
3 tablespoons raspberry jam
4 tablespoons cheap sherry

For the custard:
3 eggs
50 g (2 oz) caster sugar –
  vanilla sugar if you have it,

otherwise add a few drops
  of vanilla essence
575 ml (1 pint) milk

To finish:
250 ml (10 fl oz) whipping
  cream
25 g (1 oz) toasted flaked
  almonds

Serves 6–8

Split the sponge cake and sandwich with the jam or sandwich the fingers together in pairs then cut them up into smaller pieces. Put the pieces of sponge into the base of a serving dish – a pretty glass one is nice – and pour the sherry over them. Leave on one side while you make the custard.

Whisk the eggs and sugar together in a bowl; put the milk into a saucepan and bring it just to the boil, then pour it over the egg mixture and whisk again. Strain the mixture back into the saucepan and stir over a gentle heat for just a minute or two until it thickens. Don't let it over-cook or it will separate. (If this does happen I've found if I put it in the liquidizer for a moment and blend it at a high speed, amazingly, it seems to be all right again.) Pour the custard over the sponge pieces and leave on one side to cool. To finish the trifle whisk the cream until it's softly thickened, then spoon it over the top of the trifle. Chill the trifle then sprinkle the almonds over the top just before you serve it, so that they're still crisp.

VANILLA ICE CREAM

ITALY

Home-made ice cream sounds like hard work but it isn't really all that much effort and the result is so delicate and creamy that it's well worth it. My recipe is a fairly modest economical one but I

292

think you'll find the flavour and texture are good. Actually home-made ice cream isn't really extravagant when you consider what a useful source of protein it is and plan the meal accordingly. It's excellent, for instance, after a simple pasta, rice or vegetable-based meal.

2 eggs or 4 egg yolks
275 ml (½ pint) creamy milk
75 g (3 oz) vanilla sugar, or
   caster sugar plus a few

drops of vanilla essence
250 ml (10 fl oz) whipping
   cream

Serves 4

Turn the fridge to its coldest setting. Whisk the eggs in a medium-sized bowl. Put the milk and sugar into a heavy-based saucepan and bring just up to the boil, then slowly add it to the eggs, stirring all the time. Strain the eggs and milk back into the sauce-pan, put back on the heat and stir for just a minute or two until the mixture thickens – this happens very suddenly and the custard soon goes lumpy and curdled if you're not careful. Don't worry if it does; I've found that this doesn't affect the ice cream. Cool.

Whisk the cream until it has thickened and is standing in soft peaks, then fold this gently but thoroughly into the cooled egg custard. Pour the mixture into a suitable container (don't cover with a lid) and freeze until it's setting well round the edges. Then scrape the ice cream into a bowl and whisk it thoroughly. Put the ice cream back into the container and freeze it until it's firm

It's a good idea to put the ice cream into the main part of the refrigerator at the beginning of the meal so that it can soften a little. Don't forget to turn the fridge setting back to normal.

YOGHURT

Chilled and served in small bowls, yoghurt makes a delicious, refreshing pudding. It's particularly good for a special occasion if you use evaporated milk or even single cream or a proportion of single cream. It's also used in a number of other recipes in this book; I find it particularly useful in salad dressings. It's not difficult to make; all you need is a suitable warm place in which to put the yoghurt while it sets. I stand my yoghurt on the gas cooker by the pilot light; alternatively you can use an airing cupboard or find a corner near a radiator.

575 ml (1 pint) milk
2 rounded tablespoons skim
  milk powder
1 teaspoon fresh natural

yoghurt – from a carton or
from your last batch
A little demerara sugar to
serve

Serves 4–6

Put the milk into a saucepan and bring up to the boil, than leave it to simmer, without a lid on the saucepan, for 10 minutes. This reduces the milk a little and makes the yoghurt thick and creamy. Take the saucepan off the heat and leave it until it has cooled to lukewarm. While you are waiting for the milk to cool select a bowl or two jars big enough to take the milk and sterilize them by swishing them out with warm water with some household bleach added, then rinse them thoroughly again in hot water.

Whisk the milk powder and yoghurt into the milk then pour it into your clean sterilized bowl or jars, cover with foil and leave in a warm place for a few hours or overnight until it's firm. Cool, then put the yoghurt into the fridge where it will firm up even more and be thick and creamy to eat. To serve spoon the yoghurt out into individual dishes and sprinkle with sugar just before taking to the table.

If you prefer you can make the yoghurt directly into little individual dishes, as you would egg custards. I think it's particularly attractive done like this because you can dig your spoon into the firm, creamy mixture.

Sweet Pastries, Biscuits and Cakes

This is quite a varied collection of goodies. There are some mouthwatering pastries such as the apple tart from France, the cheese cake and raisin sour cream pie from the USA, the yoghurt tart from Greece and *linzertorte* from Austria, which all make delicious puddings after a light main course or salad. Then there are a few cakes, such as Madeira cake and Dundee cake which are probably mainly useful for tea-time, although a slice of Dundee cake can be nice after a salad instead of a pudding, and slices of Madeira cake are good with fools and fruit salads. Also good as accompaniments to puddings are the various biscuits which is the main reason I've included them: a little dish of crumbly home-made shortbread, crunchy coconut biscuits or crisp macaroons provide the final touch when you're serving a special fruit salad or compote and they're not difficult to make.

As you will have gathered by now I am keen on using wholewheat flour and some of the recipes are made entirely with wholewheat flour while in others I suggest using a mixture of wholewheat flour and white flour (try to get unbleached white flour from the health shop). You can of course use just wholewheat flour or just white flour if you prefer; but the proportions I've suggested in the recipes are the ones which I've found to work in practice, bearing in mind the sometimes conflicting aims of healthiness on the one hand and taste and appearance on the other!

APPLE TART   FRANCE

This tart looks so appetizing with its glossy golden rings of apple slices on a crisp pastry base. If you have time bake the pastry base before you put on the topping because the pastry is then lovely and crisp, a delicious contrast to the soft apple slices and moist golden apricot glaze. I make this tart on one of those big round ceramic pizza dishes measuring 30 cm (12 in) across but any big flat ovenproof plate or tin would do.

For the pastry base:
200 g (8 oz) plain wholewheat
    flour
2 teaspoons baking powder
50 g (2 oz) soft margarine
50 g (2 oz) white vegetable
    fat
2 tablespoons water

For the topping:
900 g (2 lb) apples – Bramleys
    or Golden Delicious

For the glaze:
350 g (12 oz) apricot jam
4 tablespoons water
2 teaspoons cornflour

Serves 6

First set the oven to 200°C (400°F), gas mark 6, then make the pastry. Sift the flour into a large bowl, adding also the residue of bran left in the sieve. With your fingertips rub the fats into the flour until the mixture looks like breadcrumbs, then add the cold water and mix a dough. Turn the dough on to a floured board and roll it out to fit your plate or tin. Turn under the edges of the pastry to make it fit the dish neatly then decorate the edge by pressing it with the prongs of a fork. Prick the pastry all over then bake it in the preheated oven for 15 minutes, until it's golden brown. Take the flan out but leave the oven on.

While the flan is cooking prepare the apples. Cut them into quarters, then remove the skin and core with a sharp knife and cut the apples into thin slices. Arrange these slices on the pastry base, overlapping them a bit to get a nice even pattern. When the apple is all arranged put the tart into the oven and bake it for 30 minutes, until the apple feels tender when pierced with the point of a knife.

Towards the end of the cooking time prepare the apricot glaze. Heat the apricot jam in a small saucepan with 2 tablespoons of the water. Mix the remaining 2 tablespoons with the cornflour in a small bowl or cup. When the jam is boiling, pour some of it over the cornflour mixture, stir, then return it to the saucepan and stir over the heat for about 2 minutes until it has thickened. Take the saucepan off the heat and pour the glaze evenly over the top of the hot tart; try to make sure that all the apple is covered with the lovely shiny apricot glaze, then leave it to cool slightly before serving. We like it best hot, but you could equally well serve it cold.

BRANDY SNAPS

GREAT BRITAIN

Crisp brandy snaps with their filling of brandy-flavoured whipped cream are really sheer indulgence and a very French-tasting British contribution. This is an easy recipe for brandy snaps because it doesn't contain golden syrup and so you have more time to get the brandy snaps off the baking tray and curl them up before they harden. They are really quite easy, and lovely for serving for a special occasion, perhaps to accompany a fruit salad or purée. You can also keep them flat and serve them without cream as crisp biscuits, or roll them up tightly into 'cigarettes'. Like this they're good with gooseberry fool.

50 g (2 oz) soft margarine
50 g (2 oz) soft brown sugar
50 g (2 oz) plain flour – I use
   white for these
¼ teaspoon ground ginger

To finish:
150 ml (5 fl oz) whipping
   cream
A little icing sugar
1–2 teaspoons brandy

Makes 12

Put the margarine and sugar into the bowl and cream them together, then sift in the flour and ginger and mix to a smooth dough. If you've got time to cover the bowl and leave it on one side for an hour or so before using, I've found this helps the brandy snaps to cook better.

When you're ready to cook them, set the oven to 190°C (375°F), gas mark 5. Grease a large baking sheet with butter. Roll teaspoons of the brandy snap mixture into balls and place them well apart on the baking sheet. You will probably have to cook them in two batches. Bake the brandy snaps for about 15 minutes, until they're golden brown in the middle, deeper brown at the edges. Take the baking sheet out of the oven and let it stand for 2 minutes, then ease the brandy snaps off the baking sheet with a palette knife. (As there is quite a lot of fat in the mixture it's not difficult to get them off the tray and I find I don't have to grease it again between batches.) Roll the brandy snaps around the handle of a wooden spoon and leave them to cool. As they cool they will get crisp. Keep them in an air-tight tin until you want them.

Whip the cream until it's standing in soft peaks. Stir in the icing sugar to taste and the brandy and whip again. Then spoon or pipe the cream into the brandy snaps. Serve them as soon as possible after this, while they're still crisp.

CHEESE CAKE   USA

This cheese cake looks most impressive if you make it in a small-ish, deep tin – an 18 cm (7 in) spring cake tin with removable base is ideal – so you get a good layer of the lovely white creamy mixture above the crumb base. Alternatively you can use a cake tin lined with foil or a fluted porcelain flan dish, but with the flan dish, of course, the sides of the cheese cake are hidden, and I think then a topping of fruit, such as strawberries with a shiny glaze of red-currant jelly, is a nice finish.

I've experimented a good deal to find the right combination of cream cheese and cream and I think this mixture of low-fat quark (or cottage cheese if you can't get it) and soured cream gives the best result – light but creamy. If you prefer a richer cheese cake you could use cream cheese or half cream cheese and half quark or cottage cheese. On the other hand, you can make a very good low-fat cheese cake by using cottage cheese or skim milk quark with natural low-fat yoghurt instead of the soured cream.

125 g (4 oz) digestive biscuits	½ teaspoon vanilla extract
50 g (2 oz) butter, softened	or essence
225 g (8 oz) low-fat quark or	75 g (3 oz) caster sugar
cottage cheese	1 tablespoon lemon juice
2 eggs	150 ml (5 fl oz) soured cream

Serves 6–8

Set the oven to 150°C (300°F), gas mark 2. Put the digestive biscuits on a board and crush them with a rolling pin, then mix them with the butter. Press the biscuit mixture evenly into the base of your chosen container. Leave on one side while you make the filling. To do this, if you've got a liquidizer, just put everything into the goblet and blend for a minute until smooth. Alternatively, push the cottage cheese through a sieve into a large bowl, or just put the quark straight into the bowl, then add the eggs, vanilla, sugar, lemon juice and soured cream and beat thoroughly to a smooth creamy consistency. Pour the mixture into the tin or flan dish on top of the crumbs.

Bake the cheese cake towards the bottom of the oven for 1–1¼ hours (depending on the size of the tin) or until it looks set and feels firm to a very light touch. Cool, then chill. If you've used a cake tin with a removable base, slip a knife round the sides of the cheese cake and unclip the spring on the tin. Stand the tin on something like a jam jar and carefully slip the sides of the tin down, leaving the cheese cake standing clear. If you've used a foil-lined tin, lift the cheese cake out of the tin then flatten the edges of the foil and carefully lift the cheese cake off the foil using a fish slice.

If you want to top your cheese cake with fruit you'll need 350–450 g (12 oz–1 lb) strawberries and about 4 tablespoons of redcurrant jelly. Wash and dry the strawberries then arrange them on top of the chilled cheese cake. Melt the jelly in a small

saucepan then pour it evenly over the strawberries to glaze them.
Leave to set before serving.

HONEY CHEESE CAKE   GREECE

I think this cheese cake, like the one from the USA, is best made
in one of those deep spring cake tins, 18 cm (7 in) diameter, with
a loose base, because this gives a nice thick luscious layer of
filling. You can of course also use a cake tin with a layer of foil,
or a 20–23 cm (8–9 in) fluted china flan dish, although with the
flan dish the layer of filling will be thinner.

For the flan case:
150 g (6 oz) plain flour – use
  wholewheat or half wholewheat
  and half white
100 g (4 oz) butter
1 egg yolk

For the filling:
450 g (1 lb) low-fat quark or
  cottage cheese
125 g (4 oz) sugar
175 g (6 oz) honey
2 eggs
1 teaspoon powdered
  cinnamon
1 egg white

Serves 6

First set the oven to 190°C (375°F), gas mark 5, then prepare
your container by greasing it lightly with butter. Next make the
pastry. Sift the flour into a bowl (adding any residue of bran left
in the sieve), then rub in the butter until the mixture looks like
fine breadcrumbs. Add the egg yolk and knead the mixture
gently together to form a dough. Turn the dough out on to a
lightly floured board, knead it a little until it's smooth, then roll it
out and gently ease it into your baking tin or flan dish. I find the
best way to do this with the crumbly wholewheat pastry is to tip
the pastry straight from the board to the tin, holding the board
with one hand and easing the pastry into the tin with the other.
Leave on one side while you make the filling.

301

The easiest way to make the filling is to put everything into the liquidizer goblet except the egg white and blend until it's smooth. Alternatively, push the cottage cheese through a sieve (no need to sieve quark), then gradually beat in all the other ingredients except the egg white. Whisk the egg white until it's stiff and fold it in, then pour the mixture into the pastry case and smooth the top gently. If you're using the deep tin it may be necessary to trim the pastry a little so that it's practically level with the filling. Put the cheese cake into the oven to bake it for 30 minutes then turn the oven down to 160°C (325°F), gas mark 3 and cook for a further 50 minutes.

Let the cheese cake cool before serving. It can be served just warm or chilled – I think this is best as the chilling firms the cheese cake up and makes the filling luscious and creamy to eat. This is an ideal pudding to serve after one of the low-protein stuffed vegetable main courses, with perhaps *hummus* to start the meal.

CHOCOLATE BROWNIES
USA

These chocolate slices are quick and easy to make and don't need any icing as they're lovely and gooey. I like them particularly because you can use brown sugar and wholewheat flour to make them and they're all the better for it. You can use other nuts instead of pecans if you like – walnuts are probably the obvious substitute but I think hazel nuts are especially good because they make the brownies taste rather like nutty chocolate!

225 g (8 oz) butter or
   vegetable margarine
25 g (1 oz) cocoa
200 g (7 oz) brown sugar
2 eggs
75 g (3 oz) plain wholewheat
   flour

½ teaspoon baking powder
½ teaspoon vanilla extract
75 g (3 oz) roughly chopped
   pecan nuts – or use walnuts
   or hazel nuts

Makes 18

Set the oven to 180°C (350°F), gas mark 4. Lightly grease a Swiss roll tin. Put the butter or margarine into a saucepan with the cocoa and sugar and heat gently until melted. Remove from the heat and cool to lukewarm, then beat in the eggs one by one. Sift the flour and baking powder into the mixture, adding the bran left in the sieve as well, and mix well, then stir in the vanilla extract and nuts. Pour the mixture into the prepared tin, pushing it into the corners. Bake in the centre of the oven for about 30 minutes, until the mixture springs back when touched lightly in the centre.

Allow the brownies to cool in the tin, then cut them into 18 pieces.

COCONUT BISCUITS   SOUTH AMERICA

These crunchy coconut biscuits are lovely with creamy fools and fruit salads, especially the exotic fruit salad which comes from South America too.

50 g (2 oz) butter, softened
100 g (3½ oz) caster sugar
100 g (3½ oz) plain
  wholewheat flour

1 teaspoon baking powder
3 tablespoons beaten egg
25 g (1 oz) desiccated coconut
Extra coconut to finish

Makes 24

Set the oven to 180°C (350°F), gas mark 4. Put the butter and sugar into a bowl and sift the flour and baking powder on top. Also add the beaten egg and coconut then just mix everything together to a soft dough. Sprinkle a board with desiccated coconut and turn the dough out on to this; knead it lightly into a long sausage shape, then flatten the sausage a bit. Cut 6 mm (¼ in) slices off the sausage to make roughly finger-shaped biscuits and place these on a greased and floured baking sheet. Don't put them very close together as they will almost double in size.

Press a little more coconut on to the top of each biscuit and bake them for 15–20 minutes until they're golden brown. Let them cool for a few minutes on the baking sheet, then transfer them to a wire cooling rack.

DUNDEE CAKE   SCOTLAND

You can make this traditional Scottish cake very quickly if you use the modern all-in-one method. I've included it partly because it's irresistible, with its luscious fruit inside and topping of crunchy almonds, and also because it makes a very acceptable 'pudding' after a salad lunch or supper.

275 g (10 oz) mixed dried fruit
125 g (4 oz) glacé cherries
150 g (5 oz) plain wholewheat
  flour
Pinch of salt
2 teaspoons baking powder
1 teaspoon mixed spice

125 g (4 oz) butter, softened
125 g (4 oz) soft brown sugar
2 eggs
1 teaspoon grated orange rind
2 tablespoons orange juice
25 g (1 oz) flaked almonds

Makes one 15 cm (6 in) cake

Prepare a 15 cm (6 in) round cake tin by lining it with a strip of greaseproof paper round the edge and a circle in the base. Set the oven to 160°C (325°F), gas mark 3.

Wash the dried fruit in warm water then dry it well in a clean cloth. Rinse the cherries under hot water to wash off the syrup, then halve them. Sift the flour, salt, baking powder and mixed spice into a bowl, adding also the residue of bran which will be left in the sieve. Add all the ingredients except the almonds and beat them until they're light – this is of course easily done with an electric mixer. The mixture should be light, thick and fluffy looking.

Spoon the mixture into the prepared tin, sprinkle the flaked almonds on top and bake in the centre of the oven for 2 hours or until a skewer pushed gently into the centre of the cake comes out clean. Remove the cake from the oven and cool it on a wire rack. Strip off the paper when the cake is cool.

LINZERTORTE

This light, crumbly tart is delicately flavoured with spices and lemon rind and melts in your mouth. I experimented many times with this recipe until I came up with this version which we think is just right. With one of my later efforts my husband said he liked the flavour but the tart wasn't thick enough to get his teeth into, so I increased the amount of pastry to the present quantity. If you'd like to make a thinner tart you could try using only 125 g (4 oz) of flour, almonds and butter and 25 g (1 oz) sugar or alternatively use a larger tin.

175 g (6 oz) plain wholewheat flour
1 teaspoon powdered cinnamon
Pinch of ground cloves
175 g (6 oz) ground almonds – or whole unbleached almonds pulverized in a liquidizer

Grated rind of $\frac{1}{2}$ lemon
40 g ($1\frac{1}{2}$ oz) sugar
175 g (6 oz) butter
1 egg yolk
175–225 g (6–8 oz) raspberry, cherry or blackcurrant jam – the raw sugar conserves from health shops are ideal
A little icing sugar

Serves 6

Sift the flour, cinnamon and cloves into a bowl; add also the residue of bran left in the sieve. Mix in the almonds, lemon rind and sugar then rub the butter into the dry ingredients as if you were making pastry. Gently mix in the egg yolk to make a soft dough. If possible wrap the dough in a piece of foil or polythene and chill it in the refrigerator for 30 minutes or so. If you have time for this the dough will be easier to roll out but it isn't essential if you're in a hurry.

Set the oven to 200°C (400°F), gas mark 6. On a lightly floured board roll out three-quarters of the dough to fit a 20–23 cm (8–9 in) fluted flan dish – one of those pretty porcelain ones is ideal for this recipe. Spread the jam evenly over the pastry. Roll out the rest of the pastry and cut into long strips; arrange these strips in a lattice over the jam, then fold the edges of the pastry down and press them in to make a sort of rim round the edge of the tart. Bake the tart for 25–30 minutes, until it's slightly risen and golden brown.

You can serve the tart hot, cold or, my choice, warm. Sieve a little icing sugar over the top of the tart before taking it to the table; the red jam looks very appetizing glistening underneath this snowy topping. It's nice with single cream.

MACAROONS FRANCE

Crisp macaroons are lovely for serving with cold, creamy puddings. Although they might seem a bit extravagant they are in fact rich in protein and so not completely frivolous.

1 egg white	Rice paper
125 g (4 oz) ground almonds	12 whole blanched almonds
125 g (4 oz) caster sugar	

Makes 12

Set the oven to 180°C (350°F), gas mark 4. Put the egg white into a good-sized bowl and whisk lightly, just to break it up. Stir in the ground almonds and caster sugar and mix to a paste. Lay the rice paper on baking sheets and put spoonfuls of the macaroon mixture on it, leaving room for them to spread a little. Smooth the macaroons with the back of a spoon dipped in cold water and place an almond in the centre of each. Bake for 15–25 minutes.

Transfer the macaroons to a wire rack, tearing the rice paper roughly; trim off the remaining paper when the macaroons have cooled.

MADEIRA CAKE ENGLAND

This cake used to be served in England to accompany a glass of Madeira wine but I think it is useful for serving with some desserts, especially the Russian *pashka*. But really it's such a beautiful, delicately flavoured, smooth-textured cake that it's useful on all sorts of occasions. In my family it has formed the basis of a number of birthday cakes ranging from an enchanted house to a teddy bear which I literally carved out of an oblong block of cake. Normally I just bake the cake in a loaf tin and serve it unadorned except for the piece of peel baked into the top. I like to use a loaf tin as it is easier for cutting and you can arrange the peel all down the centre so that everyone gets some on top of their slice.

150 g (5 oz) plain flour – half wholewheat, half white is best for this
½ teaspoon baking powder
125 g (4 oz) butter, softened
125 g (4 oz) caster sugar

1 tablespoon grated lemon rind
2 eggs
2 tablespoons milk
Piece of citrus peel

Makes one 450 g (1 lb) cake

Set the oven to 160°C (325°F), gas mark 3. Line a 450 g (1 lb) loaf tin with a strip of greaseproof paper and brush with softened butter, then sprinkle with a little flour

Sift the flour and baking powder into a large bowl or the bowl of your mixer, adding also the residue of bran left in the sieve and all the other ingredients except the citrus peel. Beat everything well together to make a light, fluffy mixture. Spoon the mixture lightly into the prepared tin and level the top. Place in the oven and bake for 25 minutes, then without taking the cake out of the oven, very carefully lay the citrus peel along the top of the cake, and bake it for a further 35 minutes.

Cool the cake for a few minutes in the tin, then turn it out on to a wire rack to cool completely. Take off the greaseproof paper when it's cold.

BABY MERINGUES   FRANCE

Crisp little meringues make a very nice accompaniment to smooth
fools and ice creams. They're also a pretty garnish to use on a
pudding such as a trifle or an egg custard if you don't want to use
cream.

2 egg whites
125 g (4 oz) caster sugar

Makes about 24

First prepare a couple of baking sheets by covering them with
greaseproof paper then brushing the paper with cooking oil. Or
use non-stick baking paper.

Whisk the egg whites until they're very stiff. Add half the sugar,
and quickly whisk it into the mixture, then fold in the remaining
sugar using a metal spoon.

The best way to put the meringues on to the baking sheets is to
use a piping bag fitted with a 1 cm ($\frac{1}{2}$ in) shell nozzle, but if you
haven't got one a teaspoon will do. Pipe or spoon the mixture on
to the baking sheets, leaving a little space between the meringues,
as they will spread slightly and I find they bake best if they are not
too close together. Put the meringues into the oven and set it to
its lowest temperature – 110°C (225°F), gas mark $\frac{1}{4}$.

They will take about 1$\frac{1}{2}$ hours to dry out. Test one by taking it
off the tin and tapping it on the base to see if it feels and sounds
firm and dry. Let the meringues cool on the trays, then take them
off and store them in an air-tight tin. In theory they keep well in
a tin for a week or so but in practice I find they never get the
chance to do so!

PARKIN   ENGLAND

This is one of those cakes in which you can use wholewheat flour,
brown sugar and black treacle without any problems at all and
the result is delicious as well as nutritious. It's moist and gooey,

particularly if you wrap it in foil and keep it for a few days before you eat it.

125 g (4 oz) butter or margarine	1 teaspoon baking powder
225 g (8 oz) black treacle	1 teaspoon ground ginger
125 g (4 oz) dark brown sugar	1 teaspoon mixed spice
125 g (4 oz) plain wholewheat flour	125 g (4 oz) medium oatmeal
	6 tablespoons milk
	1 egg

Makes 15–18 pieces

Preheat the oven to 160°C (325°F), gas mark 3. Put the butter or margarine into a small saucepan with the black treacle and sugar and heat gently until melted, but don't let the mixture boil. Cool. Sift the flour, baking powder and spices into a bowl and stir in the residue of bran left in the sieve and the oatmeal. Make a well in the centre of the dry ingredients and pour in the treacle mixture and the milk, then add the egg and mix everything until smooth. Brush an 18 cm (7 in) square tin with softened butter or margarine, then pour in the parkin and put it in the oven.

Bake it for 55–60 minutes, or until it has shrunk away from the edges of the tin and feels firm to the touch. Cool in the tin, then cut into slices when it's cold.

Note: As treacle is rather a nuisance to weigh out, if you like parkin you can get around this by making up a double batch of parkin at a time using a whole 450 g (1 lb) tin of treacle and keeping one lot of parkin either in the deep freeze, or if you want it to get all nice and gooey, wrapped in foil and stored in a tin until it's needed.

PUMPKIN PIE   USA

An American friend gave me this recipe which I've adapted to give the right quantity for a 20–22 cm (8–9 in) flan dish. It makes a lovely autumn pudding, smooth and warmly spiced. I think it's best when it's hot but you can also serve it cold; it's nicest with cream. Sometimes I scatter some roughly chopped walnuts over the top of the pie which makes it look specially interesting and is a pleasant variation.

For the flan case:
175 g (6 oz) plain wholewheat flour
1½ teaspoons baking powder
125 g (4 oz) white vegetable fat and margarine, mixed
1 tablespoon cold water

For the filling:
1 kilo (2¼ lb) pumpkin, weighed in the shop with skin and pips
4 tablespoons water
125 g (4 oz) soft brown sugar
½ teaspoon ground ginger
½ teaspoon powdered cinnamon
A little grated nutmeg
Pinch of cloves
150 ml (5 fl oz) single cream
2 eggs

Serves 6

Set the oven to 200°C (400°F), gas mark 6. Sift the flour and baking powder into a bowl and add the residue of bran left in the sieve. Rub in the fats until the mixture looks like fine breadcrumbs then add the water and mix to a dough. Roll the pastry out on a lightly floured board and put into a 20–23 cm (8–9 in) diameter flan dish. Prick the base, then bake the flan in the oven for about 15 minutes until it's browned and crisp. Take it out of the oven and let it cool slightly while you make the filling. Reduce the oven setting to 180°C (350°F), gas mark 4.

Peel the pumpkin and remove the pips. Cut the pumpkin into even-sized pieces, put them into a heavy-based saucepan with the water and cook gently, with a lid on the saucepan, until the pumpkin is tender – about 10 minutes. Put the pumpkin into a colander and drain it very well indeed, pressing gently with a spoon to extract as much water as possible. Put the pumpkin into a bowl and add the sugar, spices, cream and eggs. Mix well, then pour into the flan case and bake in the preheated oven for about 50 minutes, until it's set.

RAISIN SOUR CREAM PIE   USA

The friend in the USA who kindly gave me this recipe serves it
as an alternative to pumpkin pie at Thanksgiving. I think it also
makes an excellent alternative to mincemeat pie at Christmas
because it's got a spicy, festive flavour. It's a nourishing, protein-
rich pudding with the wholewheat flour, eggs and nuts. If you
can't get pecan nuts you can use walnuts instead, or flaked
almonds which I like best of all; and an alternative to the soured
cream is natural yoghurt.

225 g (8 oz) seedless raisins –
or use sultanas
150 ml (5 fl oz) soured cream
¼ teaspoon ground cloves
¼ teaspoon grated nutmeg
1 teaspoon powdered
cinnamon
2 eggs
50 g (2 oz) soft brown sugar
50 g (2 oz) pecan nuts or

walnuts, chopped; or flaked
almonds

For the flan case:
100 g (4 oz) plain wholewheat
flour
1 teaspoon baking powder
50 g (2 oz) butter or soft
vegetable margarine
1 tablespoon cold water

Serves 6

First start making the filling by putting the raisins or sultanas into
a bowl with the soured cream and the spices; mix well, then leave
on one side while you make the flan case.

Set the oven to 200°C (400°F), gas mark 6. To make the pastry
sift the flour and baking powder into a bowl and also add the
residue of bran left in the sieve. Rub in the fat until the mixture
looks like breadcrumbs, then mix in the water and gently press
the mixture together to form a dough. Roll out the dough on a
lightly floured board and use to line a 20–23 cm (8–9 in) flan dish.
Trim the edges and prick the base of the flan, then bake it in the
oven for about 15 minutes, until it is set and golden brown. Take
the flan out of the oven and reduce the temperature to 180°C
(350°F), gas mark 4.

Finish making the filling: beat the eggs, then add them to the

311

soured cream and fruit mixture, together with the sugar and nuts. Mix everything together well, then pour the filling evenly into the flan case – it doesn't matter if this is still warm – and smooth the top gently with a knife or the back of a spoon. Bake the flan in the oven for 35–40 minutes, until the filling is set. You can serve the flan hot or cold but I think it's nicest hot.

SHORTBREAD FINGERS   SCOTLAND

These crisp little biscuits melt in your mouth and are so useful for serving with fruit salads, fools and creamy puddings as well as being popular at tea-time.

125 g (4 oz) plain wholewheat flour
125 g (4 oz) plain white flour
2 teaspoons baking powder

75 g (3 oz) caster sugar
200 g (7 oz) butter, softened
Caster sugar

Makes 18–20

Set the oven to 160°C (325°F), gas mark 3. Sift the flours and baking powder into a large bowl or the bowl of your mixer, and tip in the bran from the sieve too. Add the sugar and butter, then beat everything together to a soft dough. Turn the dough out on to a floured board and knead it a little, then roll the dough out 6 mm ($\frac{1}{4}$ in) thick and cut it into fingers. Put these on a lightly floured baking sheet then prick them all over with a fork and bake them for about 20 minutes, until they're golden brown.

Let them cool on the baking sheet as they're fragile while they're still hot. Sprinkle them generously with caster sugar before serving them.

SPONGE FINGERS

FRANCE

These are useful for serving with fools and creamy puddings where you want something crisp but not as rich as shortbread. You really do need an electric mixer for these and they're best made the day you want to eat them.

1 egg
40 g (1½ oz) granulated sugar
40 g (1½ oz) plain flour – white is best for the small quantity needed for this recipe
Extra granulated sugar to dredge

Makes 12–15

Set the oven to 190°C (375°F), gas mark 5. Prepare a baking sheet by covering it with a piece of greaseproof paper and brushing with oil. Put the egg and granulated sugar into the bowl of your mixer and whisk at top speed until it's very thick and pale and able to hold its shape. Gently sift the flour over the top of the egg mixture and carefully cut and fold it in with a metal spoon. Pipe or spoon thin fingers of the mixture on to the prepared baking sheet, allowing space for them to spread – they will roughly double in width. Sprinkle the tops of the fingers thickly with sugar, then bake them for about 12 minutes until they're golden brown and firm to a light touch. Let the fingers cool slightly, then carefully ease them off the baking sheet and put them on a wire rack to finish cooling.

STRAWBERRY TARTLETS

FRANCE

The combination of crisp pastry, creamy filling and shiny strawberries makes these little tartlets very delicious. You can vary the flavour of the filling; I like it with rose essence or rosewater as a change from vanilla. The tartlets are also good made with other fruit toppings: I particularly like them with those little green seedless grapes or halved and seeded black grapes, with lemon-flavoured filling and apricot jam to glaze.

For the pastry cream:
25 g (1 oz) flour
1 egg yolk
200 ml (7 fl oz) milk
25 g (1 oz) sugar – vanilla
   sugar is best if you have it
15 g (1½ oz) butter

For the pastry:
175 g (6 oz) plain whole-
   wheat flour – or you could
   use a mixture of white and
   wholewheat

1½ teaspoons baking powder
75 g (3 oz) butter or vegetable
   margarine
1½ tablespoons cold water

For the topping:
225 g (8 oz) small ripe
   strawberries
125 g (4 oz) redcurrant jelly
2 tablespoons water
½ teaspoon cornflour

Makes 12

First make the pastry cream. You can do this a day or two in advance if you like because it will keep perfectly in a covered container in the fridge. Put the flour into a small bowl with the egg yolk and enough milk to make a smooth paste. Put the rest of the milk and the sugar into a small saucepan and bring to the boil, then pour it over the egg and flour mixture, stirring. Tip the mixture back into the saucepan and stir over a moderate heat. It will go lumpy, but go on stirring hard and after a few minutes you will have a thick, smooth sauce. Take the saucepan off the heat, turn the mixture into a small bowl and add a little vanilla essence or any other flavouring you fancy to tone with the fruit. Dot the butter over the top of the mixture – this will prevent a skin from forming – cover with a piece of foil and leave on one side. When the pastry cream is cool, store it in the fridge until you need it.

Next make the tartlet cases. Set the oven to 200°C (400°F), gas mark 6. Sift the flour and baking powder into a bowl; if you're using wholewheat flour add also the bran which will be left in the sieve. Rub the fat into the flour using your finger-tips, then mix to a dough with the cold water. Roll the dough out on a lightly floured board then use it to line 12 tartlet tins. Prick the base of each tartlet lightly with a fork, then bake them in the preheated oven for about 15 minutes, until they're golden brown. Leave on one side to cool.

When you're ready to fill the tartlet cases whisk the pastry cream to blend in the butter and make the mixture smooth and light, then put about a teaspoonful of pastry cream in each tartlet. The exact amount will depend on how deep the tartlets are and you may find you don't need quite all the pastry cream. Hull and wash the strawberries and halve or quarter them unless they're really small. Arrange the strawberries on top of the pastry cream.

To make the glaze melt the redcurrant jelly with 1 tablespoonful of the water. Mix the cornflour to a paste with another tablespoonful of water and add this to the redcurrant jelly in the saucepan, stirring until you have a smooth slightly thickened glaze. Spoon the glaze over the strawberries on the tartlets then leave them to cool. Eat them the same day.

YOGHURT TART   GREECE

In this tart the combination of creamy, fresh-tasting filling and crisp wholewheat pastry is delicious, and it couldn't be simpler to make as the filling is uncooked.

For the flan case:
100 g (4 oz) plain wholewheat flour
1 teaspoon baking powder
50 g (2 oz) butter
1 tablespoon cold water

For the filling:
225 g (8 oz) low-fat quark or cream cheese
150 ml (5 fl oz) natural yoghurt
1 tablespoon honey
1 tablespoon sugar
A few chopped walnuts

Serves 6

Set the oven to 200°C (400°F), gas mark 6. Sift the flour and baking powder into a bowl, adding the bran in the sieve too. Rub the fat into the flour then mix to a dough with the cold water. Roll the pastry out on a lightly floured board then put the pastry into a 20–23 cm (8–9 in) flan dish; trim the edges and prick the base. Bake the flan for about 15 minutes until it's set and golden brown. Leave on one side while you make the filling.

Put the quark or cream cheese into a bowl and break it up with a fork, then gradually beat in the yoghurt, honey and sugar until you've got a light, creamy mixture. Spoon the mixture into the flan case and smooth the top. Chill the flan for 1–2 hours, then scatter a few chopped nuts over the top just before serving. The filling will be fairly soft at first but it will firm up as it chills.

Breads, Scones and Sandwiches

You will see I suggest wholewheat flour for most of these recipes; as I'm convinced of the value of wholewheat flour I was determined to try to make good wholewheat versions of some of the traditional international breads and scones. I'm particularly pleased with the wholewheat version of pitta bread which we think is nicer than the type you can buy in the shops. If you want to use wheatmeal flour or white flour instead of some of the wholewheat flour you can of course do so. As wholewheat flour absorbs less water than white or wheatmeal you will probably need to add a little extra liquid to the recipe.

For the yeast recipes I suggest dried yeast because that's what I normally use – mainly because I can keep a large drum of it in my cupboard and it's one less thing to have to remember to buy, or, with me, forget to buy! You can certainly use fresh yeast for the recipes, though, if you prefer; simply use double the amount and crumble it into the liquid without adding the $\frac{1}{2}$ teaspoonful of sugar, then continue with the recipe as described.

These breads and scones can make the basis of very nourishing meals; a bowl of lentil soup and wholewheat rolls, or some lovely hunks of home-made wholewheat bread with cheese and fruit may be simple to prepare but they contain as many nutrients as a cooked meal and always seem to be popular.

CHAPATIS   INDIA

These circles of unleavened bread are delicious with any curry dish; they can also be rolled round salad fillings or stuffed and baked in a similar way to the tortillas in the pasta and pancakes section of the book.

250 g (9 oz) plain wholewheat flour
1½ teaspoon oil, melted butter or *ghee*

1 teaspoon sea salt
About 150 ml (¼ pint) cold water

Makes 12

Sieve the flour into a bowl, adding also the bran which will be left in the sieve. Mix in the fat, salt and water to make a firm dough. When the dough has formed turn it out on to a very lightly floured board and knead it for about 5 minutes. Then if possible cover it with a damp cloth and leave it to rest for 2–3 hours before kneading it again.

Divide the dough into 12 pieces, form each into a ball with your hands, then roll them out with a rolling pin so that they are 15–20 cm (6–8 in) across. Fry the chapatis both sides in an ungreased frying pan. Pile them up on a plate as they're done and cover them with a piece of foil to prevent them from drying out.

If you like you can brush them over with a little oil, melted butter or *ghee* before serving them.

CHEESE SCONES   SCOTLAND

Light and savoury, cheese scones are delicious both with creamy dips and with hot soups, especially if the scones have come straight from the oven. As they're quick and easy to make it's not difficult to mix up a batch while the soup is finishing cooking and they really make it into a meal, with just some fruit to follow.

225 g (8 oz) plain wholewheat flour, or use half wholewheat and half white if you prefer
2 teaspoons baking powder
½ teaspoon mustard powder
½ teaspoon sea salt

50 g (2 oz) softened butter or soft vegetable margarine
125 g (4 oz) finely grated cheese
75–100 ml (3–4 fl oz) milk

Makes about 12

Set the oven to 200°C (400°F), gas mark 6. Sift the flour, baking powder, mustard and salt into a large bowl adding also the residue of bran left in the sieve. Using your fingertips rub the fat into the flour until the mixture looks like fine breadcrumbs. Lightly mix in the grated cheese, then enough of the milk to make a soft but firm dough. Turn the dough on to a lightly floured board and knead briefly, then roll it or press it out to a thickness of about 1 cm (½ in). Use a plain 5 cm (2 in) pastry cutter to cut the dough into rounds. Place the rounds on a floured baking sheet and bake in the preheated oven for about 10 minutes until the scones are risen and golden brown.

VARIATION

Cheese and walnut scones are delicious. Add 50 g (2 oz) chopped walnuts to the mixture with the grated cheese.

CHRISTMAS FRUIT LOAF   DENMARK

The candied fruits make this a pretty, jewelled loaf. It's nice for Christmas because it's festive without being too rich. The best way to get the crushed cardamom is to buy some cardamom pods at a health shop or Indian shop and crush them in a pestle and mortar or with the back of a spoon – the seeds will come out of the pods as you crush them and you keep the seeds and discard the pods. If you can't get it leave it out, but it does give a beautiful flavour and cardamom is a useful flavouring for curries and spicy rice dishes, too.

100 ml (3½ fl oz) lukewarm
  milk
½ teaspoon caster sugar
2 teaspoons dried yeast
450 g (1 lb) plain flour – I
  use half wholewheat, half
  white for this recipe, or you
  could use wheatmeal
Pinch of salt
50 g (2 oz) soft brown sugar

125 g (4 oz) softened butter or
  soft margarine
½ teaspoon crushed cardamom
2 teaspoons vanilla essence
Rind of ½ lemon
225 g (8 oz) mixed candied
  fruits, chopped – try to get a
  nice variety of colours
2 eggs, beaten

Makes 1 large loaf

First grease a 1 kilo (2 lb) loaf tin with butter. Then put the milk
into a small bowl, stir in the caster sugar and yeast and leave on
one side to froth up. Meanwhile mix together the flour, salt and
sugar and rub in the butter or margarine; add the cardamom,
vanilla, lemon, fruit and eggs. Make a well in the centre and
pour in the yeast mixture. Mix to a soft dough, adding a little
more flour if necessary, then knead for 10 minutes. Put the dough
into an oiled bowl, cover with a clean damp cloth then with a
polythene carrier bag and leave it in a warm place until doubled
in bulk – about 1 hour.

Punch the dough down, knead it again lightly, form into a loaf
shape and put into the prepared tin. Cover the loaf with the cloth
and polythene bag again and leave in a warm place for about 30
minutes to rise. Set the oven to 180°C (350°F), gas mark 4. When
the loaf has come up to the top of the tin, bake it until it's golden
and crisp. The loaf should sound hollow when turned out of its
tin and tapped on the base. Leave on a wire rack to cool. It's nice
served with a rich pudding, like *pashka* or *crème brûlée*, or sliced
and buttered for tea.

DANISH PASTRIES DENMARK

Light, crisp and not-too-sweet, Danish pastries are ideal for
serving with coffee on a special occasion. They take time to
make, but are not difficult; I found it particularly satisfying
to produce a wheatmeal version that was light and delicious.
They freeze well, but leave the final icing until just before serving.

150 g (5 oz) butter
225 ml (8 fl oz) warm water
1 teaspoon sugar
15 g ($\frac{1}{2}$ oz) dried yeast
40 g ($1\frac{1}{2}$ oz) butter
275 g (10 oz) plain wheatmeal
  flour
1 egg

For the fillings:
50 g (2 oz) mixed dried fruit

Makes 15

40 g ($1\frac{1}{2}$ oz) caster sugar
1 teaspoon mixed spice
125 g (4 oz) marzipan

To finish:
Beaten egg to glaze
Glacé icing made from 175 g
  (6 oz) icing sugar and a
  little water
50 g (2 oz) flaked almonds

Beat the 150 g (5 oz) of butter to make it soft then spread it
out into a square about 20 cm × 20 cm (8 in × 8 in) and place it
in the refrigerator to get really hard while you prepare the dough.

Put the water into a small bowl and stir in the sugar and
dried yeast; leave on one side for 10 minutes to froth up. Rub the
40 g ($1\frac{1}{2}$ oz) of butter into the flour, then make a well in the
centre, pour in the frothy yeast mixture and add the egg. Mix
everything together to make a soft dough, then knead it until it
feels smooth and pliable. Put the dough into a polythene bag and
leave it in the fridge to rest for 15 minutes. Roll the dough 6 mm
($\frac{1}{4}$ in) thick into an oblong 30 cm × 20 cm (12 in × 8 in). Place
the square of butter on the dough covering two-thirds of it.
Fold the remaining third of the dough over the butter-covered
part and then fold the remaining pieces of butter-covered dough
over so that you have the un-buttered piece in the centre.

Seal the edges by pressing with a rolling pin, then chill the dough in the fridge for 15 minutes. Roll the dough into an oblong again and fold in three as before, then chill in the fridge for 15 minutes. Repeat the rolling and folding 3 or 4 times more, then roll the dough out 1 cm ($\frac{1}{2}$ in) thick and cut into 3 pieces.

Roll one of these pieces into an oblong about 30 cm × 20 cm (12 in × 8 in), sprinkle the dried fruit, caster sugar and spice over the top of the dough and press it in lightly with a rolling pin. Roll up the dough from the long side like a roly-poly pudding. Cut the roll into 6 even-sized pieces, then make two deep cuts in each piece and open them out slightly. Place them on a baking sheet.

Cut both the remaining pieces of dough into 6 pieces. Roll each piece into a square roughly 10 cm × 10 cm (4 in × 4 in). Cut the marzipan into 12 pieces. Form 6 of the pieces of marzipan into 2·5 cm × 10 cm (1 in × 4 in) strips. Place a strip of marzipan at the top edges of 6 of the squares of dough. Roll the dough over then make cuts all down the length, almost through to the edge, and curl the dough round to make a cock's comb. For the remaining pieces of dough fold the corners to the centre and press down. Form the remaining marzipan into rounds. Place one round in the centre of each piece of dough.

Brush all the pastries with beaten egg. Set the oven to 220°C (425°F), gas mark 7. Place the pastries on top of the cooker to get the heat of the oven as it warms up. When the pastries are puffy looking, after about 20 minutes or so, place them in the oven and bake for 20 minutes. Cool the pastries on a wire rack, then ice them and sprinkle with toasted flaked almonds. I think they're best warmed through before serving.

To freeze Danish pastries, open-freeze the cooled pastries. When they're firm store them in a polythene bag. To use them, put them on a wire rack to de-frost – allow about 2 hours for this – then ice them as usual.

GARLIC BREAD   FRANCE

Hot bread oozing with melted butter and garlic is a wonderful
accompaniment to soups and creamy dips, particularly those
containing lentils and beans. French bread is of course the type
that is normally used for garlic bread, and there's no doubt
that this is delicious, with a crisp crust and tender crumb, but
wholewheat bread can also be used very successfully. Although
the loaf is a different shape you treat it in just the same way,
but allow a little longer for it to heat through. For quick wholewheat garlic bread for just one or two people you can spread
slices of wholewheat bread with garlic butter, lay them out
individually on a baking sheet or grill pan without any foil
covering and heat them in the oven or under the grill until the
butter has melted and the bread is just crispy round the edges.

1 French loaf or 1 small wholewheat loaf	Salt
	125 g (4 oz) butter, softened
3–4 cloves of garlic	

Serves 4–6

Set the oven to 200°C (400°F), gas mark 6. Slice the French loaf
almost through into chunky pieces – they should just hold together
at the base. Cut the wholewheat loaf right through into slices –
don't make them too thick. Make the garlic butter by peeling the
garlic and crushing it in a little salt, then mixing it into the butter.
Spread this butter on both sides of the slices of bread. Pile the
wholewheat bread back into the loaf shape. Wrap the loaf in foil
and place it on a baking sheet in the oven. Bake it for about
20 minutes, until it's heated right through and crisp on the outside.
Serve at once.

MELBA TOAST
FRANCE

Wholewheat Melba toast is delicious. crisp and nutty-tasting. This is the method I've found most successful for making Melba toast with wholewheat bread.

8 thin slices wholewheat
  bread

Serves 4

Preheat the oven to 200°C (400°F), gas mark 6. Cut the slices of bread as thin as you can; it helps if the bread is a couple of days old. Lay the slices on baking sheets and place in the oven. After about 7 minutes turn the bread over and bake it for a further 7–10 minutes, or until lightly browned. As soon as the bread comes out of the oven cut it diagonally across, then cool the slices on a wire rack – they'll crispen as they get cold. Melba toast is particularly good with the creamy dips.

OATCAKES
SCOTLAND

Oatcakes are easy to make and crisp and nutty-tasting to eat. Try them for breakfast or tea with butter and clear honey, or serve them with a creamy dip or Scottish cream cheese.

225 g (8 oz) medium oatmeal
½ teaspoon baking powder
½ teaspoon salt

25 g (1 oz) butter or margarine,
  melted
6 teaspoons hot water
A little extra oatmeal to finish

Makes 24–28

Set the oven to 200°C (400°F), gas mark 6. Put the oatmeal into a bowl with the baking powder, salt and butter or margarine.

Mix them together lightly, then stir in enough warm water to make a dough – you'll need about 6 teaspoonsful.

Sprinkle some oatmeal on a board and turn the dough out on to this, kneading lightly, then roll it out to a thickness of about 3 mm ($\frac{1}{8}$ in), sprinkling the surface with a little extra oatmeal if necessary to prevent it from sticking. You can either roll the mixture into a circle and then cut it into wedges, or stamp it into rounds using a pastry cutter. Transfer the oatcakes to a baking sheet and bake them for about 15 minutes until firm and lightly coloured. Let them cool on the tin for a few minutes, then transfer them to a wire cooling rack. Or serve them straight from the oven, all warm and crumbly.

OPEN SANDWICHES DENMARK

A tray of colourful open sandwiches looks really mouthwatering and is a surprisingly practical way of feeding a large group of people. If you want to make the meal more substantial serve mugs or bowls of soup as well with a choice of different puddings laid out on a separate table for people to help themselves. Medium-sized plates and forks will be needed for eating the sandwiches and plenty of paper napkins are advisable.

It's fun to make the open sandwiches and not difficult to make them look pretty. I think the easiest way to do them is to prepare a really good assortment of different ingredients and spread them all out in front of you so that you can create different combinations as you go along.

For the base:

Wholewheat bread, rye bread
 or pumpernickel
Butter
Crisp lettuce leaves

For the toppings:

Finely grated cheese mixed to a
 paste with mayonnaise,
 cream or milk
Sliced hardboiled egg
Chopped hardboiled egg mixed
 with mayonnaise or low-fat
 quark
Cold scrambled egg
Peanut butter
Cottage cheese
Quark or cream cheese
Any of the dips on pages 65–73
 (*hummus*, mock caviar, Liptauer
 cheese and avocado dip are
 particularly good)
Cold bean or lentil salads
 are also excellent

For the garnishes:

Slices of lemon, tomato,
 avocado (tossed in lemon
 juice) onion, red and green
 pepper, cooked beetroot,
 cucumber, radishes, spring
 onions
Sprigs of parsley, mint or
 watercress
Chopped chives
Pineapple cubes or rings
Chopped apple, sliced banana
 tossed in lemon juice
Raisins, dates, chopped dried
 apricots
Black or green grapes
Black or green olives
Chopped walnuts and flaked
 almonds
Chopped stem ginger
Mango chutney
Olive oil
Mayonnaise
Paprika pepper

Butter the bread fairly generously and place it on the tray from which it will be served. Cover each piece of bread with a lettuce leaf, pressing it down so that the butter sticks it on to the bread. Now arrange your toppings and garnishes on the lettuce leaf, covering each as generously as possible whilst making them practical to eat. Here are some ideas for different combinations:

1. Avocado (dipped in lemon juice), watercress, a spoonful of mayonnaise, quark or cottage cheese, chopped walnuts.
2. Peanut butter, coarsely grated carrot, green pepper rings, sliced onion.
3. Quark or cottage cheese, pineapple rings, black grapes, toasted flaked almonds.

4. Sliced cooked beetroot, onion rings, chopped walnuts, cream cheese or quark.
5. Cold lentil salad, mango chutney, chopped apple, parsley.
6. *Hummus*, onion rings, paprika, sliced tomato, parsley,
7. Mock caviar or aubergine and sesame pâté, sliced tomato, onion rings, olive oil.
8. Liptauer cheese, tomato, black olives, parsley sprigs.
9. Goat cheese and herb spread, sliced cucumber and radishes.
10. Avocado dip, coarsely grated carrot, sliced tomato, chopped walnuts.
11. Cubes of cold spicy fritters, mango chutney, tomato, onion rings, garlic mayonnaise.
12. Quark or cream cheese, apple, chopped stem ginger, walnuts.

PEAR BREAD
SWITZERLAND

Slices of this pear bread, *birnbrot,* are lovely served warm with coffee, or if you serve it hot with single cream it makes a very good pudding. I think it goes rather well after a fondue because it's sweet without being rich. You can leave out the kirsch and wine but they do give a beautiful flavour for a special occasion. You will probably be able to get dried pears at a health shop; they're also nice in fruit compotes.

5 tablespoons lukewarm milk
$\frac{1}{4}$ teaspoon caster sugar
1 teaspoon dried yeast
150 g (5 oz) plain wholewheat flour
150 g (5 oz) plain white flour
Pinch of salt
50 g (2 oz) butter or soft margarine
50 g (2 oz) soft brown sugar
1 egg, beaten

For the filling:
275 ml ($\frac{1}{2}$ pint) water
125 g (4 oz) dried stoned prunes
225 g (8 oz) dried pears
50 g (2 oz) seedless raisins
Rind and juice of $\frac{1}{2}$ lemon
50 g (2 oz) soft brown sugar
A little ground cinnamon
Grated nutmeg

1 tablespoon each of dry red
  wine and kirsch (optional)

To glaze:
A little beaten egg

Makes 1 large loaf

Grease a large baking sheet with butter; leave on one side. First make the dough. Put the milk into a small bowl and stir in the caster sugar and yeast. Leave in a warm place for the yeast to froth up. Put the flours and salt into a large bowl; rub in the butter or margarine and add the sugar. Make a well in the centre and pour in the yeast and milk, together with the beaten egg. Mix everything together to make a smooth, soft dough, adding a little more flour if necessary. Turn the dough on to a floured board and knead it for 10 minutes, then put the dough into a clean, oiled bowl, cover it with a clean damp cloth then put the bowl inside a large polythene carrier bag and leave it in a warm place for about an hour or until it has doubled in bulk.

While this is happening make the filling. Put the water, prunes, pears and raisins into a small pan and heat gently until soft, thick and dry. Sieve, finely chop or liquidize the mixture, then add the lemon and sugar and some cinnamon and nutmeg to taste – about $\frac{1}{4}$ teaspoonful of each – and the wine and kirsch if you are using them. Don't make the mixture too liquid – it should hold it's shape.

To assemble the pear bread take the risen dough and knead it for a minute or two, then put it on to a lightly floured board and roll out into a large square, about 38 cm × 38 cm (15 in × 15 in) and not more than 6 mm ($\frac{1}{4}$ in) thick. Spread the fruity filling over the square to within about 2·5 cm (1 in) of the edges. Fold the edges over to enclose the filling, then roll it firmly like a Swiss roll and put it on to the prepared baking sheet. Prick the pear bread all over, cover it with a clean cloth and put it into a warm place for 30 minutes to rise. About 15 minutes before the pear bread is ready, set the oven to 180°C (350°F), gas mark 4. Then brush the bread over with beaten egg and bake it in the centre of the oven, for about 35 minutes, or until it's golden brown and crisp. Serve warm.

PITTA BREAD

MIDDLE EAST

These long thin bread 'pockets' are very popular with my children who irreverently refer to them as 'Arabs' feet' on account of their shape! They're no more trouble to make than rolls and fun to eat because you can fill them with lots of crunchy salad, dips, cottage cheese etc., when they make a delectable lunch or supper. The only problem is you do need one or two large baking sheets to cook them on as they take up rather a lot of space.

300 ml ($\frac{1}{2}$ pint) hand-hot
    water
$\frac{1}{2}$ teaspoon sugar
2 teaspoons dried yeast
450 g (1 lb) plain wholewheat
    flour

2 teaspoons salt
1 teaspoon sugar
1 tablespoon oil

Makes 12

Put the water into a jug and stir in the yeast and the $\frac{1}{2}$ teaspoon of sugar; leave on one side to froth up. Meanwhile put the flour, salt, the sugar and the olive oil into a bowl and mix together. Add the yeast mixture and mix to a dough. Knead for 5 minutes until smooth. Put the dough into an oiled bowl, cover with a damp cloth, cover the bowl with a polythene carrier bag and leave it in a warm place for 1 hour to rise. When the dough has doubled in size, punch it down and knead it lightly. Set the oven to 230°C (450°F), gas mark 8.

Divide the dough into 12 pieces and roll each into an oblong about 18 cm (7 in) long and 7 cm (3 in) wide. Put the pieces on to oiled baking sheets and leave them in a warm place or on top of the cooker for 15 minutes to rise a bit.

Put them in the oven and bake them for 5 minutes, then turn the oven heat down to 200°C (400°F), gas mark 6 and bake for a further 10 minutes or so, until the pitta are golden brown. When they come out of the oven they'll be light and puffed up; cool them on a wire rack and make them into pouches by inserting the point of a sharp knife into one of the long edges and sliding it along.

That's proper pitta bread, but when I was working out this recipe I made a batch which I rolled out rather longer and thinner and baked for a bit longer at the higher temperature and they came out thin and very crisp and that is how my children always ask me to make them now.

SODA BREAD   IRELAND

Soda bread is quick to make, an ideal standby when the bread-bin is empty and there is no time to make yeast bread. It only takes about 40 minutes from start to finish and is delicious served slightly warm. It's particularly good with runny honey. Although I'm very much a wholewheat bread fan, I think this particular recipe is best made with half wholewheat and half white flour, or with wheatmeal flour. Alternatively, an Irishman I met while writing this book told me that although no one ever made bread like his mother he thought the most authentic-tasting loaf was made with scofa flour and buttermilk.

450 g (1 lb) plain wholewheat and white flour mixed; or plain wheatmeal flour; or scofa flour

1 teaspoon salt

1 rounded teaspoon bicarbonate of soda

Makes 1 loaf

25 g (1 oz) butter or vegetable margarine

275 ml ($\frac{1}{2}$ pint) buttermilk, sour milk or milk warmed with a tablespoon of cider vinegar or lemon juice to sour it

Set the oven to 220°C (425°F), gas mark 7. Flour a baking sheet. Sift the flour, salt and bicarbonate of soda into a large bowl. With your fingertips, rub in the fat until the mixture resembles fine breadcrumbs. Make a well in the centre and pour in the milk, then gradually mix everything together to make a dough. Turn the dough out on to a floured board and knead it lightly, then form it into a round loaf. Put the loaf on the prepared baking sheet and using a sharp knife cut a cross shape in the top. Bake the loaf for 30–35 minutes until it's risen, golden and crusty, then leave it to cool on a wire rack.

Soda bread doesn't keep well; it's really best eaten the same day.

TORTILLAS

MEXICO

In Mexico tortillas are eaten as we would eat bread. They're easy to make and versatile. You can eat them as they are, with butter or other toppings; you can roll them round salad mixtures such as cottage cheese, lettuce and tomato or mixed bean salad, watercress and onion to make a kind of hearty rolled sandwich. If you fry them in hot oil they become crisp like poppadums and can be served with creamy salad dips. They can also be treated like pancakes, filled with savoury mixtures, covered with a well-flavoured sauce and baked · there are two recipes for this in the pancakes and pasta section of this book.

100 g (4 oz) maize flour – you get this from health shops, or use plain wholewheat flour
150 g (5 oz) plain wholewheat flour

1 teaspoon sea salt
About 150 ml ($\frac{1}{4}$ pint) cold water

Makes 12

Sift the flours into a bowl, tipping in any extra bran left in the sieve, then stir in the salt and enough water to make a dough that's soft but not sticky – like a scone dough. Turn the dough on to a floured board and knead it slightly to make it smooth, then divide it into 12 pieces. Roll each piece into a ball, then use a rolling pin to roll each into a thin round – about 15–20 cm (6–8 in) diameter.

Heat a frying pan without any fat in it and fry the tortillas in this, one at a time: keep the heat fairly low. When the underside is set turn the tortilla over and cook the other side. Put them on a plate when they're ready and cover them with a piece of foil because they quickly become dry and brittle.

Serve the tortillas with salads instead of bread. A pile of freshly cooked tortillas and bowls of spicy avocado dip, sliced tomatoes, quarters of hardboiled egg, grated cheese, red bean salad and shredded lettuce makes a lovely easy-going buffet lunch or supper.

TOSTADAS   MEXICO

A *tostada* is a tortilla that has been fried in oil so that it becomes crisp, like a poppadum. *Tostadas* are particularly good with creamy dips and salads because their crispness is such a pleasant contrast.

12 tortillas – see page 332
Oil for shallow frying

Makes 12

Make the tortillas as described - this can be done in advance if more convenient. Heat a little oil in a frying pan and fry the tortillas until they're crisp on one side then turn them over and fry on the other side. Drain them well on kitchen paper.

Tostadas make an excellent 'edible plate' for a salad – allow a *tostada* for each person and arrange the salad on top, making it as colourful and mouthwatering as you can. Lettuce makes a good foundation – make sure it's well dried so that the *tostada* remains crisp – followed by some or all of the following: sliced tomato, grated carrot, red bean salad, grated cheese, cottage cheese or quark, watercress and spring onion, piled up well and finished off with a generous dollop of spicy avocado dip or mayonnaise.

WHOLEWHEAT BREAD ENGLAND

So many recipes for bread-making start off 'bread-making is easy' – and it really is – but still many people say they find the prospect daunting! I must admit that what recipes should say is 'bread-making is easy when you do it often'. If you make bread twice a week or so you learn a lot about the behaviour of the yeast and the dough and the effect of heat on the mixture. But for everyone there has to be a first time and so I'm going to try and put down all the things I've discovered and I hope this will be helpful and make it as easy as possible for you.

If you're baking for a family, or have a deep freeze, I don't think it's worth making up less than a 1·5 kilo (3 lb 5 oz) bag of flour. You can use all wholewheat flour, or, if your family isn't used to wholewheat flour, you might find it best to use wheatmeal flour, which is flour which has been sieved once by the millers to remove the coarsest part of the grain, and contains 85–90% of the grain, whereas wholewheat flour consists of 100%. Or you might find it best to use wheatmeal flour or wholewheat flour with a proportion of strong white bread flour (preferably unbleached) – half and half is a good mixture to start with.

I use dried yeast, largely because it's handy – one of those large tubs lasts ages and so I don't have to keep remembering to buy it; also it's more predictable, and I think, easier when you're learning. But it is important that the dried yeast should be fresh, so buy it from a shop which has a quick turnover and, unless you know you're going to do a lot of breadmaking, it's best to buy a small quantity to start with.

If you've got a warm place like an airing cupboard you can put the bread to rise; I stand mine near the pilot light on my gas cooker. But the bread will rise just as well but more slowly standing on the working surface in the kitchen; you don't especially need to put it into a warm place, and it's important not to let it get too hot.

300 ml ($\frac{1}{2}$ pint) hand-hot
  water
$\frac{1}{2}$ teaspoon sugar
2 tablespoons dried yeast
1·5 kilo (3 lb 5 oz) bag of
  wheatmeal or wholewheat
  flour; or a mixture of

wholewheat flour and
  strong white bread flour
2 tablespoons sugar
4 teaspoons fine sea salt
50 g (2 oz) butter or margarine
600–700 ml (1–1$\frac{1}{2}$ pints)
  hand-hot water

Makes five 450 g (1 lb) loaves

Put the 300 ml ($\frac{1}{2}$ pint) of water into a small jug or bowl and
stir in the $\frac{1}{2}$ teaspoonful of sugar and the dried yeast. Leave
on one side for 5–10 minutes to froth up. While this is happening
grease your loaf tins by brushing them with a little oil or softened
butter, then leave them on one side too, in a warm place if
there's one handy, but this isn't essential.

Now put your flour into a large bowl – the bowl of your
electric mixer if the mixer has a dough hook attachment –
and add the 2 tablespoons of sugar and the salt. Rub in the
butter with your fingers. By this time you should find that the
yeast has frothed up quite dramatically into a lovely volcanic
mass and you can add it to your flour, together with the water,
but don't add quite all the water; start off with 600 ml (just over
a pint), and leave the rest for a moment. Mix the flour, yeast and
water together until the dough forms – add the remaining
water now if the dough seems too stiff. It should be firm, but soft
enough to handle pleasantly, rather like soft well-worked Plasti-
cine. If you've got a dough hook on your mixer – and I must say it's
since I got one that I've managed to make our bread regularly –
you can now leave it to knead the dough for 5 minutes. Otherwise,
turn the dough out and knead it by hand, pushing and pummell-
ing, folding and refolding it, for 5 minutes or even 10 minutes
if you can manage it. As you knead the dough you'll feel it
change from a coarse, lumpy and slightly sticky texture to a
beautiful smooth, supple, silky one.

Put the dough back in its bowl, cover it with a damp tea-towel
then stand the bowl in a polythene carrier bag and leave it to

double in size. I find this takes an hour in a warm place, perhaps slightly longer if the bowl is just standing on the working surface and up to 2 hours if the kitchen is cold.

Now punch down the dough with your fist and knead it again a little – just 1–2 minutes this time, to wake the yeast up again. Cut the dough into 5 equal-sized pieces and shape them to fit the tins. I find the best way to do this is to flatten each piece with the palm of my hand, then gently roll it up and pop it into the tin with the fold underneath. Then I press the sides and corners down so that the centre of the loaf is higher, coming up into a nice dome shape. Put the loaves on top of the cooker or in a warm place, cover with the damp cloth again and set the oven to 240°C (475°F), gas mark 9. (If you put the loaves on top of the cooker the heat of the oven as it warms up will help them to rise.)

They'll take about 30 minutes to rise: as soon as the dough is just peeping over the tops of the tins put them into the oven. Don't let them over-rise or they'll collapse in the oven: if there is still some rise left in them the heat from the oven will give them a final boost and they'll have a lovely domed crust.

After 10 minutes turn the heat down to 200°C (400°F), gas mark 6 and bake the loaves for a further 25 minutes. Turn the loaves out of their tins straight away – they should sound hollow when you tap them on the base with your knuckles – and leave them on a wire rack to cool.

You can of course make 2 large loaves and 1 small loaf if you'd prefer; large loaves take about 10 minutes longer to bake.

WHOLEWHEAT ROLLS   ENGLAND

Warm home-made rolls are useful for serving with so many dishes and they're really not difficult to make. This recipe is based on half one of the new metric bags of flour containing 1·5 kilos, which is why the amount looks rather strange in the Imperial measurements.

200 ml (7 fl oz) hand-hot water
1 tablespoon dried yeast
½ teaspoon sugar
750 g (1 lb 10½ oz) wholewheat
   flour
2 teaspoons salt

1 tablespoon sugar
50 g (2 oz) butter
200 ml (7 fl oz) milk
1 egg, beaten
A little extra flour to finish

Makes 24

Put the water into a small bowl and stir in the yeast and the ½ teaspoon of sugar. Leave on one side for 10 minutes to froth up. Meanwhile put the flour, salt and the 1 tablespoon of sugar into a bowl and rub in the butter. Pour the frothed-up yeast into the centre of the flour and add the milk and egg; mix together to make a firm but pliable dough. Turn the dough out and knead it for 10 minutes, then put it back into the bowl, cover with a damp cloth, stand the bowl inside a polythene carrier bag and leave until it's doubled in size. This takes about an hour in a warm place, 1–2 hours just standing on a working surface, depending on how warm the room is.

When the dough has risen set the oven to 220°C (425°F), gas mark 7. Punch down the dough, knead it again lightly then divide it into 24 pieces. Form the pieces into rounds then flatten them with the palm of your hand and place them on greased baking trays, allowing room for them to spread. Cover them with a damp cloth and leave in a warm place for 20–30 minutes to double in size – I put mine on top of the cooker so that they get the benefit of the heat of the oven as it warms up. Sprinkle the rolls with a little flour then bake them for 15 minutes. Cool on a wire rack.

Recipes Classified under Countries

AUSTRIA
Beetroot and horseradish salad
Gnocchi in mushroom sauce
Linzertorte

BULGARIA
Chilled cucumber soup
Lentil and red pepper stew
Red kidney bean stew

CARIBBEAN – see also Jamaica
Banana fritters with lime
Courgettes stuffed with cheese
  and onion
Red bean rice

CHINA
Chop suey
Fried wheat protein with sweet and
  sour sauce
Mushrooms and tofu
Stir-fried Chinese cabbage

CZECHOSLOVAKIA
Yellow split pea soup

DENMARK
Christmas fruit loaf
Danish pastries
Open sandwiches
Red fruit pudding
Rice and almond pudding

ENGLAND
Crème brûlée

Gooseberry fool
Leek pie
Macaroni cheese
Madeira cake
Mint sauce
Parkin
Pouring custard
Trifle
Wholewheat bread
Wholewheat rolls

FINLAND
Apple snow
Mushroom salad
Mushrooms in soured cream

FRANCE
Aïoli with crudités
Apple tart
Baby meringues
Carrots *à la Vichy*
Celeriac salad
Cheese sauce (*sauce Mornay*)
Cheese soufflé
Chick peas and vegetable
  mayonnaise (*aigroissade*)
Coeurs à la crème
Cold *gougère* with cream cheese
  filling
Courgettes with fresh herbs
Crêpes suzette
Garlic bread
Gougère with mushrooms, onions
  and red wine
Green salad

338

FRANCE – *cont.*

Green salad with Gruyère cheese
Haricot bean salad
Individual asparagus tarts
Individual cheese soufflés
Leek flan
Leek soufflé
Lentil salad
Lettuce soup
Little coffee custards
Macaroons
Mayonnaise
Melba toast
Mont blanc
Mushroom flan
Mushroom soufflé
Mushrooms *à la Grecque*
Omelettes
Onion flan
Onion soup
Pancakes stuffed with mushrooms
  and artichoke hearts
Pears baked in wine
Peas braised with lettuce
Pipérade
Potato soup
Potatoes Anna
Potatoes baked with cream (*gratin
  dauphinoise*)
Pumpkin baked with butter and
  garlic
Ratatouille
Red cabbage and chestnut
  casserole
Red cabbage stuffed with
  chestnuts
Rice and artichoke heart salad
Salade Niçoise
Salsify with parsley and butter
Sponge fingers
Strawberry tartlets
Stuffed aubergines *à la duxelles*
Stuffed tomatoes à la Provençale
Sugar-glazed parsnips

Tian
Tomato, cheese and olive salad
Tomato salad
Tomato soup
Vinaigrette
Watercress soup
White sauce (*sauce Béchamel*)
Wine sauce

GERMANY

Carrots with apples
Dried fruit compote
Haricot beans with apples
Mushroom soup
Potato pancakes
Potatoes with apples
Rice and peas with tomato sauce
  (*Schoten*)
Stewed red cabbage
Yellow split pea purée with
  vegetables

GREAT BRITAIN

Apple sauce
Baked potatoes
Brandy snaps
Gravy
Pease pudding
Roast potatoes

GREECE – see also Middle East

Cauliflower in tomato sauce
Cheese pie
Honey cheese cake
Stuffed aubergines in béchamel
  sauce
Stuffed vine or cabbage leaves
Tomatoes stuffed with rice
Yoghurt tart

HOLLAND

Brussels sprouts with cheese
Green split pea soup
Lemon whip
Potato bake
Potato and watercress soufflé

HUNGARY
Chilled cherry soup
Green pepper and tomato stew
  (*Lecso*)
Liptauer cheese
Potato and mushroom stew with
  soured cream

INDIA
Biriani
Chapatis
Cheese curry
Curried stuffed eggs
Curry sauce
Fried rice
Ghee
Khitchari
Samosas
Spicy okra
Vegetable curry

IRELAND
Soda bread

ITALY
Asparagus pudding (*sformato*)
Aubergine bake (*parmigiana*)
Cheese and onion soup
Chestnut soup
Chick peas and vermicelli
Coffee *ricotta* pudding
Fennel baked with cheese
Fennel and cucumber salad
Fresh fruit salad
Fresh orange salad
Fresh peach salad
Fried *gnocchi*
Gnocchi alla Romana
Lasagne with spinach and cheese
Pasta and beans
Pasta with cream cheese and
  walnuts
Pineapple sorbet
Pizza
Quick non-yeast pizza (*al tegame*)

Red peppers with tomatoes and
  onions (*peperonata*)
Rice and peas (*risi e bisi*)
Rice croquettes
Ricotta gnocchi
Risotto bianco
Spaghetti with *pesto*
Spinach *gnocchi*
Stuffed cucumber salad
Stuffed onions
Stuffed peaches
Tomato sauce
Vanilla ice cream

JAMAICA – see also Caribbean
Pumpkin soup

MEXICO – see also South America
Avocado dip (*guacamole*)
Pancakes stuffed with cheese
  and baked in spicy tomato sauce
Pancakes stuffed with spicy red
  beans
Tortillas
Tostadas

MIDDLE EAST – see also Greece,
  Turkey, North Africa and
  Morocco
Avocado and carrot salad
Aubergine and sesame pâté
Bean pâté
Bulgur wheat pilaf
Bulgur wheat and cheese pilaf
Bulgur wheat, tomato and parsley
  salad (*Tabbouleh*)
Butter bean salad
Cabbage salad with mint and
  pomegranate
Cold cooked spinach salad
Cucumber and yoghurt salad
Hummus
Lentil soup
Pasta with lentils
Pitta bread

MIDDLE EAST – *cont.*
Spicy fritters
Spinach pie
Yoghurt

MOROCCO – see also Middle East
Couscous

NORTH AFRICA – see also Middle
  East
Orange and radish salad

NORWAY
Cabbage with soured cream
New potatoes baked in butter
Prune delight
Rhubarb compote

POLAND
Red cabbage salad
Vegetable and bean salad (*salata mehania*)

PORTUGAL
Kidney beans with tomatoes, onions and cumin
Red kidney bean stew
Tomatoes stuffed with cheese

RUMANIA
Goat cheese and herb spread
Mixed vegetable stew (*ghiveci*)

RUSSIA
Baked stuffed eggs
Beetroot soup (borsch)
Blini
Cauliflower, egg and potato bake
Cucumber salad with soured cream and hardboiled eggs
Little cheese tartlets (*vatrushki*)
Mock caviar
Pashka

SCOTLAND
Cheese scones
Dundee cake
Oatcakes
Shortbread fingers

SOUTH AMERICA – see also
  Mexico
Chilled avocado soup
Coconut biscuits
Exotic fruit salad
Hot potato salad with peanut dressing
Pumpkin in orange syrup

SPAIN
Chick pea soup
Chocolate and orange mousse
Gazpacho
Green salad
Paella
Stuffed courgette bake
Stuffed peppers

SWEDEN
Apricot and almond pudding
Baked creamed swedes
Creamed spinach

SWITZERLAND
Cheese fondue
Cheese and onion tart
Fruity muesli
Pear bread (*birnbrot*)
Stuffed tomato salad
Swiss fried potato cake (*rösti*)

TURKEY – see also Middle East
Chilled cucumber soup
Ground rice and rosewater pudding

USA
Cauliflower and apple salad
Cheese cake

USA – *cont.*

Chocolate brownies
Coleslaw
Cranberry sauce
Cream cheese and soured
  cream dip
Creamed onions and peas
Glazed sweet potatoes
Potato salad
Pumpkin pie
Raisin sour cream pie
Red bean salad
Spinach salad

Sweetcorn fritters
Sweetcorn pudding
Three-bean salad
Vichyssoise
Waldorf salad

WALES

Bread and cheese pudding
Glamorgan sausage
Welsh rabbit

YUGOSLAVIA

Aubergines stuffed with cheese

Index